OTHER BOOKS BY T. R. MALLOCH

Beyond Reductionism (Praeger, 1982)

Where Are We Now? with William A. Harper eds.,
(University Press of America, 1980)

Issues in International Trade and Development Policy
(Greenwood Press, 1984)

Unleashing the Power of Perpetual Learning, with Donald Norris
(SCM Press, 2003)

Renewing American Culture, with Scott T. Massey (Scrivener, 2006)

Being Generous (Templeton Foundation Press, 2006)

Spiritual Enterprise (Encounter, 2009)

Thrift: Rebirth of a Forgotten Virtue (Encounter, 2009)

Doing Virtuous Business (Thomas Nelson, 2010)

America's Spiritual Capital, with Nicholas Capaldi
(St. Augustine Press, 2012)

The End of Ethics and a Way Back, with Jordan Mamorsky
(Wiley, 2013)

Practical Wisdom for Management (Greenleaf, 2015)

PRAISE FOR DAVOS, ASPEN & YALE

"Laird Malloch is my kind of life tour guide. Recounting decades of his exotic experiences, his bold and irreverent storytelling plunges us into vastly different worlds, making us laugh, wince, and simply marvel at the highs and lows of postmodern global elites."

—PROF. DANILO PETRANOVICH, YALE UNIVERSITY

"This is the ultimate WASP coming-of-age saga by the world's best spreader of bull. Read it and laugh out loud! This book is fabulous. Not since Korda's *Power! How to Get It* has a book so accurately described how to live a productive life!"

—F. SKIP WEITZEN, AUTHOR OF HYPERGROWTH

"Like the proverbial Chinese fire drill, Ted Malloch has done just about everything, changing positions while teaching us how to find true happiness and prosperity.

—FENGGANG YANG, DIRECTOR, CENTER ON RELIGION AND CHINESE SOCIETY, PURDUE UNIVERSITY

"There may well come a day when a new-and-improved obsession with equality will grind down the very last of the better things. In the meantime, Malloch's hilarious memoir will serve as a map of the true landscape of unequal men and their unequal things. And perhaps some future "equalitarian" will, upon reading it, suddenly remember the great truth: that things and men can be divided between better and worse, between good and evil—and that, for the sake of their sanity, men would do well to rank things as their ancestors once did."

—KENNETH BICKFORD, BOARD MEMBER, ETHICS & PUBLIC POLICY CENTER

"My very dear friend Ted Malloch has, as the saying goes, been everywhere and met everyone, and *Davos, Aspen, and Yale* tells us about them in staggering, graphic detail—in truly rollicking fashion."

—PAUL MARSHALL, SENIOR FELLOW, HUDSON INSTITUTE

"An honest life, honestly told! One of the many things that has always impressed me about Ted Malloch is his integrity. It's tough to convey this in pithy fashion, but he accomplishes it in this amazing life story."

—NICHOLAS CAPALDI, LOYOLA UNIVERSITY, SCHOOL OF BUSINESS

"Don't be fooled by this lighthearted memoir. While humorous, its pages reveal an indefatigable Renaissance man who, like his namesake [Theodore Roosevelt], 'is actually in the arena' in every way imaginable. Moreover, we not only meet a Malloch 'who strives valiantly,' 'who knows the great enthusiasms, the great devotions,' and 'who spends himself in a worthy cause' but we also find inspiration in a life that embodies "the triumph of high achievement."

—ROBERT W. PATTERSON, COLUMNIST, *PHILADELPHIA INQUIRER*

"This book is full of it — humor, wisdom, pomposity, and humility—all in equal doses. A must read!"

—PRASAD KAIPPA, AUTHOR OF *SMART TO WISE*

"Ted Malloch—bon vivant, scholar, diplomat, businessman, sportsman—has been, roughly speaking, everywhere and met, roughly speaking, everyone, and in this rich memoir he brings us along on some of his greatest adventures."

—LINDA BRIDGES, EDITOR-AT-LARGE, *NATIONAL REVIEW*

Bully! When shot in the chest, preparing to make a campaign speech as Bull Moose candidate for president, the author's ancestor Teddy Roosevelt shouted, "It'll take more than that to kill a bull moose!" then proceeded to read his bullet-punctured speech while blood oozed an expanding red patch on his shirt. The luckily well-positioned metal cigar box and thick folded-up speech in Teddy's jacket pocket proved the health value of cigars and bullets-be-damned rhetoric, in which context this memoir will fit in perfectly . . .

—CHARLES L. HARPER JR. FORMER SENIOR EXECUTIVE, TEMPLETON FOUNDATION

"Movie star good looks, an acerbic wit, and a giant intellect . . . Ted Malloch's memoirs are a fascinating, and at times disturbing, glimpse into the oft-transecting worlds of academia, corporate finance, and realpolitik. . . . While Professor Malloch captures the zeitgeist of postmodernity, he reminds his readers that virtuous cultures require more than just great leaders—they need a soul, and he isn't afraid to suggest where they should start searching for it."
—DR. KENNETH J. BARNES, FRSA, DEAN, RIDLEY COLLEGE, MELBOURNE, AUSTRALIA

"Ted Malloch's wonderful memoir is a splendidly written chronicle of a unique and unforgettable American life, as writer, intellectual, philosopher, teacher, diplomat, sportsman, bon vivant and boulevardier: truly a man for all seasons. A rollicking good read."
—JOSEPH F. JOHNSTON JR., BOARD MEMBER, LIBERTY FUND

"Theodore Roosevelt (Ted) Malloch is witty, poignant and insightful. His lectures, writings, and relations pull back the curtain on truth in a most winsome, delightful way."
—TED BAEHR@THEMOVIEGUIDE

"Finally a witty, honest, insightful, and unapologetic account of a successful WASP life. Ted Malloch shares his life, opinions, and cultural pride in a refreshing tone that may be politically incorrect but which will delight those who enjoy authenticity."
—MAGETTE WADE, CEO, TIOSSAN

"Wonderful! Ted is not just global; he is intergalactic. I think the wit and verve he brings to this story will be a welcome addition to the publisher's list. The only question I have is: So who will play Ted and Beth in the film version?"
—ISABELLA BUNN, REGENTS PARK COLLEGE, UNIVERSITY OF OXFORD

"This book is a MUST read for anyone interested in a Big Tent Conservatism!"
—MALLORY FACTOR, CONTRIBUTOR, FOX NEWS

DAVOS ASPEN &YALE

MY LIFE BEHIND THE ELITE CURTAIN AS A GLOBAL SHERPA

THEODORE ROOSEVELT MALLOCH

 WND Books

DAVOS, ASPEN, AND YALE

Published by WND Books, Washington, D.C. WND Books is a registered trademark of WorldNetDaily.com, Inc. ("WND")

Book designed by Mark Karis

WND Books are available at special discounts for bulk purchases. WND Books also publishes books in electronic formats. For more information call (541) 474-1776 or visit www.wndbooks.com.

Hardcover ISBN: 978-1-944229-04-7
eBook ISBN: 978-1-944229-05-4

Library of Congress Cataloging-in-Publication Data

Names: Malloch, Theodore R., author.
Title: Davos, Aspen, and Yale : my life behind the elite curtain as a global
  sherpa / Theodore Roosevelt Malloch.
Description: Washington, D.C. : WND Books, [2016]
Identifiers: LCCN 2015035115| ISBN 9781944229047 (hardcover) | ISBN
  9781944229054 (e-book)
Subjects: LCSH: Malloch, Theodore R. | Economists--United States--Biography.
  | Businesspeople--United States--Biography. | Leadership. |
  Entrepreneurship. | International relations.
Classification: LCC HB119.M253 A3 2016 | DDC 330.092--dc23
LC record available at http://lccn.loc.gov/2015035115

Printed in the United States of America
15 16 17 18 19 20 MVP 9 8 7 6 5 4 3 2 1

TO MY PROGENY:
Ian, Trevor, Nigel, and Morgan,
truly wonderful children,

and

ALL MY DOGS OVER A LIFETIME:
Duke (cocker spaniel); Ming Yen (Pekinese); Jason (Irish setter); Bo, Duke II, Duchess, and Heidi (Vizlas); Stanley (Wheaten Terrier); and Clare, Liberty, and Justice for All (Kerry blue terriers)—man's best friends and my partners in the game

CONTENTS

FOREWORD

When Peter Drucker died in 2005 the world lost its management soul and self-described "social ecologist."

The father of modern management left a long trail of books and articles covering private enterprise, government, and the not-for-profit sectors of society. Over decades he seemed to have the knack to predict just about everything—from privatization to flatter organizations and from the rise of Japan to the emergence of the information society; and most important the value of knowledge workers.

Dr. Drucker taught at Claremont University in California where the values-based School of Management is now appropriately named after him. His profound skepticism of macroeconomic theory made him more interested in practices, processes, and always objectives than grand theories. With his thick Austrian accent Drucker is still peering down over all of us mere mortals.

No one will likely ever take Drucker's place or have his fame in management circles. Until now . . .

Enter front stage . . . Theodore Roosevelt Malloch, who Lady Margaret Thatcher dubbed a "Global Sherpa" already in 1992 is emerging as the heir apparent. His refreshing thinking crosses disciplines as diverse as economics, decision-making, philosophy, and theology. Ted Malloch teaches at Yale University and is best known for his strategy work with over 150 multinational companies.

He has led the PricwaterhouseCoopers CEO Learning Partnership for ten years, touching over seventy-five thousand CEOs worldwide, who want to "invent the future." Having served on dozens of boards of directors in venture capitalist companies, mutual funds, and universities as well as on foundations and charities, he is no stranger to corporate governance. He has become an authority on reputation capital and the father of something dubbed, "spiritual capital."

As his name suggests his political connections are many and somewhat bipartisan. He has at an early age served in the US State Department, US Senate on Foreign Relations, as an ambassador in the United Nations during the cold war. He was on Wall Street in capital markets during *Liar's Poker*. He was also on the executive board of the famous, Davos World Economic Forum. Recently he helped start the new Zermatt Summit to humanize globalization.

Traveling to some 145 countries, Malloch is a pioneer of globalization who coined the term, "thought leadership." His books on everything from trade and development in policy circles to perpetual learning in the academy to *Doing Virtuous Business* (Thomas Nelson, 2011)—which was even made into an Emmy-nominated PBS documentary.

The documentary focuses on how fourteen leading companies embody different virtues to succeed in the competitive arena of international business. As a virtue-ethicist, Malloch is indeed providing for a whole new way of doing business that he calls "virtuous capitalism." He has a ton of followers, big name CEOs among them. Larry Kudlow of CNBC says on the cover of the new book, "Every CEO should read this book and regain the moral energy to lead both their firms and the global economy." The former CEO of Wal-Mart says, "The owl of Minerva takes flight in Malloch's work—he provides an entire framework for the values and virtues of a good corporation."

With big business under attack everywhere, Dr. Malloch's work provides, as Drucker's did, a light on a different road ahead. He has penned many books on counterintuitive notions like—thrift (before the crash) spiritual enterprises, and being generous. His latest project, with the European Academy of Business, asks what is the practical wisdom for management of the world's six great historic faith traditions? His recent book, *The End of Ethics*, attempts to bring back the arc of trust so critical to global markets.

No small assignment, and no small mind. Move over Peter, your new counterpart may have arrived.

—SKIP WEITZEN, JOURNALIST AND AUTHOR OF *HYPER GROWTH*

Men go abroad to wonder at the heights of mountains, at the huge waves of the sea, at the long courses of the rivers, at the vast compass of the ocean, at the circular motions of the stars, and they pass by themselves without wondering.

—*ST. AUGUSTINE*

PREFACE

White Anglo-Saxon Protestant (WASP) has in recent decades become a derogatory term for a closed group of high-status Americans mostly of British Protestant ancestry. In some circles it is a term of derision.

The accolade applies to a group believed to (have) controlled disproportionate social, political, and financial power. WASPs, it was said, control a degree of "privilege" held by few others. However few people bragged about their cuisine of overcooked, bland foods; boring, Brooks Brothers fashion; or their décor, which was notably "shabby chic." They are no better or worse than anyone else, *truth* be told.

Many scholars agree that the group's influence has waned since the end of World War II, with the growing influence of Jews, Catholics, African-Americans, and other former outsiders.

Historically, "Anglo-Saxon" has been used for centuries to refer to the Anglo-Saxon language (today more correctly called "Old English") of the inhabitants of England and much of modern Scotland before about 1100, and since the nineteenth century has been in common use in the English-speaking New World, but not in Britain itself, to refer to all Caucasian people of British descent, who were mostly Protestants. The *W* and *P* were added in the 1950s in the United States to form a witty epithet with an undertone of so-called *waspishness*.

The first published mention of the term was provided by a political scientist, Andrew Hacker, in the 1957 article "Liberal Democracy and Social Control," in *American Political Science Review*, indicating it was already used as common terminology among American sociologists:

> They are "WASPs"—in the cocktail party jargon of the sociologists.

That is, they are wealthy, they are Anglo-Saxon in origin, and they are Protestants (and disproportionately Episcopalian). To their Waspishness should be added the tendency to be located on the Eastern seaboard or around San Francisco, to be prep school and Ivy League educated, and to be possessed of inherited wealth.

While WASP culture and influence may be on the decline, it is impossible to appreciate American or indeed world history without a proper comprehension of our influence for more than a thousand years— and most prominently in the American founding and the institutions then spawned and which survive to this day. But please note: this is *not* about any kind of racial supremacy, ethnic gloating, gender power, or religious exclusion. *WASP* is herein just a cultural euphemism. It is also part of my story.

So years ago at a Christmas brunch and with plenty of mimosas, my sons asked me the perplexing question, "Dad, what is it exactly that you have done?"

THE MALLOCH GUIDE TO SINGLE MALT SCOTCH[1]

The term *single* has a precise meaning. It indicates that *all* of the whiskey in the bottle was made in the same distillery. It has not been blended. The term *malt* indicates the raw material, as whiskey is made exclusively from malted barley, no other grain. It is infused with water (Scottish waters are distinct) and fermented with yeast and distilled in a pot still. There are more than 150 malt distilleries in Scotland. Their products are the *only* malts that may be called *scotch*.

Each single malt represents a place, which also provides a name. These places are grouped into regions: Lowland, Highland, Campbeltown, and Islay. Each embraces certain characteristics. The tasting of whiskeys notes their color, nose, body, palate, and finish. Malts are rated with a score to 100.

Here are a few of my own favorites cultivated from living in Scotland, visiting often, and by trial and error—from my personal collection of some one hundred different single malts, which were housed in a separate bar in the Bear's Club. Note drinking is to be in moderation and can be harmful to your health!

1. *Lagavulin* is my first choice. Classic Islay, it has a sustained peaty/smoky power and great complexity, with a dry, pungent bouquet and astonishingly long finish. The sixteen-year version has a sherry character but costs more than one hundred dollars a bottle.

2. *Edradour* is the smallest distillery in Scotland, near Pitlochry and hidden in a glen. The color of its single malt is golden, and it is spicy and creamy. Its finish is mellow and warming.

---

[1] Probably the most valuable thing I will ever give you.

3. *Glenmorangie* is light, sweetish, flowery, spicy, and an easy taste to embrace. It comes from Tain in the eastern Highlands (near my favorite links golf course, Dornoch) and uses bourbon wood in aging.

4. *Glenturret* is the oldest distillery in Scotland, near Crieff, in Perthshire. Its single malt is dry, fresh, young, soft like toffee, and best as an aperitif.

5. *Highland Park* is in the Orkneys, way up north, offshore. Its malt has a distinct smokiness with a heather and honey accent, maltiness, and a smooth and deep, round, and full flavor. Lovely.

6. *Tomintoul* is from Speyside, in the shadow of the Cairngorm mountains. It has a light palate and a delicate, grassy, perfumy nose, with a lively, long finish.

7. *Scapa* is very peaty, even oily, with vanilla notes, and salty water.

8. *Talisker* is from Skye. It has a powerful palate and emphatic island character. Talisker is pungent, with volcanic water, seaweed, brine, and sweet maltiness, along with some peppery qualities. It warms the heart.

9. *Oban* is from the western Highlands. Its nose has a whiff of the sea. Oban is smooth and firm, with a smoky dryness, almost gingery.

10. *Ardbeg* is an Islay malt. Smoke and peat dominate, with bonfires of tar. Ardbeg has a hefty character, earthy and robust. It is a perfect bedtime malt.

11. *Caol Ila* is another Islay, from the north shore. It is distinctive for its attack. Caol Ila has an olive-like, pale color, seaweedy but peaty in taste, with a very warming finish.

12. *Rosebank* is a classic Lowland malt with a potpourri aroma and a flowery palate. It is light, aromatic, and has hints of clover.

13. *The Macallan* is the Rolls Royce of malts, made with golden barley from Speyside, which utilizes sherry aging. Macallan is full of flavor, big bodied, oaky, and satisfying. It is great after dinner.

INTRODUCTION

Thou, O Lord, shalt endure for ever; and thy remembrance unto all generations
—PSALM 102:12 KJV

Nearly all of us have heard or used the phrase "Been there, done that," to the point of exhaustion. I suppose in popular culture it has become commonplace for saying you have experienced the topic under discussion, to the extent of boredom or complacency. It also has a kind of geographical or even intellectual heritage about the places or states of mind you have visited, inhabited, or collected over time. In that sense this, then, is my personal memoir. People on reading or hearing my résumé recited typically say, "Really, um, you've been to all those places and done all that stuff? So many countries (145 and still counting); all those luminaries and world-changing events? How old are you, anyway?"

This catchy notion of "having been there" is a phrase that actually began life in the early 1970s, in the short form—"Been there." It was not a put-down so much as an expression meaning that you had had the experience and learned from it—expressing a sort of psychic empathy.

The first known use of the longer phrase dates from 1983. It appeared in newspapers, and about a decade later, "got the T-shirt" or "got the hat" was added for effect or for extra emphasis.

A very wise, old, famous person, who shall remain nameless, said to me, "At some point you really have to put your life's experiences down; they are quite unbelievable." Like Malcolm Muggeridge's, these are my *Chronicles of Wasted* (or at times, not so wasted) *Time*.

I was challenged to collect that experience (or, I suppose, plural, experiences), since they cross public, private, and social sectors and crisscross academe, politics, diplomacy, philanthropy, corporate life, and finance, and make a record. So here it goes, long title and all. The title was my publisher's idea, so blame him! I should also thank Chip MacGregor, my literary agent, and especially John Bloom, a writer from *The Daily Show*, who worked with comedian Jon Stewart, for his editorial comments on this text. Jerome Corsi brought this book to life and is to be credited for that, and thanks to my editor, Geoffrey Stone.

This is not going to be the typical autobiography. "Born on a blustery yet bright fall day on September 22, 1952, as a first child Virgo perfectionist and into a prosperous Presbyterian family of some pedigree in the city of . . . blah, blah, and blah." No. Everything I've ever written—all fourteen books and hundreds of articles, reports, and even more speeches—has been, well, serious, deadly serious; scholarly and well researched; thoughtful and overly analytical. Even the footnotes were acts of erudition. But not this one!

Oh no, this represents my other side, not necessarily darker side but cynical, and perhaps flippant side, where the real truth in its entire candor can be spoken. No holds barred, which in the original Old English meant that there were no restrictions. The term was likely derived from a wrestling analogy meaning that no holds were disallowed. I can picture the kind of fighting implied. Picture it in your mind when reading on.

I've had the good fortune (some say "blind ambition"; I say good personnel; if there is such a thing, it is a French military term and they didn't do particularly well), you see, to be at the right place, at the right time in my so-called brilliant career, to steal a trite phrase made famous in a novel by Miles Franklin, written in 1901. WASPs like to do philology and name the source of things—sort of like being a member of the DAR (Daughters of the American Revolution) or the Mayflower Society.

As a result, there are many stories to tell, a few holes to cover, and some bubbles to burst. Most of all, there are lessons to glean. All the names and events herein are real and remembered to the best of my human (therefore fallible) ability. They are true, not fabricated, but highly prejudicial and seen entirely through my rose-colored lenses. Some are indeed rosy scenarios; others outright scandalous! They are also edited to ensure there is nothing close to political correctness.

None less than Her Majesty, Queen Elizabeth, has knighted me into the Order of St. John, and to my family and closest friends, I am therefore known as Sir Ted or "aka Sir Ted." I was even given a jewel-encrusted "Sir Ted" white belt by my wiseass sons one Christmas as a prank that is distinguished in the way that the music of 50 Cent is distinguished. I also had the moniker on my Mercedes G55 AMG military vehicle along with the Lion Rampant license plate on the front, which does, I have to admit, cast a kind of *Braveheart* spell on casual observers.

But alas, Americans, even aristocratic ones, are not permitted the use of titles in our overly egalitarian society. Which is one reason why I suspect we are so enamored with the notion of royalty and all its outward trappings and doings. But since our own George Washington, old boy, turned down a kingship early in our founding, we are stuck with a republican form of government and a nonhierarchical society. Thank God or Jefferson (I guess it was Madison, come to think of it, in Federalist nos. 10 and 51) for all those checks and balances!

We do have our dynasties, Adams, Tafts, Kennedys, Clintons-almost (not yet), Bushes (again?), and my own preference, of course, the Roosevelts. The two presidents, my relatives and namesake, were related and intermarried and together held the Oval Office for longer than any other family—thereby defining both the twentieth century and modern world history.

Here, in a giant panoply, a sort of Golden Age Dutch landscape painting, if you will, is the story of where I've been and the actors involved in this all-too-human drama: *bene thema*, as the Latins would have phrased it. This is my bully pulpit.

Is it a tragedy? Or a comedy? Perhaps, some of each? I'll let you decide. And be sure to check out the takeaway(s), although there is no final exam. My thirteen favorites after each chapter contain a lifetime of collected wisdom or memories, for your edification.

I was recently asked what I am going to do *next*, since I've been precocious and done much and so soon (I was a preemie). Other than retire and die, which would surely be bad to accomplish prematurely. I would quote Gorbachev as my antiauthority, "[we] are born, [we] suffer, and [we] die."[1] I want to do more. Since I am not Russian in the least, my answer is instead typically, modern, entrepreneurial American: I will start all over again, just at a higher level—until the evening comes.

In a speech to the Palm Beach pundits, a caste of old, wealthy, yes, only Waspy men, on the topic of economics, I got their attention (some are hard of hearing) by stating rather loudly up front that I was close, very close, to working out a way (soon to be patented) whereby we could all "take it with us." In other words—transfer your wealth and who knows what else, maybe prominence or reputation capital (not wives), into the next life. They liked the idea a great deal, loved it—but truth be known, I haven't patented the quixotic formula quite *yet*.

1

THE GREATEST RACE

I can do all things through him who strengthens me. —PHILIPPIANS 4:13 (NASB)

White Anglo-Saxon Protestants don't have an ethnic pride day. It's not really a Waspy thing to do. We fly the flag every day.

But if they did have one, it would be the closing round of the Henley Royal Regatta.

I got there early.

It is the Fourth of July, in the millennium year of 2000, and the WASPs foregathered on the sceptered isle are about to witness the greatest sporting event in the history of the English-speaking world. I don't say this lightly. I've been to the Super Bowl, to the NBA Championship, to various international golfing events, including the British Open at St. Andrew's, but today I'm both nervous and exhilarated as never before—or at least as exhilarated as a WASP can be, since we're not, as a rule, an excitable species. I want someone to cue the *Chariots of Fire* theme. I'm like a pilgrim on his lifetime hajj to Mecca, and as the late afternoon start time approaches, I apprehensively quaff Brakspear ale with my raw oysters on the half shell. It is a rich, creamy milk shake of a beer known as the local pride of Henley-on-Thames.

For that's where I've come, to Henley, the little hamlet thirty-nine miles due west of London, where the Regatta is staged. This is the World Cup for WASPs, even though, yes, I know, *WASP* is an American term.

Question: What do you call a White Anglo-Saxon Protestant male in England?

Answer: A male.

Although my joke is no longer strictly true—England, like all other European countries, grows ever more multiethnic—it certainly seems that way during the week, when the hordes pour into Berkshire for the races. Henley is an elaborate $3 million party thrown by bluebloods in cravats, bonnets, stripped blazers, and flannel trousers, who would be appalled to take a single dollar for commercial advertising (my ale is poured into a sleek, twenty-ounce pub glass, sans insignia), much less resort to something as déclassé as a television contract.

I am surrounded by British upper class of the old school—you might say of the oldest school—and I, too, wear formal clothing despite it being one of the hottest, muggiest days of the year. In the tony Stewards' Enclosure, there are cantilevered women's hats the size of small topiaries, which they resemble, and there are men in Edwardian suits not seen since . . . well, since the Edwardians. There are one hundred thousand more spectators ranged up and down the ten-and-a-half-furlong course on the River Thames, where the regatta has been contested for almost two centuries. (The Olympic standard for a rowing course is two thousand meters, or 122 yards and four inches shorter than Henley. WASPs don't do metric. The length of the race, like everything else at Henley, is unchanged since 1839: 1 mile, 550 yards).

The whole event seems frozen in time. During the regatta you might not find any social type who couldn't also be found in, say, 1833, the year Tennyson wrote "O earth, what changes hast thou seen!" The cerebral cortex of Henley is contained entirely within the Stewards' Enclosure, which, despite having a name that sounds like a livestock pen, is in fact an exclusive canopied preserve marked out for the scions of Olde England to consume their expensive champagne, strawberries, scones, and petit fours, but not before a panel of grey-haired matriarchs have passed judgment on young ladies to ensure proper skirt length and punish violations of the no-culottes-or-short-skirts rule. The standard drink is a pint of Pimm's, which I use as a chaser to my Brakspear's. Strong mead for the coming battle royale. I feel *tribal*.

In the twenty-first century, it has rarely been "cool" to be a WASP. Supposedly, we are the last lingering remnants of a dead white European male culture that has come and gone, withering on the vine. When the sporting press condescends to write about Henley, they inevitably describe it as a "throwback." But to me it looks rather robust. Here we have the mingled bloodlines of the Saxons, the Angles, the Jutes, the Picts, the Normans, the Frisians, the Danes, and all the other palefaces of Europe, engaged in their original sport, which happens to be the oldest sport in the civilized world—rowing. (I use the term *civilized* loosely, since the original competitive rowers were Viking raiders, my less-refined ancestors. What I can say in their favor is that they all did their own rowing, as opposed to, say, the Romans, who, as we know from *Ben Hur*, used slave sculling.) What could be more athletic than this purely amateur pursuit that requires a training regimen more rigorous than professional boxing? What could be more thrilling than an ancient competition that is, in fact, the oldest continuous race of any sort on any continent? You don't have to answer. That was a WASP rhetorical.

Today's final race, in which I have a keen interest, will pit the heavy-weights of Oxford Brookes University against the lightweights of Yale University, who are well known at Henley because Yale's was the first collegiate boat club in the United States in 1843. (Obnoxious WASP aside: Although the Rutgers–Princeton football game of 1869 is frequently cited as the beginning of intercollegiate sports in America, the actual date is seventeen years earlier, 1852, when Yale rowed against Harvard in the regatta, which has been staged annually ever since. This is why I will refrain from shouting, "Boola Boola!" at Henley, as that would be a cheer invented for Yale football and, therefore, an anachronism.)

The Oxford heavyweight crew is heavily favored, not only because lightweights almost never defeat heavyweights (and would never even compete against each other except at Henley, which maintains the same open-class knockout-draw format from the nineteenth century instead of Olympic six-lane competition), but because Oxford is undefeated for years, the number one team in Europe, and holds the record for the Henley course. Yale is fresh from an upset victory at the national collegiate championships a few weeks earlier, but no one really expects the Americans to challenge.

I am here to wave the red, white, and blue of the United States (25 percent WASP) as well as the dark-blue pennant of the Yale Bulldogs (until recently 95 percent WASP). The fact that a British crew and an American crew are competing on English soil on the day of American independence from England is an irony that goes entirely unnoticed by both sides. That's because I and my fellow American spectators are such unregenerate Anglophiles that we regard the Revolutionary War of the late eighteenth century as little more than a spat among cousins that has long since been patched up. The Brits who are present regard it not at all.

In fact, like most WASPs, I'm an Anglophile to the core, a proud stereotype of the species. I was born into the Presbyterian Church, which my grandfather would have called the Church of Scotland, and at some point I grew so enamored of the Book of Common Prayer that I eased into Anglicanism, which is why you will find my final resting place already marked out among Colonials in the front row of the historic Old Wye Episcopal Church graveyard in Maryland. I am a golfer, a single malt scotch drinker, a member of many clubs, and a lover of yachts, Ivy campuses, and the hermetic rituals of secret societies. I grew up in Philadelphia and could have been the prototype for the Dan Aykroyd character in *Trading Places*, complete with girlfriends who, if not named Muffy, should have been. My parents christened me Theodore Roosevelt, after my paternal WASP ancestor, who remains one of the finest exemplars of the breed.

But I have even more personal reasons for being at Henley, as will shortly become apparent.

Umpire J. A. Stephenson calls Race Number 19 to the starting line at precisely 5:20 p.m. It is to be the final match of the meet, the conclusion of hundreds of two-boat duels over the past five days. There are nineteen different competitions in the regatta, but the Temple Challenge Cup, for eight-man undergraduate crews, is among the most popular because it attracts so many athletes from around the world, and as such it always concludes the racing.

The cup is named after the starting point for the race, "the Temple," an odd structure located on a tiny island of the same name, and inevitably described as a "folly" because it doesn't seem quite elegant enough for Henley. It was built in 1771 as a fishing lodge, based on designs unearthed at the ruins of Pompeii—now, *that's* lineage—and today is used for formal luncheons and, more to the point, picturesque watercolor representations of the splendors of the regatta. (It's not clear what the object of veneration in the temple was supposed to be, other than the gods of fishermen, or, to use the proper term, anglers.) Victorian silversmith Charles Fox, in 1835, made the trophy itself even though the regatta was not raced until 1839 and the Temple Challenge Cup was not added until 1990. Nevertheless, the Henley high sheriffs saw fit to commission an engraving of the Temple on the side of the cup, apparently to give Henley's most modern event a tinge of history. This, by the way, is a very Waspy thing to do. So is giving the complete history of a trophy.

And now the race has begun.

It is one of the peculiarities of the sport of rowing that you can't actually witness most of the race. The coveted Stewards' Enclosure is located at the finish line, so spectators must wait for the contestants to come into view at about the halfway point, called the Fawley mark, named for Fawley Court, a baronial estate on the left bank of the river, lately used as a school for Polish boys and a Roman Catholic retreat. (Don't ask.) Still some twelve football fields distant, the individual rowers remain invisible at Fawley mark, and the competing shells are mere specks, but thanks to the regatta's one concession to modernity—loudspeaker announcements relayed from the referee's chase vessel—there are periodic updates as to which team is ahead.

At the Fawley mark, on this, the greatest day of the Henley Regatta, Yale is ahead by an astounding boat and a half. The announcement is met by utter gasps from the polite but decidedly pro-British crowd. Since the eight-man shells are sixty feet long, this is a huge lead indeed.

Yale's only hope had been for a lightning start against the Oxford rowers, and that's exactly what coach Andy Card has ordered. Card is a bundle of intensity, 150 pounds of lean muscle, and a technical genius in race planning, and he calls his approach "bats out of hell." For the first quarter mile, the Yale crew has rowed forty-three strokes a minute, a vigorous but not unheard-of pace, but one they obviously can't maintain for the entire six- to seven-minute race. Card knows that the Oxford men, who weigh an average of fifty pounds more than the Yalies, will gain speed as the race progresses, and so, psychologically, he wants the other team to be pressing. He has used the technique several times already, trying to get larger opponents to over-stroke and flounder to catch up.

Rowing is the supreme team sport; it's more important for all eight men to row at the same rate than to row at the fastest rate. A strong crew is almost eerily unhurried; from a distance it appears that the oars are hardly moving, with no splashes and no effort beyond what seems natural. In fact, the coxswain is keeping the men at the maximum steady rate, so that all row at the full capacity of the weakest oarsman. If one crew member starts to pull a little ahead of the others, the entire boat slows down. This is why any trailing boat, especially in a two-boat race, requires maximum concentration from the crew. Using the same psychology employed in match play golf, Yale is hoping to knock Oxford off its game.

Yale has already been tested several times. Earlier in the week the Elis cruised into the quarterfinals, but then had slightly more difficult victories against Bath University and Manchester University. The day before this final match, they had a scare against an old rival, Columbia University, eager for an upset, and just pulled it out by half a length. The penultimate race was earlier on this final day—against Exeter University, a top English rowing school that had already defeated the South Africans, the Irish, and the French. In a mid-morning matchup, Yale was once again the underdog, but defeated Exeter by a full boat length, surprising the pro-British crowd. Card, ever the strategist, sensing the chance of a lifetime, spirited the team away from the hubbub and forced them to rest up for Oxford. To everyone's surprise, the Americans had made it to the finals.

And now they were not simply basking in the honor of competing against the Oxford men; they had the effrontery to be trying to win. Rowers are probably the best-conditioned athletes in the world–certainly the best-conditioned amateurs, since there is no such thing as a pro rowing contract. They get up at 5 a.m. every day of the year and sometimes practice five hours during the day, spread over two sessions. Yale even took yoga lessons. They obviously have powerful upper bodies, but eight-man rowing depends just as much, if not more, on leg strength.

Fortunately, the fifth seat (known as the engine room) in the Yale shell was occupied by a superior athlete named Ian Malloch, known to his teammates as "Our Patton," famed for sometimes willing crews to win. Andrew Morley anchored the team in the all-important stroke (eighth) seat, setting the rhythm for the others. The remaining six rowers were named Tyler, David, Thad, John, Patrick and, yes, another Andrew. Did I mention that rowing is a WASP sport?

The elements favored Yale as well. The wind was slight from the south, an almost nonexistent quartering crosswind. When heavyweights face lightweights against a steady headwind, the lightweights lose. Today's race would be won or lost with muscle and discipline, not because of the weather. At the Barrier, the first mark on the course, Yale had already broken the record for a quick start at 1 minute, 56 seconds. (The Barrier comes at roughly three-tenths of the total distance.) As they settled into a rhythm, both crews were keeping up a strong thirty-seven-stroke-per-minute pace, but that meant that as time went on, the strokes of Oxford men would count for more power. There were a few murmurs in the crowd when the Barrier time was announced, but when the two crews finally came into view, there were loud gasps. Up until now the guests from New Haven had been greeted with polite applause, but a boat and a half seemed too much for comfort.

The Oxonians are well aware that it is too much and start to make up the distance. The Oxford coxswain calls for a "power 10"—ten strokes at the crew's warp speed—and the course champions shift into overdrive. A few hundred yards beyond Fawley, the Oxford prow catches up to the Yale stern, and a hundred yards after that, Yale's lead is a mere two-thirds of a boat length. It's now a real race, and the question is how much Yale has left. A fast start always has consequences in the late stages of a race. After a mile of racing, at the Remenham Club marker, where both banks are teeming with crowds, Oxford has pulled to within a third of one boat length, or just two seats. Because the Henley course is longer than standard, Yale has reason to think it's only a matter of time.

And then, the impossible: Yale's coxswain calls for a "power 10" of his own, Yale starts to match the faster pace of Oxford, and with less than a minute to go, Yale is suddenly rowing thirty-eight strokes per minute, Oxford only thirty-six.

The screams are absolutely deafening as the two boats pull into the last hundred-yard stretch, all within the realm of the Stewards' Enclosure. And by some miracle—here is where I'd cue the *Chariots of Fire* music—Yale continues to increase the pace!

At the finish, the Yale crew is rowing at forty-one and a half strokes per minute, and Oxford actually loses ground. The final edge is two-thirds of a length, at a time of six minutes, thirty-seven seconds. When Umpire Stephenson records the official result, he adds, with precise and classic British understatement, that it was "a superb race and a fitting final and last race of the entire Henley Regatta."

The Yale crew has accomplished the equivalent in rowing of what the American amateur hockey team did against the Russian professionals in the 1980 Olympics. It is the first time that a collegiate lightweight crew has won any event at Henley since 1974. The aforementioned Ian

Malloch, rower number 5, my eldest son (All-Ivy three times; captain, Yale Crew; Leander Club [Pink Hippos]; and given the Yale Oar at graduation '02, as the winningest rower in Yale history, S&B, nickname: "Our Patton") celebrates by standing up in the shell and pumping his fist with intensity, a gesture that's a definite no-no in rowing, and especially at Henley. I ignore this breach of WASP protocol and run from the finish line, where I have been doing some obnoxious-American fist pumping of my own, all the way to the boathouse. I see Ian on the dock and he runs to me with a warm, embracing hug. And then he says something that no father would ever in a lifetime forget: "Great genes, Dad!"

There is champagne and feasting well into the night, but Ian's words are what make it the greatest sporting event in history. My Inner WASP can relax.

The lesson: the bloodline is secure.

MY THIRTEEN FAVORITE BOATS I HAVE OWNED

1. **40-foot CABO**, the BMW of sport fishing, from which I could catch many trophy fish, from marlin to wahoo to sailfish to tuna to dorado to sharks and barracuda. A CABO is the best platform for offshore fishing in the world.

2. **42-foot Cruiser**, a slow Cadillac of a family boat good for over-nighting and cruising in places like the Chesapeake Bay or the Intracoastal Waterway.

3. **60-foot Ocean**: my relative Bill Roosevelt and I kept this one at the Sailfish Club in Palm Beach, and we ran over to his place in the Bahamas and to fishing spots that are very secret. A real diesel hog.

4. **36-foot Luhrs**, with tuna towers as high as the sky, which my kids used to climb up and jump off of. Lots of rockfish were caught on this one.

5. **28-foot MAKO**: these boats are rugged and can take a beating. This one even had a cuddy, and we kept it in our boathouse on Spa Creek in Annapolis.

6. **42-foot Benateau sailboat**: I had a partial interest in this sleek one-sheet boat with my pal Charlie, who was a psychologist on and off the water. We made many trips together, including a few to the British Virgin Islands.

7. **22-foot Tanzer sailboat**: this was my father's gift. He and I sailed it together in his retirement all over the shores of Maryland and Delaware, and up every tributary. It was kept on the Wye River.

8. **19-foot MAKO CC**: my first Mako sold me on the make for life, and we took it far offshore and caught many a striped bass on the rocky shores of Massachusetts, especially during a full moon.

9. **17-foot Boston Whaler and Mastercraft**: these were wake-boarding exercises for my kids. Occasionally they even let me drive, but I was not fast enough for their taste.

10. **Yamaha jet ski**: we had this for only two years in Palm Beach and raced it all over the Jupiter Yacht Club—and got stopped by the marine police more than once.

11. **52-foot Morgan sailboat**, my captained yacht. We loved to have someone captain us while we snorkeled and went ashore.

12. **14-foot Sailfish**, my earliest sailing experience on lakes, and always tacking to get back—all wet.

13. **16-foot Old Town Canoe**, my first boat, which my dad and brother and I used every summer in the lakes of the Adirondacks, in upstate New York.

2

BURSTING THE TECH BUBBLE: IT'S FREE MONEY ANYWAY

And my God will meet all your needs according to his glorious riches in Christ Jesus.

—PHILIPPIANS 4:19

The stock market experiences a "bubble" when the price of stocks rises and becomes overvalued by any reasonable measure of valuation. Such stock market bubbles are at odds with the assumptions of efficient market theory, which assumes rational investor behavior. The behavioral finance textbooks say that cognitive biases can lead to groupthink and herd behavior. Often these kinds of markets become contagious. It is also said that when the taxi driver in New York City tells you about "hot" stocks to buy, things are near the top.

In the mid to late 1990s, the NASDAQ Composite Index spiked and then fell sharply as the result of what became known as the dot-com bubble. There have been a number of earlier bubbles, including the tulip bulb bubble in Holland centuries ago, the Mississippi scheme in France, and the South Sea bubble in England. These were all sev-enteenth- and eighteenth-century scandals bankrupting thousands of unfortunate investors. One author wrote about them as "extraordinary popular delusions and the madness of crowds."[1]

I'm no sports writer, so fortunately this is not a book about rowing or any of the other WASP sports (lacrosse, anyone?), but I wanted to begin with that story because, in a way, it reveals all the major themes of what this book *is* about: enterprise. Just as that finely tuned Yale crew was a victory of organization, dedication, skill, teamwork, diligence, and planning, so there are examples in nature of the opposite—people so caught up in the zeitgeist that they decide all of those virtues are no longer needed and what's called for is "the next big idea," the inside lane to nirvana, or the quick buck. Consider this next tale the *yang* to my son's *yin*. But first let me introduce myself.

Like the man in the Hank Snow song, I've been everywhere: 145 countries and counting.

I've got a passport that looks as if Rorschach threw up on it. I have enough frequent-flier miles to transport the population of Cleveland to Sydney, with first-class upgrades for the city council and a side trip to Adelaide. I've stayed in hotels in countries that don't *have* hotels, or even airports. For the past twenty-odd years I've been in the business of staging executive forums and meetings for the most prominent people in the world, so there's no concierge I haven't befriended or bribed. You name the city and I can tell you the top conference center, the best resort, the most entertaining "celebrity academic" at the best local university, two bartenders who know how to mix a Sazerac, and at least one joint that serves a ham sandwich at 4 a.m., even in countries that don't eat ham.

Before I got into this business, I was a high-level United Nations diplomat, a Wall Streeter, a political economy professor, and a policy wonk for both the US Senate and the State Department, so if we were to play the game "Six Degrees of Kevin Bacon," I would have to give you a four-degree handicap. Maggie Thatcher once introduced me as "our global Sherpa," which pretty much sums it up. I can not only show you how to get to the summit of Everest; I can arrange to get the bags of everyone in your company up there as well.

I've had wanderlust from boyhood. It's another WASP thing. My people were, after all, the first ones to get on the boat, as well as the first ones to get tired of the boat and convert to the covered wagon. The WASPs don't just travel, though; we expect the trip to make our lives better. Every place I've gone has been an education, and the third and fourth visits to the same place have been even richer than the first. After you've seen all the cathedrals and castles and marvels of nature on all the continents, you start to realize that it's your traveling companions who make mere trips into real journeys. I've dined and fraternized with several thousand very smart and accomplished people—and about seventeen who were absolute dumbbells—and the old adage coined by John Henry Faulk turns out to be true: if you know twenty different people well, you know the world.

One of those people I got to know well is the irascible and eccentric mouth of the South, Ted Turner. (By the way, that's the last time I'll describe anyone in this book as irascible or eccentric. Since most of my friends are professional dealmakers and/or professional thinkers, half are irascible and the other half eccentric. Ted happens to be both.)

We are now entering a world of high-stakes poker. There are no timid people. Ted Turner really is not very religious, but he respects people who are and he knows his Bible. He used to say that he agreed with the Ten Commandments, but he would feel a whole lot better if God had made them the Ten Suggestions. It's in a similar spirit that I'm offering the principles enumerated in this book (there are thirteen of them—WASPs aren't superstitious), trying to distill down into nuggets of practical wisdom what all the world's most successful people have in common—a sort of natural law, in Aquinas's definition.

An Australian television hack named Rhonda Byrne purported to do the same thing in a book called *The Secret*, in which she claimed that the movers and shakers of the planet have hidden away the first principles of the universe and perpetuated their own health, wealth, and success by exploiting this hidden knowledge—hidden, that is, until she revealed it on *Oprah*. But since I've spent most of my life with the very people that Ms. Byrne would call the "gatekeepers," I can attest that the guy they left in charge of the secret apparently got drunk and left the gate wide open. The people at the top are, for the most part, eager to share everything they've learned, with the possible exceptions of the formula for Coca-Cola and the code for the Google search engine. And what they have to share is less about observable principles than about character. Moreover, Ms. Byrne would be distressed to find out, I think, that 99 percent of those character lessons come, not from their various victories and successes, but from their failures.

Which brings me to the dot-com bubble. I was there. It was rich in character building.

Bubble is such a gentle word, though. It is reminiscent of my young daughter's friends, with their colorful, plastic bubble wands, creating birthday party fun with gentle waves of their hands. If we're going to get all metaphorical about a business failure, shouldn't we have a more relevant expression, like the Dot-com-Holy-Cow I'm-Broke Festival? How about the Dot-com Sherman's March Through Georgia Role-Playing Exercise? Or the Dot-com Godzilla Stomps Tokyo Episode? When used in economics, *bubble* would be better translated as "everybody going collectively insane and setting fire to all their cash." In the case of this particular bubble, which I was intimately involved in from 1996 till about 2001, more than $3.5 trillion magically appeared and then just as magically disappeared. I did my part.

Capitalism is a marvelous thing. It holds out the irrational hope that we can all be richer than the rest, which, if true, would mean there was no rest to be richer than. At its best, it's the foundation of civilization itself. At its worst, it's little better than a lottery. There have been many madnesses in its history, beginning in the 1630s when European speculators drove up the price of Dutch tulip futures—yes, contracts guaranteeing the delivery of flowers—and the entire nation of Holland was seized with "Tulip mania." (It ended the same way a tulip bouquet normally ends.) Then there was the South Sea bubble of the early eighteenth century, when thousands went broke buying stock in the slave ships of a British trading company. (Sometimes justice *is* poetic.) Closer to home, we had the Mississippi scheme, in which Scotsman John Law deluded both the French and the English public into investing in a derelict company that supposedly would have a monopoly on the vast wealth of the American West, thanks to his new gateway town of New Orleans. (John Law had never seen western Kansas, or, for that matter, New Orleans in the summer.) Speculation in shares of the Mississippi Company was so frenzied in 1720 that it had a paper capitalization seven times larger than the nation of France itself. All that fizzled in about thirty days' time, Law was forced to flee France, and tens of thousands were completely ruined.

The dot-com collapse of the late nineties was part of this tradition of collective lunacy, but, unlike most others, it was based on assumptions that turned out to be true—namely, that we were in the midst of a technological revolution, that the Internet would change the way we publish and communicate forever, and that certain pieces of broadband real estate would be worth billions in the future.

Unfortunately, the devil is in the details. Knowing there's a revolution going on and knowing what to do in the midst of the revolution are two entirely different things. And here's where it gets personal.

As an investor, the advantage of dwelling among the "first movers," as I do, is that you know what the first moves are. As Martha Stewart famously, and fatally, said, "Isn't it nice to have brokers who tell you these things?"

The disadvantage of dwelling among the first movers is that you know what the first moves are.

I was in the vortex. I was not only an investor; I was frequently consulting for these companies, setting up high-level strategic think tanks for technology CEOs and handling their relations with the business press and their best clients. I was swamped with insider information. And almost every single person who brought me into an Internet venture was smart, experienced, business savvy, and hard-nosed.

There were no starry-eyed neophytes in this saga. Paul Dietrich, a tall good-looking Republican lawyer with black horn-rimmed glasses, from the "Show-Me" state, for example, brought the first company I invested in, to me. And he showed me! When I look today at the prospectus for Meridian LLC, even knowing that it fizzled, crashed, and burned, it still doesn't look that bad! The idea was that there were fifty-six stock exchanges in so-called emerging markets—Third World countries testing the capitalist waters—that would need to be monitored and tracked electronically for those exotic traders who wanted to find stock plays in, say, Kazakhstan utilities, Pakistani pharmaceuticals, or Estonian perfumeries. Meridian would provide real-time electronic trading services for all these marginal markets so that if you needed to chart a Malaysian commodity at 4 a.m. in Columbus, Ohio, you could.

I knew a lot about these markets from my days as a Cold War diplomat at the United Nations office in Geneva, and later as one of the top executives at the World Economic Forum, famous for its annual summit in Davos, Switzerland (we'll get to that saga later). Still, it wasn't so much the basic idea that drew me into the party; it was the assembled dignitaries who were putting in their own money. Dietrich himself had been editor and publisher of *Saturday Review* during the last of many attempts to revive that middlebrow bastion of American letters in the mid-eighties, and since then he had held court at a white-shoe Washington legal firm where, among other things, he represented Mikhail Gorbachev. (If you think about it, Gorbachev is the *first* emerging marketeer.) Paul looked the part of a studious and responsible gentleman—he reminded me of Clark Kent, complete with the horn-rimmed glasses—and he had credentials out the wazoo, including being the author of the *Emerging Markets Guides* for Reuters. He was on the board of the Catholic University of America, was an editor of *A Guide to American Foreign Policy*, and was known as a critic of the World Health Organization, which, in my circles, always counted for intelligence.

Paul's elevator pitch was an easy one to make. In the nineties, the formerly Communist world was still trying to figure out capitalism, and there were so many companies being created every day that everyone was looking for a trusted source of fast, reliable data. Someone was going to provide it, and we had a head start. He offered me a substantial stake and a board position in return for one hundred thousand dollars and some of my own know-how getting the company launched. He also introduced me to some of the other board members, who had the kind of résumés that, in the rarefied circles of high-flying Washington deal making, were household names:

- Frank Bonsal, sometimes called "the godfather of venture capital," a Baltimore-based start-up and IPO specialist who had created some five hundred companies, many of them in the medical field. A Princeton grad, he was on the board of Johns Hopkins Hospital.

- Ed Matthias, one of the founders of the mysterious Carlyle Group, located five minutes from the White House in opulent offices where we had our initial meetings, with the kind of catering normally not found this side of the Four Seasons. The Carlyle Group had so many Pentagon, CIA, and defense contracts (its former chairman was Donald Rumsfeld's bunk mate at Princeton), and so many offices in foreign countries, that it had long been a bugaboo of conspiracy theorists trying to plumb the depths of the military-industrial complex. Matthias was the ultimate Washington insider—double Ivy (Penn and Harvard Business), a Penn trustee, a National Gallery trustee, and on the committee managing Carlyle's $85 billion in investments. With his wire-rims and receding hairline, he was like a shadow CEO, offering his hospitality while looking for the entire world like the ultimate K Street fixer and brain trust.

- Richard Burt, onetime ambassador to Germany, chief negotiator at the SALT talks, partner with Henry Kissinger in a consulting firm, member of the Council on Foreign Relations, onetime security correspondent for the *New York Times*, member of the

Aspen Institute's Middle East Strategy Group—should I stop now or enumerate the other thirty-seven bullet points on Rick's curriculum vitae?

- Harlan Ullman, a naval commander who invented the military theory of "shock and awe" while teaching at the National Defense University, where Colin Powell was one of his students. Harlan was the type of two-fisted guy you loved to have in any board room—150 combat missions in Vietnam, a national security consultant, a PhD in international affairs, finance, and economics. He could talk about the destroyer he commanded in the Persian Gulf, but he could also describe several spectacular venture capital successes he'd had in Asia while serving on the board of the Wall Street Fund. He allegedly got caught up in the "DC Madam" scandal in later years.

I won't bore you with the whole list, but suffice it to say that this was an assemblage of titans, backed by investors such as Novak Biddle Venture Partners, who specialized in early-stage information-technology companies. Meridian LLC was heavily capitalized, had all the right players, had all the right ideas, and was perfectly poised at the beginning of an explosion of international stock market activity.

And it was a complete and utter failure. All that real-time data turned out to be not such great data after all, and usually not in real time. There were just fundamental problems in getting quality information from, say, the Baku Stock Exchange, much less getting it on the day it happened. Dietrich had left his law job at Jones, Day, Reavis & Pogue because he believed in the venture, so it wasn't a matter of the principals not being committed. Dietrich even assembled his own team of high-powered geeks to assemble raw data from every emerging market in the world. Ron Readmond, the former head of Charles Schwab, had come on board as chairman, partly because the strategy was to ramp it up and then after three years sell it to Thompson or Reuters or one of the big aggregators and walk away ten times richer. That was always the price point for selling: ten times your investment. (This was the early days of the dot-com boom. Later deals were greedier and wanted even a hundred times an investment.)

But the data coming in from the overseas markets was never as good as we thought it would be. The timeliness issues were costly to solve. The technology required constant upgrading. We would need thousands more geeks than we had to solve the specific problems of stock exchanges in places such as Kyrgyzstan that, not too many decades ago, were dusty trading posts on the Silk Road frontier. As more and more capital was required, egos got bruised. There's nothing more painful than being in a boardroom where a dozen people, all accustomed to being told how right they are, are attempting to define why they're apparently wrong. The meetings became less cordial. At one gathering it was suggested that we had a marketing problem. The solution: hire one of the board member's mistresses to solve it. We did. She sucked at marketing. Finger-pointing ensued. Additional rounds of equity raises failed to make any difference. The company finally sold for pennies on the dollar, and there were no longer any catered lunches at the Carlyle Group. We went our separate ways. Or most of us did, anyway. As Ron Readmond, a real take-no-prisoners tough guy said to me at the time, "You find out who your real friends are when you lose money together."

Ron proved what a real friend he was. He showed me several more ways we could lose money together.

By the time Meridian collapsed, Ron and I were socializing a lot at his farm near Goose Cove on Maryland's bucolic eastern shore. We shot geese, we drank together, we ate crabs, we talked about his world-class French bulldogs—and soon another Internet venture loomed. Readmond felt bad that I had lost money in the Meridian deal, but the next one was closer to his bailiwick. He was known as a pioneer in the nascent world of online financial services (the other pioneer, of course, was, ahem, Bernie Madoff), and in the course of doing business with his old Charles Schwab cronies, Ron had run into a New York whiz kid named Andy Klein. Together they had formed a company called Wit

Capital—the "wit" part referring not to scintillating intellect but to the Belgian ale called *witbier*. For Andy Klein, a securities lawyer, was also a beer lover. Klein had started Spring Street Brewing Company in 1993, but needed capital to extend distribution of his exotic neo-Belgian brew beyond the confines of lower Manhattan. He found that capital through the sale of shares over the Internet. He essentially spammed his way to success, launching the first-ever Internet IPO (initial public offering) and raising $5 million by getting beer lovers to pony up small amounts of capital in exchange for equity. Readmond and Klein thought the same idea could be applied to dozens, if not hundreds, of other companies, and Wit Capital was formed to be a sort of online retail investment bank, taking small companies to the lucrative IPO market. Wit would be an eBay for new stocks.

From its offices over the legendary Strand Bookstore in Greenwich Village, Wit quickly gained attention and traction. Goldman Sachs put in $25 million in return for 22 percent of the company. Another $25 million came from a venture capital firm called Capital Z. When Bob Lessin, who ran the investment banking division at Morgan Stanley, came over to be board chairman, it started to look like a can't-fail prospect. Ron got me in early as the thirteenth "original" investor, and this is how crazy things were: he had to argue with his partners to *allow* me to give them a million dollars. The first investors were called "friends and family," and they got the best price. Ron's argument to his partners was that my particular expertise would help with their dog-and-pony shows (grueling one-city-per-day trips to sign up investors), and since I was friendly with all the business publications and editors, they needed me for public relations as well. Reluctantly, the others conceded and agreed to take my mere million.

When Wit finally went public in June 1999, it opened at $9 a share. My shares had been purchased for $1, so I made $8 million that day. Two weeks later the stock was trading at $38. You do the math. It would eventually rise to $48. I could retire. I could move to a remote foreign island, my own island. Ron started negotiations with me to merge my own company with Wit Capital in an arrangement that would cost me nothing; just some stock trades when the market had hiccups.

And then Wit itself had a hiccup. It went down a little bit, for no apparent reason, stayed there for a few days, then went back up. We noticed that Wit had competition now, an indication that the idea was sound. Charles Schwab, Datek, E*TRADE, Intuit, and Merrill Lynch were all announcing Internet IPO services. Was that a good thing or a bad thing? Nobody knew. Then the stock went down some more.

Call me a wimp, but I was nervous. I told Ron I was thinking about selling a few of my shares, just to protect myself. No one likes to hear that from an insider. You either drink the Kool-Aid or you don't. Ron was not very happy. I dropped the subject.

But the stock wasn't bouncing back. I knew I was going to need a good excuse if I wanted to sell anything. That excuse came when Ron said he wouldn't be able to do the merger with my company at the moment because of "accretion." I'm not sure exactly what accretion is—especially since this company was accreting, it was SEcreting dollars—but all I could think at the time was, *Thank God for accretion!*

My shares had not yet been registered—which would have locked me in and made me subject to insider rules—so I sold them as quickly as I could and got a good price. Everyone else rode the pony down to zero. I was fine with being a wimp.

Should I have taken my newfound millions and moved to St. Barts? Of course.

Did I? Of course not. Twenty million dollars, give or take, was a lot of money, but in the Internet world of the late nineties, it was not considered "the end zone," as we used to call it. After you've played in Washington, and played in New York, there was still one big ocean of money left to frolic in, and that was Tokyo.

And I already knew the Nipponese landscape. I was, in fact, wired at the top, having served for a while on the board of a Japanese merchant bank called Zeron. Zeron was run by the mercurial Shigeru Masuda, one of those larger-than-life Asian investors who was not just bicoastal, or bi-continental, but bi-hemispheric, and, in true Japanese style, divided his time equally between New York and Tokyo on a strict unvarying schedule, flying between the two cities precisely twenty-six times per year. In America he lived in a swank New York City Fifty-Seventh Street condo, drove exotic sports cars, and lavished attention on blondes. In Tokyo he was the protégé of the shadowy Akio Morita, chairman of Sony and godfather of Japanese business. Shig ran the investment arm of Zeron, called Zeron Capital, as well as several other funds with military names, such as the Shogun Fund, that put money into play from Sony, Toyota, Fuji, and other Japanese *samurai* business titans. These were the days when the Japanese were investing all over the world, onshore, offshore, any shore, and routinely expecting 35 percent returns.

Shig and I had become fast friends. I went on his board as vice chairman, and he started offering to bring me in on his various can't-miss Internet deals, many of them long before the IPO was announced. Shig had been a famous equities trader on the Japanese stock exchange and had been parlaying that reputation into deals with United States firms that wanted a Japanese partner. What made Shig such a genius was that he could talk the language of both countries. There were quite a few Japanese investors who could explain the Americans to the Japanese, but very few who could make the Americans feel chummy with the Tokyo *shiretsu*. Shig could turn on the loose Western charm when he was in America, and return to the reserved hierarchical system of Japan when he was in Tokyo. He wore his hair in a distinctly non-Japanese Michael Boltonesque shag, right on the edge of being a mullet, and he favored silk jackets sans tie. If you didn't know who he was, you might mistake him for the best-dressed doorman at the trendiest downtown dance club, complete with the designer shades. As a result, Shig had brought Japanese capital to everything from a Las Vegas sports medicine clinic to the QVC shopping network. He "got" America in a way most Japanese didn't, which may be one reason he was famous for being one of the few Japanese heavyweights who did *not* invest in Hollywood movie studios in the eighties. (The Japanese now regard those plays as some of the dumbest they ever made.) Shig also loved to play golf—even at the famed Pebble Beach course for which his cronies had paid too much.

To illustrate how connected he was, Shig once asked me to conduct a private seminar in the Theodore Roosevelt Suite of the Willard Hotel in Washington for one person—Shoichiro Toyoda, chairman of Toyota and of the Japan Business Federation. It's not really possible to express the stature of this man in American terms; he would be like a Bill Gates, a Warren Buffett, and a Donald Trump all rolled together in a regal personality that in many ways was more respected than the prime minister. Needless to say, I did my homework. But I can't say that the great man retained much of what I presented. The imperious Toyoda, silver-haired, with his trademark wire rims and big grin, ignored almost everything I said and kept asking about the dollar–yen rate, then proceeded to make a speech about how unfair it was, chopping the air karate-style and raising his voice in a military staccato. Eventually he pronounced the presentation finished. Toyoda may not have liked the exchange rate, but he trusted Shig for investment advice. Toyoda is the only person I ever met, by the way, with a doctorate in "fuel injection."

Shig, on the other hand, had a PhD in enthusiasm injection, and his pet Internet project near that time was a company that would revolutionize both the construction and the aviation industries by selling access to data needed by businesses in those fields. It was such a sure thing that they had already acquired tens of millions in venture capital, and once again, they could "get me in" if the CEO liked me. I was taken to a meeting near Dulles Airport with the CEO by Sam Pai, a Chinese-born Internet banker who was tall, thin, dressed like a rock star, and always had a new chick hanging off his arm, a cell phone for an office, and after the introductions were made and the sake consumed, the CEO did indeed say that I could certainly get in on the "friends and family" level. What he didn't tell me was that he didn't know the first thing about construction *or* aviation. In a now-familiar pattern, the company was gone within a year, and so was my money. Shig shrugged. To him it was no big deal, not enough money to matter. That kind of money, to Shig, was a rounding error. He consoled me by saying that was chump change compared to what was coming next.

And what was coming next was by far the biggest play I ever got sucked into—the infamous Kozmo.com. It started when Shig invited me to dinner with Kozmo founder Joseph Park at his favorite restaurant in New York's Chinatown. Over dim sum and egg rolls, the twenty-six-year-old Park told the story of how, as an analyst at Goldman Sachs, he had tried to order a book from Amazon.com one night, couldn't make his way through all the delivery options, got frustrated, and ended up going to the bookstore to get it. If Amazon.com had a delivery service, he thought, he could have had the book within thirty minutes. And if that was true of books, it was equally true of every other product sold over the Internet. Park's vision for Kozmo.com was to provide one-hour delivery of anything, anywhere, and to do that he had PowerPoints and spreadsheets and flow charts showing how it was the same way that FedEx had begun, just on a different scale. FedEx was all about planes; his company was all about bicycle messengers. Kozmo's intense army of cyclists would be decked out in bright green and orange, partly for safety and partly because the distinctive safety helmets looked really cool in orange, making the bike squads resemble a squadron of Tour de France racers instead of delivery guys.

I can't say that Park was a charismatic salesman, although that was his reputation at the time. He was short, nerdy, and a little scary in his ability to down twelve courses of dim sum. But that was the kind of guy who ran all the hot Internet companies of the late nineties—the kind who, as one of the Kozmo execs put it, "always got beat up in high school." Park apparently liked me, he wanted me in, and this time they even said they would "kick somebody else out" if necessary to make room for my $10 million. (Whoever got kicked out can thank the chef and me that night.) The exit strategy, this time, was to ramp the company up, take it public, then sell when it got to a price of fifty times investment. That would mean $250 million for me, which would qualify (just barely) as the end of the end zone.

Did you miss my end-zone dance? So did I. Park and his partner, Yong Kang (his real name), who was described as the Spock of the team, went into business, established bicycle-delivery teams in twelve major American cities, and eventually had thirty-five hundred employees delivering everything from videos to snack foods to—the single most requested item—yes, condoms. Kozmo.com became the go-to place for stoners, agoraphobics, couch potatoes, and the merely lazy. The company was so big that Starbucks was in for $25 million and Amazon, Park's inspiration, came in for $60 million. The capital raise eventually started to approach $300 million when, along about April 2000, some pesky analyst—one of Park's former cubicle-mates at Goldman?—pointed out that revenue was not even approaching $2.5 million per year and, by the way, Kozmo was losing money on every single delivery.

The crash came overnight. Diehards held on for a year—although the board kicked Park out three months after the stock tanked—and everyone lost their jobs. Then everyone lost their money. Park went off to Harvard Business School. (Aren't you supposed to go to Harvard Business School *before* you raise $300 million?) Yong Kang was last seen stoically reboarding the starship *Enterprise*. And almost a decade later, the only evidence of Kozmo's presence are the hundreds of orange bicycle helmets, which can still be seen late at night on the streets of New York City, now used by City Harvest, which pedals from restaurant to restaurant, collecting leftovers for the homeless.

If you've been paying attention, you probably want to ask me a question now, and that question would be, "Why did we all stay in? It's interesting that everyone who writes about the dot-com bubble seems to know that the companies were overvalued and that the crash was inevitable. If you listen to the idle talk at a cocktail party, no one invested in the dot-coms anyway—everyone passed on it." In fact, almost the exact opposite is true. Everyone invested, and everyone thought the valuations were fair—until April 12, 2000, the day the NASDAQ changed everyone's mind for us. I wasn't the only person who invested in one Internet deal after another.

But to take a little longer view of the matter, we were all under the spell of certain intellectual trends of the day, many of them birthed by Nicolas Negroponte's book *Being Digital*, which had defined how the world was changing (e-everything). The other aspect that's difficult to grasp from the outside is that these deals were not necessarily sequential but overlapping, so that the enthusiasm of one carried you into the next. Yes, we knew there were failed companies. Yes, we knew that things were moving a little too fast for safety. That's why we attached ourselves to the big names and the big ideas.

Besides, the successful dot-coms—and there were some—were so wildly profitable that you had to go back to the days of the nineteenth-century robber barons to find examples of that much wealth concentrated in those few hands. Mark Cuban, the unruly Dallas Mavericks owner, is an example of someone who got in early, got out early, and took his cash to places far, far away from anything involving the Internet. Nobody today even remembers the source of his wealth, a company called broadcast.com that Cuban sold to Yahoo! before anyone realized how worthless it was. Many investors knew that the market was unstable, but they were managing their money like a Hollywood studio, knowing that the next twenty movies might be flops, but the megahit that comes in on the twenty-first play is worth two hundred times what you invested on all the others.

And we had real-life examples. Much bigger than Cuban, for example, was David Wetherell of Boston's "Silicon Alley." Wetherell had become one of the fifty richest men in America as the high-flying founder of CMGI. Nobody talks much about CMGI anymore, but as late as 2002 Wetherell's company still had naming rights to the stadium of the New England Patriots. That's how big it was. The stadium was actually advertised as the new CMGI Field, although, by the time it opened, CMGI had unloaded that asset to a shaving cream company, so the Patriots today play in Gillette Stadium.

Wetherell's Internet success story was a little atypical. Raised on a chicken farm in Connecticut, he was a math major at Ohio Wesleyan who was precocious about computers. In 1986 he founded a little technology company called CMG Information Services, and it developed a sort of proto-Amazon, called BookLink, by which books could be ordered and sold with a PC and a modem. (This was the days before people went to commerce websites.) He made his first fortune when he sold BookLink to AOL. Then, when the Internet really broke out, he was one of the few guys who already had credentials for the thousands of investors who wanted in. As a result, CMGI became an Internet conglomerate, eventually holding stakes in more than fifty companies, including AltaVista, Lycos, Tribal Voice, iChat, Spamfish, AuctionWatch.com, CarParts.com, MotherNature.com, Geocities, and many others. By the late nineties he was routinely making billion-dollar deals. "We have companies growing at a rate of 1 percent a day," he told *Time* magazine. "The internet is growing at a rate of 3 percent a day. If you can't make money in this business, then you might as well go pick oranges."

I almost got burned up in the CMGI comet.

My introduction to CMGI came through a friend named Carol Vallone, who was the CEO of North Shore Boston-based Universal Learning Technology, a pioneer in online education that later merged with WebCT. I had been an adviser to WebCT and helped them raise start-up capital, and she was right there with CMGI on Boston's Route 128, the epicenter of the East Coast tech business. Carol thought I should do business with CMGI, thought, in fact, that CMGI should purchase my company. So on a certain day she met me at the airport and drove me over to the opulent headquarters in Andover at a time when CMGI was a $40 billion company. Wetherell, the balding, mustachioed impresario of tech's brave new world, greeted me in his trademark black T-shirt and grey suit. I got the usual speech about "viral growth," or I should say "VIRAL GROWTH!" because Wetherell spoke with all the zeal of Vince Offer pitching the ShamWow! Wetherell's game plan was to acquire real estate on the web and worry about profit later. He wanted portals, content sites, advertising ventures, marketing ventures—he was creating a company that was both vertically and horizontally integrated, as though he intended to own the entire Internet. Things were happening so fast that Wetherell had his board on "emergency status," meaning they all had to be available 24/7 to approve his deals. And one of those deals, he hoped, would involve my own company, which he wanted to buy, thanks to the recommendation of an MIT professor who was on their board and another friend of mine.

The only thing I didn't like about his offer was . . . his offer. There was no cash at all, just $7.5 million in CMGI shares. The employment agreement didn't inspire much confidence either. It looked as though David Wetherell could end up as the president of my company if he ever so desired. Everything was on the come. I was already inclined to regard it as a wasted trip, but on my way back to Logan International Airport, my cab driver sealed my opinion. Apparently he had made many trips to CMGI headquarters and he had seen "many things." Forty billion dollars can buy a lot of hookers and drugs. The onetime manager of Genesis (a factoid the press never failed to mention when talking about Wetherell) apparently still lived like a promiscuous rock star.

But he did have his run. As early as 1997 both Intel and Microsoft were major investors in CMGI. In the year 1999, Wetherell sold Geocities to Yahoo! for a billion-dollar profit. In June of that same year, CMGI paid $2.3 billion for 83 percent of the AltaVista search engine, then owned by Compaq. But by October 1999, Wall Street was starting to get nervous. As with many other high-flying Internet companies, nothing was showing up on the monthly profit ledgers. CMGI announced a "burn rate" of $63 million per month, with $654 million cash on hand. Those numbers aren't terrible, but when you use the term "burn rate," that means somebody has finally asked the question, "What's your burn rate?" Doubt has crept in. Wetherell gave tours of his multimillion-dollar Cape Cod mansion and was blithely optimistic when anyone would question the fundamentals of his business plan. "It would be sinful to be making money on the Internet right now when it's growing this fast," he told *Business Week*. (Hmmmm. What happened to "If you can't make money, you should be picking oranges"?)

Reality struck home for Wetherell in April 2000, the same month it struck home for Kozmo, when CMGI's stock price went from $163 to $10. Downsizing began, including a decision *not* to do the planned AltaVista IPO. In retrospect that decision seems odd, since AltaVista was at that time the most sophisticated search engine and had all the bells and whistles that would eventually be monetized by Google. The rest of CMGI's failed ventures were just failed ventures. Furniture. com bankrupted after burning through $45 million. BizBuyer.com ran through $70 million. In 2002 the stock price of CMGI itself fell below $1, a fact that didn't prevent Wetherell from ordering a $23 million private jet. He closed down company after company, but most of the next few years would be spent picking through the bones of a carcass. Fortunately, thanks to intuition and a gabby cabbie, that carcass didn't include my company.

My final brush with the Internet cash-devouring monster—at this point they were brushes instead of full-scale scalpings—involved the fabled Internet Capital Group, which was the king of technology for a few years as its stock soared past an astronomical $400 a share. Years before dot-coms existed, I had met their founder, Pete Musser, at the crusty old Merion Country Club in suburban Philadelphia. Pete had run the legendary Safeguard Scientifics out of Wayne, Pennsylvania, and Safeguard was known as one of the top tech incubators in the world. When Safeguard later morphed into ICG, the investor list included IBM, General Motors, AIG, Dartmouth, Comcast, Compaq, BancBoston— you get the idea. In fact, by 1999 the company was valued at $60 billion—larger than GM.

One of the scores of ICG companies was one called eMarketWorld, headquartered in Richmond, Virginia, and they too were interested in a merger with my firm. I had several meetings, and they seemed very confident about their business plan, which was to vertically integrate a number of businesses by doing conferences online and off and then using some proprietary systems to capture their e-business. They wanted my company and its clients mainly to give them access to CEOs. We had a three-month courtship in early 2000, with many lawyers coming and going, with both sides doing their due diligence. They didn't want to give me much cash, but they were offering $9 million worth of their soon-to-be-publicly-offered ICG-backed stock. We were within days of closing the deal when the bubble burst forever. ICG had been worth $212 a share in December 1999, but on February 1, 2000, it dipped to $106 as all the insiders sold their shares. By April it was down to $40, by November $10, and by 2001 it was under $1. That's about when they called back, begging me to join them and help run what remained of their business. They eventually filed for bankruptcy. Not even Pete Musser escaped. The old-school Main Line billionaire who had sold Comcast its very first cable TV franchise in 1963 had to sell his twenty-four-acre estate in Bryn Mawr to satisfy the alimony demands of a trophy wife who was thirty-eight years his junior. Things were tough all over.

The question I asked earlier—why did so many go so wrong?—is not easily answered, but it's a common scenario when all the rules seem to change very quickly. In this case, the people who understood the technology didn't necessarily understand business, and the businesspeople who wanted to invest in the tech boom didn't necessarily understand computers and software. Why did Google eventually succeed where Alta Vista had failed? Google wasn't really a better mousetrap; it was just a mousetrap that wasn't run by David Wetherell. Why did pets.com self-destruct, whereas today petmeds.com thrives and the online website for Petco makes money hand over fist? In part it's simply a matter of scale. Just as hundreds of railroad companies in the nineteenth century went bankrupt, only to be consolidated into one big, healthy company by J. P. Morgan and his cronies, so there were hundreds of Internet companies that miscalculated both the scale and the timeline. People assumed that the Internet was a game changer, and it was, but it didn't guarantee any advantage for first movers, nor did it guarantee monopolies for people who had proprietary technology. Everything was much more complicated than anyone could ever know. Joseph Park, the boy genius of Kozmo, used to make apocalyptic predictions such as "No one will ever go to a physical store ever again" and "You have to play to win it all; you can't play not to lose" and "Internet stocks are all about momentum," and—who knows?—if he'd had another $300 million and two more years to spend it, maybe he would have cornered the market on delivery services forever and made trips to the mall obsolete. After all, there were not that many people buying *anything* online in the year 2000, and by some estimates his numbers were no worse than Amazon's. Guys like Park had always preached, "We'll sell the idea now and figure out how it makes money later," and for a long time Wall Street indulged them. It wasn't that they had some cocka-mamie business model that was wildly inaccurate—"figure it out later" *was* precisely the business model. What might have worked better was the business model of Park's Korean parents, dry-cleaning operators in my native Philadelphia. They saved their money and expanded slowly, over a lifetime of toil and long hours.

I began my story with my son's triumph as part of the Yale crew that defeated the much larger, more famous Oxford Brookes team, to make my first point about enterprise: Goliath doesn't always win.

This chapter was about my own ups and downs, my losses, in a business world where everyone believed the hype and no one did the real homework, because there were so many geniuses around, too many smart people investing too many millions of dollars. As an economist, I knew we were going through a period of "creative destruction," to use the phrase popularized by Joseph Schumpeter and the Austrian School of Economics. Normally a period of creative destruction means a lot of young, nimble companies wipe out the companies formed by their grandfathers. But in this case it was the upstarts who, backed by the biggest investors in the world, became bigger than the companies they were designed to replace, and ended up getting spanked. Which leads to my real point about enterprise:

Goliath doesn't always win.

The first one I hope you'll find inspirational, this second one cautionary.

MY THIRTEEN FAVORITE WORKS OF ART

1. *Tower of Babel*, by Pieter Brueghel the Elder. This medieval Flemish painter strokes the conscience about vices really well. I find the Babel story all too relevant, and we never, ever seem to learn.

2. *The Garden of Earthly Delights*, by Hieronymus Bosch. What could be better than a garden of temptations? Beauty abounds, and the undercurrent is a reminder of the original garden of Eden and the sin of Adam and Eve.

3. *The Raft of Medusa*, by Théodore Géricault, the icon of nineteenth-century French Romanticism.

4. The Sistine Chapel frescoes, by Michelangelo, an awe-inspiring wonder. You can hardly believe your eyes—perhaps a glimpse of heaven on earth.

5. *The Starry Night*, by Vincent van Gogh, the original scary story, I guess, both haunting and captivating!

6. *The Birth of Venus*, by Sandro Botticelli. Is there any higher paragon of feminine beauty and delicacy than Venus?

7. *The Night Watch*, by Rembrandt, a real political statement of the Dutch Gold Age by the true master. It raises all sorts of philosophical questions about the State.

8. *David*, by Michelangelo, a sculpture exuding manly strength and heroic stature. Harvey Mansfield, the Harvard philosopher, loved it.

9. The *Isenheim Altarpiece*, by Niclaus of Haguenau and Matthias Grunewald. If you worship or are in the Christian tradition, this piece says it all.

10. *The Third of May 1808*, by Francisco Goya, the great battle picture of suffering that shows Napoleon had no mercy.

11. *The Scream*, by Edvard Munch, sort of an overarching statement about the fright of the twentieth century and its madness and insanity.

12. *The School of Athens*, by Raphael. What academic could not be drawn into the depiction of the dialogue in its first and best form?

13. The *Mona Lisa*, by Leonardo Da Vinci. Yes, she is beguiling and mischievous, and her eyes seem to follow you wherever you go.

3

THE CITY OF BROTHERLY LOVE/HATE

The fear of the LORD is the beginning of wisdom: and the knowledge of the holy is understanding.

—PROVERBS 9:10 KJV

To discover what a WASP is supposed to sound like, all you have to do is watch any Hollywood movie made in the 1930s and set in any large American city.

The city you're hearing is Philadelphia. Long before there was a Broadway theater—long before there was much theater at all in New York—there was theater in Philadelphia. And so old is the theatrical tradition in my native city that the so-called Main Line accent was the standard for all performance, including motion picture performance, until shortly after World War II. Think of Bette Davis or Katharine Hepburn in their ingénue years and you have all-but-perfect Philadelphia enunciation.

By the time of Philadelphia's own Grace Kelly, her stage manners perfected at the prestigious Stevens School in northwest Philly, standards in the motion picture industry had started to decline, and some would blame the masculine New York accent of Lauren Bacall for that decline, although more properly the opprobrium should belong to Nancy Hawks, wife of Howard Hawks, who trained Bacall to speak that way. Once Marlon Brando started mumbling on-screen, it was all over for the Main Line. But my point is that my Philadelphia is the one that doesn't exist anymore, the Philadelphia of manners, enunciation, tradition, and a belief that arts and culture are contained between the Schuylkill and the Delaware, concentrating especially around the Walnut Street Theatre and the Philadelphia Museum of Art, with afterparties at the venerable Philadelphia Club.

And yet the reason that the American accent of the twentieth and twenty-first centuries varies so greatly from the British accent that fostered it is that, mingled among those Main Line Philadelphians with a direct line back to London were equally ancient bloodlines going back to Stockholm, Berlin, Dublin, Helsinki, Cardiff, and Amsterdam. Philadelphia was the original immigrant city, thanks to William Penn, whose views on tolerance attracted not just fellow Quakers but Mennonites, Pietists, Anglicans, Catholics, and Jews who would have been ostracized anywhere else. Before the term "melting pot" had even been coined, Philadelphia had already patented the concept.

My family was the *very* essence of Old Philadelphia, and I was born into its full Presbyterian heyday. I was born at the dawn of the baby boom, bawling into existence at Temple Hospital while Harry S. Truman was president, but General Eisenhower would reign through most of my early childhood on Rittenhouse Square and then, later, in old Olney and the Main Line suburbs.

When I say we were Presbyterian, I probably need to explain that, too, since today there are so many denominations using *Presbyterian* in the name that it can mean anything from churches in the Deep South that speak in tongues (the only tongues in the Malloch household were occasional servings of beef tongue, which was unpopular because a little too east European for our WASP tastes) to assemblies so liberal that lesbians are being ordained by transsexuals (my ancestors are turning in their collective Church of Scotland graves). This was not the religion of my youth, the one found at Tenth Presbyterian Church, where the renowned Dr. Donald Gray Barnhouse taught the essentials of Calvinism. The way I was brought up in the faith, Presbyterianism was reserved, disciplined, sensible, never calling attention to itself but standing for clean, upright, decent living. It was "Old Philadelphia" that made our family rich in culture, but it was the Presbyterian Church that gave us our discipline.

That heritage colored almost *everything* we did. When I was not yet two, my younger brother, Richard, struggled into the world, almost dying at birth as an Rh-negative baby. My parents changed his middle name to Paul, because, like Saint Paul's, his life was a miracle. He spent most of his first six months in the hospital, and I was made to understand that I was to be his protector in life. Of course, I had to do my share of teasing and picking on poor Richie, to toughen him up, but anyone who ever made the unthinking decision to pick a fight with him got the holy Presbyterian crap beat out of him. I was an "enforcer" from the outset, and the role made me feel from an early age that I was on my own, that we all had to be tough and on the lookout.

It was a time when the sobriquet City of Brotherly Love still had meaning for affluent upper-middle-class Protestants, especially those with Scottish surnames and Old Dutch family roots. The advantage of being a baby during the baby boom was that the struggles and penury of the previous generations somehow got converted into dividends for us.

Whatever I wanted, I more or less got. We were in an ever-expanding boom economy, and that translated into all the predictable suburban niceties—two cars in the garage, a solid roof over our heads, a stable home life, and most important, an extended intact family that embraced us, protected us, and wanted to see that we succeeded. Our parents had survived the Depression, and they were determined that we should never have to go through anything resembling the same thing. There was a Santa Claus, and he brought many gifts, and not only in late December. Somehow this made sense to us. Every Sunday in church, we sang the doxology, praising God "from whom all blessings flow." What we didn't realize at the time is that Mom and Dad and their parents and every adult in the clan were helping God along by protecting us from want.

That's not to say we got a free ride. Far from it. The Protestant work ethic is so deeply ingrained into old-school Presbyterianism that people who don't work at least a half day on Saturday are regarded with suspicion. We retained our immigrant mind-set even into the third and fourth generations, and the children were not spared. My grandparents, especially, believed that God helped those who helped themselves, and that you basically received whatever you put in. That meant risk, sacrifice, and dedication brought riches; that effort and toil brought independence; and that yes, faith might be more important than works, but just barely. I can still see my Scottish grandfather with his wiry eyebrows and distinctive Perthshire brogue, reminding us that card-playing amounted to idleness and that anyone who refused to walk four miles to save twenty-five cents on bus fare was just plain lazy. While my grandmother was raising nine children, he had worked sixty-hour weeks, speculated in land even through the Depression, and lived to the ripe age of 102 without ever stopping working.

On the family's hundred-acre country farm in Lancaster County, in a place called Honeybrook, out among the Amish folk, they grew fruits and vegetables, raised sheep and geese, and—most tellingly—used the Yellow Pages for toilet paper. (Charmin would have been a needless expense.) Almost every weekend the extended family would travel "up the country," where we all did chores, shared meals, and spent time together. The farm had a Scottish name, *Sunny Brae*, and it did look a lot like the land of heather.

The word *thrift*—not a popular concept among children—had a real meaning for us whether we liked it or not. One of the rituals of growing up in the picturesque brick-and-stone neighborhoods of old Olney was the day you were taken down to the Market Street skyscraper that housed the Philadelphia Savings Fund Society, the oldest savings bank in the United States, where you were issued your Scotch-plaid savings account book. So ingrained was the tradition that PSFS was allowed to sponsor school pageants dedicated to the ideals of thriftiness—teaching wide-eyed first graders that it was better to sacrifice treats and movies and arcade games for the wonders of compound interest—and the program was so successful that the bank had a separate counter in its Grand Hall just for students, with handy step stools for the tiniest ones.

Since very few of us had actual jobs, it was expected that our parents would pay us what was called an "allowance," but only after we had completed our assigned chores. I was paid to do things like collect and recycle newspapers and cans, take out the trash, polish shoes, and, of course, mow the lawn. We could have afforded landscapers and handymen, but that would be all but sinful when there were two boys in the house who needed to "learn the value of things." The only time you could withdraw money from your PSFS account was at Christmas, and that was so you could responsibly purchase gifts for the other members of the family. There were other ways to make money, too—easier ones, in my case. I got paid for every A on my report card, since scholarship was highly regarded and education viewed as the only sure pathway to success. I earned almost all As right up through high school graduation and into college, and no small part of the reason was this very financial incentive. Well, maybe the fact that my father was our scoutmaster, too.

But those were not "real" jobs, and I was an upwardly mobile little pipsqueak. As soon as I was old enough to work outside the home—age eleven, in the fifth grade—I applied for and was accepted as a paperboy, for the afternoon daily, the *Philadelphia Bulletin*. I was the youngest boy in my delivery district but lucked out and got one of the very best routes—about a hundred houses in a three-street area that included my own block. Every afternoon I would race home from school, mount my bicycle with the large basket on the front, speed back to the storage garage where all the papers were dropped off, and start gathering and folding so that I could sail through the route without stopping. The faster I finished, the sooner I could get onto the athletic fields to play (depending on the season) baseball, football, or basketball—my true childhood loves. After I got good at it, I could finish the entire route in fewer than thirty minutes, throwing the papers from the bicycle with pinpoint accuracy (I never broke a window, the occupational hazard of paperboys everywhere) and getting huge tips from my pleased customers. A paperboy is actually an entrepreneur—he buys the papers from the publisher at a set price and then collects from the customer, losing money if the customer moves away without paying or otherwise stiffs him—and it was the very best early lesson in how to fend for yourself financially. I happened to have blond hair and blue eyes, and I was trained to say, "please" and "thank you" a lot, and I found that those traits translated into extra money as well, especially when the newspaper started selling accident insurance, using the paperboys as sales agents. I sold so much of the stuff that I won an all-expense-paid trip to EXPO '67 in Montreal, Canada, setting the Philadelphia record for new nickel policies.

The only problem with being such an outstanding paperboy was the recurring nightmare I had every fortnight or so. In my typical dream I would forget to deliver my newspapers, causing the equivalent of the apocalypse in my narrow Olney world. I would often wake up in the middle of the night, worried, shaken, and terrified that I had let everyone down and would now be an outcast. Nothing of the sort had happened, of course. In fact, I never missed a single day and, if I had to be away with the family, always arranged for substitutes. But to this day the dream, or at least the memory of it, still haunts me.

In retrospect I see that dream as the dark side of the Protestant work ethic. It was so ingrained in me—the idea that virtuous duty and thrift and hard work and responsibility were required of me and always would be—that it had become a permanent part of my psyche. As I came of age in the Philadelphia of the 1960s, many people my age were dropping out and dropping acid, trying to create new dreams and hallucinations, in a rebellion against everything the culture of my forefathers stood for. I experienced very little of that, but later I saw the fruit of it: a coming age of entitlement and overly pampered children who were sometimes decadent before they turned eighteen, never understanding the work ethic in either word or deed except as something to be lampooned. Elton John's "Philadelphia Freedom" was a song that could be taken several ways, but I always thought of it as a memorial written for a city that was passing away. For those of us who had grown up there, that song was part of the ethos of the soul of the city, the sort of anthem that said true freedom is something to be found in a hardworking community, whatever Philadelphia neighborhood you were from, black or white, rich or poor, Jew or Gentile, from the Brook to B&O, from the Speedboys to Germantown. We all knew what that meant.

Most of our organized family activities in the city involved either improving ourselves, helping others, or both. We went to the YMCA, we read scripture in church, we undertook missions to Delaware Avenue to dispense soup to the homeless, and I was forced to take trumpet lessons every week at Zapf's on Fifth Street. (My brother studied the only slightly less raucous tenor saxophone.) But the main ritual I remember was my father taking us—or, to be honest, dragging us—to the Free Library of Philadelphia, an imposing citadel in Logan Square that symbolized all the accumulated wisdom of the universe. We would go every other week, usually on either Friday night or Saturday morning, and each time we were instructed to choose three or four books that we had to finish reading by the time we came back. This forced reading program undoubtedly improved my vocabulary and turned me into a proto-intellectual at a very young age. I loved social studies and politics, but my favorite genre was biography. Presidents, captains of industry, generals, religious leaders from the three great monotheistic faiths, adventurers, sports stars—I must have consumed hundreds of biographies in my youth, searching perhaps for secrets as to what makes men great. I still remember books about Thomas Jefferson, Benjamin Franklin, John F. Kennedy, Babe Ruth, all the early explorers, Andrew Carnegie (who helped build the Free Library and other libraries all over America), and, naturally, Theodore Roosevelt.

Even in grade school I tended to look at life as a contest, but early in the sixth grade is when my destiny was finally set, once and for all. After all the students at my elementary school were given a standardized test, my mother was urgently summoned to the principal's office along with the parents of a chubby Jewish girl with glasses, named Michelle. We weren't in trouble. They wanted to tell our parents that henceforth we were to be regarded as gifted and talented. I later found out that the test had been the familiar Stanford-Binet, and we had both scored over 130. So we got special reading materials, a good bit more attention from teachers, and the proverbial pats on the back from our elders. We both became accustomed to the phrase "so much potential"—and an odd thing happens when you hear that over and over again. What people expect, they often get. When you're told you're bright or special, you start believing it yourself.

I was made head boy. Even more impressive, I was appointed sergeant in the toilet patrol—yes, that's what I said—as part of the principal's crusade to stamp out various nefarious incidents involving younger boys in the restrooms, incidents that are too gross to describe here. I was fairly full of myself at the time, partly because there had never before in school history been a sergeant appointed at such a young age. In terms of grade school politics, it made it all but inevitable that I would eventually be elected captain of the safety patrol in eighth grade. (And I was.) The safety patrol was overseen by a distinguished, older Jewish gentleman, named Mr. Rebber, who apparently also saw something in me, because besides the usual duties involving assigning patrol boys to each intersection and ensuring safe crossings with our flags and poles, I was charged with . . . leading. That meant I got out of school earlier than anyone else, the ultimate badge of honor for the ultimate teacher's pet. "Teddy, do this" and "Teddy, do that" became constant refrains, and my reply was always a quick and cheerful "Yes, sir" and "Yes, ma'am," and I have to admit that I loved it, even after many of my classmates started accusing me of being a perpetual brownnoser. Achievement of any sort separates you from your peers, but it was a separation I relished. It didn't help my reputation that my voice changed early and I was asked to join the All Philadelphia Boys Choir, as a baritone.

But I was not just an overachiever and a grown-up-pleaser, I was certifiable in my drive to be the biggest buck in the herd, the alpha male and, while I was at it, the omega male as well. I wanted it all. I was ambitious and driven and so over-the-top that if a kid were to do this in 2015, he might be sent to the school psychiatrist and treated for something like hyperactivity. We had none of that in North Philadelphia, though. I was timed as the fastest kid in the city in the hundred-yard dash. I anchored the four-hundred-yard relay on the track team. I was bigger than the rest of the kids my age, so I dominated the basketball league that became less white and more black with each passing year, getting most of the rebounds and dunking over the other centers. In baseball, which we played from the coldest windy March days all the way through late September, I was both the home run champion and the pitching ace. My Little League team—the Phillies, of course—won the World Series every year. And when I graduated from junior high school I was awarded the Olney *O* Award, which stood for "Outstanding" in everything. If I didn't get all As, win the championship, run the fastest, or get the prize, I felt I was either not working up to my potential or, even worse, badly disappointing my teachers and family. And the one thing I never ever wanted to do was disappoint.

Oddly enough, the United States as a country and Philadelphia as a city were preoccupied with more than the schoolboy achievements of Teddy Malloch in the late 1960s. We didn't know this at the time. For those of us in the more or less stable neighborhoods, it was a phenomenon that crept up on us. But even as I was building my reputation at Olney, Philadelphia itself was coming apart.

Back then Philadelphia was America's third-largest city, an industrial center, a center of culture, and, of course, the caretaker of the country's most cherished historical sites. But my first year in high school was full of the racial problems that were besieging the country at that time, and it started a slow decline that in some ways never got corrected. I played both football and basketball, but in basketball I was the token white kid as we traveled to every high school in the city from the northeast to the slums of West Philly. And many of the gyms we played in were poor, dilapidated, even dangerous places. At some our coaches wouldn't even allow us to shower—we were sent directly back to the bus as soon as the game ended. After one game someone shot a referee with a staple gun, so all the remaining games at that school were played in a silent gym, with no spectators. Race had now become the defining feature of everyone's identity. The city that had welcomed all races, all religions, and all creeds was about to be torn apart by its own diversity.

The year was 1968, and after Martin Luther King's assassination, the wheels were coming off in cities all across the country. Political upheaval, race riots, a culture at odds with itself or, perhaps, a culture not sure that it was a culture anymore, created challenges to all authority, any authority, and then the inevitable striking back at what looked like anarchy. The world was full of hate and distrust, and nowhere was this more apparent than Philadelphia, where the mosaic of history had set side by side every race and every nationality. My parents eventually feared the inner city that had nurtured us, and we fled for the lily-white suburbs, the aforementioned Main Line.

The Main Line was actually the name of the original Pennsylvania Railroad track, the one that ran (and still runs) from Philadelphia to Pittsburgh, but in local usage the term meant all the little affluent towns along the route, from Merion and Narberth to Bryn Mawr and Villanova on out to Radnor, Wayne, Berwyn, St. David's, and Paoli. Anybody could buy a ticket, but few could afford to get off at any of those stops. That meant I was leaving behind some of my best friends, not because they wanted to stay but because their parents couldn't afford to leave. Jay Cohen, a happy-go-lucky Jewish kid, never left the city and never traveled beyond the Jersey Shore in his life. Pat Durkin and Robert Sullivan, two Irish Catholics, stayed behind but transferred to the local parochial schools. Franny Oldynski, a Polish Catholic and my best friend of all, went to La Salle University, the very urban Christian Brothers school right there in Olney, and later became a social worker in the horrible crime-ridden North Philly ghetto that the area was rapidly becoming. Ritchie Fox, another classmate, was convicted of murder and sent to the big House. But we Mallochs were WASPs, with money, with good graces, and so our world was quite different—we had the resources to adapt and, like our immigrant forefathers, to take our culture with us.

My father was one of the civilians who ran the Philadelphia Naval Shipyard. As a decorated World War II Navy captain, he had seen a lot of action in the Philippines aboard a PT boat and still had the light, muscular build of a sailor even into his advanced years. He knew Jack Kennedy in the War and didn't think much of him as a showboat from a rumrunner family of no distinction. Besides, he drank torpedo juice and skied behind his fast boat when he should have been doing military drills. Like most of his generation, my father couldn't or didn't want to talk much about the war, although he kept a souvenir bag with some awfully poignant pictures, as well as Jap money, a bloody Japanese flag with writing on it, and a rusty bayonet. To us children it was the stuff of folklore. All of his brothers and sisters, our uncles and aunts, had served in that war as Marines, Waves, WACs, or Navy enlistees. We were patriotic in more than words and pledges.

My mother, on the other hand, was a traditional wife and total mom, staying at home, taking care of the family and house throughout our formative years. She didn't reenter the workforce until we started high school, and her second career in credit analysis was simply an extension of her household management—she was always the best with figures and budgetary matters. She was also loving, caring, and devout. We prayed at every meal. We read devotions every night at dinner as a family. In the summer we vacationed at a faith-based camp in the Adirondacks on a lake fittingly named Lake Pleasant.

My parents had a high regard for learning and so always combined vacations with educational excursions. We went to museums; state capitals, such as Harrisburg and Albany and Dover; all the attractions of the Smithsonian Institution and the government buildings in Washington; and—more than was necessary—to Colonial Williamsburg, the capital of Virginia under British rule. In many ways we felt they were giving us the education they would have wanted for themselves—and they were getting it along with us. I will never forget or discount the investment and love my parents showered on us. The hardest thing I ever chose to do was give my father's eulogy. I loved and respected him and what he stood for so much.

The two dominant themes of my childhood—God and country—sometimes merged. One such time was during the Cuban missile crisis of 1962—the scariest thirteen days of my young life. To understand how we dealt with it, you have to return to a time when there was no separation between church and state, at least in our minds. Church attendance was never casual for us, and certainly not voluntary. Even as a boy, certain words in the catechism, like "You are marked as Christ's own, forever," struck me to the core. We were Christ's own, and we believed it. But we equally believed in America and all it stood for—liberty and freedom, the rule of law, the importance of protecting our heritage against threats.

All of this was paramount and embedded in my psyche, and it was one great thing: we were marked out for Christ and we were marked out as Americans as well. When it looked as though we were on the verge of nuclear war in 1962, we were sent to the basement at school to do drills, going under our desks with hands covering our heads—"duck and cover," as the school film instructed us. Fighting and winning the Cold War was something we had to do, and we set about that task with all our might, all our souls, and all our minds. I was an eager enlistee and, to this day, relish the thought of being a Cold Warrior. My church had a youth group that met on Sunday evenings and was called the Jet Cadets. Military and religious metaphors, though thought of as opposites, frequently mix well. I can still remember the words and music of our anthem: "We are Jet Cadets for Jesus / We are pilots for our Lord / We will bomb and strafe . . ." You get the gist. I think something of this same spirit must have still been coursing through my DNA when, almost three decades later, I was part of the diplomatic team in Europe that successfully brought down the Berlin Wall. The Jet Cadets, and Jesus, were ultimately triumphant, and young children in Olney would no longer have to duck and cover.

My Philadelphia had come and gone by 1970, the year I graduated high school at an all-white suburban palace (we did have one black running back on the football team). I had the same things I'd had in Olney—First Honor Roll on my report card, letters on my jacket in three sports—but Philadelphia, at the eastern end of the Main Line, seemed far, far away. It had become an unsafe place, crime-ridden, racially charged, sexually permissive, infested with drugs, divided according to class and economics, and just plain dirty. Far from being the city of brotherly love, it was a city at hate with itself. People tell me that today Olney is finally making a comeback, that the melting pot has returned, only this time it's not Germans and Dutch, but Koreans, Colombians, West Indians, Arabs, Chinese, Puerto Ricans and Cambodians. But the WASPs never returned.

I owe a huge debt to my own father. I am a junior, after all. My father is best memorialized for what he was—a good man and a follower of the risen Christ. He knew Him and followed His commandments. His whole life as testimony makes absolutely no sense without understanding this single fact.

My father was born on a cold winter day in 1921 in Philadelphia; he had eight siblings and graduated Northeast High School in Philadelphia. He attended college and Reformed Episcopal Seminary, although he was never ordained—he had a lay ministry besides his real job as an engineer. He was in many ways the product of the Great Depression. He served honorably as a captain in the US Navy on a PT boat in the Pacific Campaign during World War II and was decorated for his brave service. For nearly forty years he worked in a number of civilian positions at the Philadelphia Naval Shipyard, which he ended up running. He was married for just short of fifty-nine dedicated years to Dorothy, our mother, and his dear wife. I recently located a Bible he gave her on their engagement to be married in 1950 and it was inscribed with a

Bible verse, saying he would comfort and care for her at all times. And that he did.

A Sunday school teacher and superintendent, deacon, scoutmaster, and volunteer to many charities, my father is best characterized, I think, as a "lover of Christ."

About a decade ago, knowing that Pop-Pop was ill and had only so long to live, I sent him this personal letter of thanks. It was a private gesture then, but I decided to share it here.

Dear Dad,

Here are a number of remembrances and thanks I have for all you have done and given me in this life to pass down to future generations.

SACRIFICE
I still vividly remember you getting up before dawn and coming home after dark, walking up Marwood Road tired after a hard day's work at the navy yard but still having time for Mom and us and all our sporting activities, not to forget your kibitzing, horseback rides and accordion playing.

CHARACTER
I witnessed in your treatment of others, mission work and your generosity, as well as tithing, a strong Christian character, based on spiritual values.

FAITH
You always put God at the center of our lives and your own. The church was a central part of who we were and what we worshipped. I will never forget all the summers at camp and that powerful influence on each of us.

STUDY
People often ask me where I took up learning and the answer is our weekly trips to the public library on Fifth Street and all the

biographies I read as well as those homework assignments that were checked all summer long.

DISPOSITION

Your cheerfulness and smile even in times of stress and difficulty made a lasting impression on showing a Spirit-directed life of real happiness.

FAMILY

Above all else the family was the basis of our lives and it held together through holidays, sports, scouts, and visits through all these many years. I still have some of the postcards you sent us from places like Puget Sound and Rockford, IL when you missed us so much. We will always remember the simple phrase—goin' up the country—and those visits to "Sunny Brae," the family farm.

COURAGE

It has only been more recently that I have come to fully respect and honor the contribution of your "greatest generation" to what makes America truly great and a lasting hope for all mankind. I am proud of your military and public service and for valor in time of war and as a cold warrior.

GRACE

You knew your purpose in life and had the grace, common sense and good will to follow through on it.

Thank you for what you have done, who you are, and what you have practiced over a lifetime. You have left your mark on the world and in our lives. God bless.

Your son,

Teddy

When my father passed in the early morning hours of Sunday, April 19, 2006, my only and younger brother, Richard and I were fortunately able to bid farewell to his body, knowing his soul was already in glory. We read him his favorite psalm, Psalm 121.

Fortunately, I also had two excellent high school teachers who shaped my thinking and helped me deal with the changed world. One was a liberal, Ella Rhodes, the other a conservative, John Grech. Ella Rhodes mentored my senior advanced-placement social studies project on "the American Negro and the Civil Rights movement." John Grech coached the team when I represented my school on an academic TV show, answering groundbreaking questions such as, "What is the capital of Mongolia?" But increasingly everything in Philadelphia and the Main Line seemed irrelevant.

I was seventeen and feeling the eternal itch of all boys coming of age, ready to throw off the mantle of parents and relatives. So I said good-bye to everyone. I visited Aunt Thelma and Uncle Jules, who lived across the street, and Nana Banana, my loving angel of a grandmother and a prayer warrior if ever there was one, who lived down the block, and I told them all that I was going to the Athens of America. I was going to Boston and I was going to have what my family still considered a modern luxury: a college liberal arts education.

Unfortunately, the one thing you can't be guaranteed in this lifetime is that you'll receive unconditional love and support of the type I received in my childhood, so in keeping with the WASP principles of enterprise, which I will enumerate in other chapters, this one is going to be counterintuitive. I got it from Dr. Barnhouse:

God gives you unconditional love and support, whether you realize it or not. Those who realize it, reap the fruits of it.

MY THIRTEEN FAVORITE WASP MOVIES OF ALL TIME

1. *The Philadelphia Story*. It is the classic, right? The best romantic comedy, with the likes of Cary Grant, Katharine Hepburn, and James Stewart.

2. *We Were Soldiers*. Randall Wallace, the director, is a friend, and he made the all-time best, accurate Vietnam movie.

3. *Braveheart*, the ultimate story of Scottish bravery and the rally cry for "Freedom" by Mel Gibson (complete with a blue face)!

4. *The Great Gatsby*, a bit overdone, perhaps; and the remakes are not nearly as good as the original. Read the novel—it is better than either.

5. *Brideshead Revisited*. This Evelyn Waugh saga is the UK version of aristocracy gone awry.

6. *High Society*. (Well, it was.) This is the 1956 American musical comedy film directed by Charles Walters and starring Bing Crosby, Grace Kelly (a Philly girl), and Frank Sinatra.

7. *Trading Places*. This is the ultimate WASP comedy, and you won't stop laughing out loud—LOL).

8. *A Man for All Seasons*. The acting is world-class, and I find attachment to the hero—Thomas More. Henry the VIII is a bad guy.

9. *Rocky* (only because of the Philadelphia setting). I know the sequels go on and on, but try running up the steps of the Philadelphia Museum of Art on Benjamin Franklin Parkway. It will give you goose bumps.

10. All of the James Bond movies. I re-watch them every year!

11. *The Thomas Crown Affair*, a quirky jewel heist with the ever urbane, if not Waspy, Pierce Brosnan.

12. *The Best Years of Our Lives*, or not . . .

13. *Chariots of Fire*, my ultimate best and all-time favorite. A Scottish Calvinist wins the gold at the Olympics and keeps the faith.

4

THE ATHENS OF AMERICA

The fear of the Lord is the beginning of knowledge, but fools despise wisdom and instruction.

—PROVERBS 1:7

I overshot the Athens of America by a few miles and ended up in the Sparta of America, better known as the little town of Wenham, hard by the famous rustic coastline of Boston's preppie North Shore. This was the home of Gordon College, which is where they take all the stereotypical pictures next to the dictionary entry for "Small Charming New England Liberal Arts College."

The only difference is that, having been founded by a Congregationalist preacher to train missionaries in the early nineteenth century, Gordon was religious-oriented, trending toward the heavily Calvinistic, and more fond of discipline and rule making than the timekeeper in a Chinese sweatshop. Chapel was mandatory twice a week, and on Fridays, convocation. The ivory on the tower was hard and resilient. Given the turbulent times, with many mainline Protestant churches questioning their future and the nation questioning just about everything, little Gordon College was stalwart enough to resist the hedonism of the rock-and-roll drug culture, but not quite adventurous enough to foster the kind of forward-looking, open-minded humanistic scholarship I had hoped to find.

That's not to say I wasn't enthusiastic about being there. For I had, after all, come to Boston suffused with that fervent academic ambition that only an eighteen-year-old with no knowledge of the outside world can embody. What I was looking for is what Cardinal John Henry Newman, the Oxford don and later Catholic convert, had defined in 1854 as the true university (read his *Apologia Pro Vita Sua*), a place where all the knowledge of the universe and all the seekers of that knowledge are joyously conjoined. (As I said, it's an undergraduate fantasy.) "If I were asked to describe as briefly and popularly as I could, what a University was," Newman wrote in his *Apologia* or history of his religious opinions, inspiring idealists like myself, "I should draw my answer from its ancient designation of a *Studium Generale*, or 'School of Universal Learning.' This description implies the assemblage of strangers from all parts in one spot—from all parts, else, how will you find professors and students for every department of knowledge? And in one spot, else how can there be any school at all? Accordingly, in its simple and rudimental form, it is a school of knowledge of every kind, consisting of teachers and learners from every quarter. Many things are requisite to complete and satisfy the idea embodied in this description; but such as this a University seems to be in its essence, a place for the communication and circulation of normed thought, by means of personal intercourse, through a wide extent of country."

Gordon College should have been perfectly situated to realize Newman's ideal, located as it was in the greater Boston area, which has more institutions of education and more students than any other place in the world. But unfortunately the world and Gordon were moving in a different direction, a direction that continues to this day, toward the multiversity or the no-versity at all. It was the first, but hardly the last, disillusionment I would have with the over-exalted halls of academe.

But if you're going to immerse yourself in the university experience, who wouldn't want to do it in Boston? For anyone who has ever matriculated in Massachusetts, the seasons of New England remain vivid in the memory, somehow forever wrapped up with the frisson of learning new things. Continuing my obsessive study habits from high school, I finished my bachelor's degree in three years because I attended every summer session, took five courses for most terms, and signed up for independent studies on such esoteric subjects as behavioral politics, socialist realism in art, and historiography. Socially, I didn't completely fit into any of the college's demographic groups, which included students from old mainline churches, a growing number of "evangelicals" (a new term at the time, growing out of the various reform movements and social strictures), and a contingent of charismatics, or, less politely, holy (or, holier-than-thou) rollers. But that didn't matter much for a library rat who consumed books the way dopeheads devour Twinkies.

In short, I made the most out of a college that turned out to be less than it first seemed. Fortunately, there were some profoundly gifted teachers there, like the eccentric Thomas Howard, a C. S. Lewis and Milton scholar, dedicated hiker, and confirmed liturgist, who dressed in outlandish Old English garb with a cape and top hat and who eventually obliged to resign for jumping over the wall to Catholicism. Then there were Grady Spires and Malcolm Reid (a Kiwi), philosophers in the true sense of the term, including their "existential" lives.

My advisor, Bill Harper, was a very witty Christian sort of socialist in prominent black-rimmed glasses that became a close friend, and over many cold pints of bitters I witnessed his maturation beyond Fabian socialism to Kuyperian thought and everything Dutch. Stan Matson was a wonderful American history teacher and debater, but left in a huff after getting sideways with the administration. John Mason was "Econ John," a libertarian from the Austrian School and that rarest of birds in those days, a defender of the market. But it was probably Dave Franz, a classicist, who influenced me the most, through the agency of the European Seminar, which he ran. The European Seminar was sort of a "grand tour" (in the old sense of the term) and intellectual boot camp rolled into one as we spent eight weeks traveling around western Europe, starting at the (very Reformed Protestant) Free University of Amsterdam and moving every three days or so to another institution, where we would sit wide-eyed and amazed by lecturers with odd accents and foreign points of view. I first took the Seminar in 1972, and I credit it with the wanderlust that has remained with me my entire life. In later years, after becoming an academic myself, I would go on to lead that same European Seminar seven times, expanding its itinerary to the Soviet Union, Greece, and Israel.

So I'm indebted to Gordon for allowing me to see Western civilization up close and in all its gritty detail for the first and many times, but I can't sugarcoat the overall experience. Gordon had too many inferior professors, a stilted and outdated curriculum, fake zealotry, and a moral code straight out of the seventeenth century, beginning with a ban on drinking or smoking on campus, which of course meant a lot went on—just off campus.

We were not exactly the cast of *Animal House*, but we did pull the common college pranks, sent a container of human dung to a rival school, and hung out at our favorite all-night greasy spoon (super subs in Beverly, still the best cheesesteak on the planet). We keyed losers into their rooms, cut chapel, and drank too much Southern Comfort. (Actually I only drank the vile stuff once, and got so sick I swore off it forever.) I was such a professional student, though, that I was more likely to spend extracurricular hours mimicking the same sorts of things that occurred during the curricular ones. I was selected, for example, for a program intended to thaw out the Cold War, called the National Study for the Presidency, in which top students from the United States and the Soviet Union held joint symposia. (Why were the Soviet youth all forty years old? we wondered). I was awarded the usual academic honors, dean's list, Who's Who in American Colleges and Universities, but by the end of my three years was itching to move on because, in some of my classes, like those presided over by political-theory hack Phil Bom,

I felt I was teaching more than I was being taught.

And of course I fell in love. This was my own *Love Story*, as in the Oscar-winning film of that title, also set in Boston. The Gordon coed who would become my wife, Lynette (why do parents choose such fetish names), was quite attractive, and the two of us bonded at a screening of *Dr. Zhivago*—what heedless young lover could resist that movie? But we turned out to be oil and water in later years.

She grew up on a forlorn, dilapidated dairy farm in a tiny town south of Albany, New York, called Westerlo. The first time she took me home to meet her parents, I thought we were going to perish while passing over a rickety bridge as we moved back in time and into true rural poverty. The marriage was likely doomed. She had a depressive personality, whereas I pretty much take everything in stride and see the glass as more than half-full. But I rather liked the idea of a "fixer-upper." She later tended toward New Age beliefs while I stuck to the traditionalism of my youth. She studied psychology in an effort to get over her "childhood issues," and even though I helped her write her dissertation on—what else?—childhood depression, I was never convinced that she was getting her ED for the right reasons. Note to self: Beware anyone involved in psychology, as they are likely deeply flawed individuals.

Our fifteen more or less painful years together, especially the final ones, nonetheless had three wonderful results. Ian (middle name St. Andrew) is our oldest. Trevor our middle son, is the great fly fisherman; the largest salmon caught each year in Scotland wins the Malloch Challenge Trophy, named after our Scottish relative, P. D. Malloch. Nigel, our youngest and the black sheep, who majored in being a playboy at preppy Rollins College in Florida, excelled at lacrosse. The Scottish names weren't accidental, of course.

I remain active to this day in the St. Andrew's Society; was made a laird by Lord Lyon of Scotland and given a personal coat of arms with a fancy Latin inscription (*Veniut Veritatem Attest*); knighted into the Sovereign Order of St. John by the Queen, Elizabeth II herself; and proudly claim the tartan of Clan Gregor (yes, I wear a kilt). I belong to the University Club, Oxford-Cambridge Club in London, to Beefsteak (don't ask) and the Pilgrims.

By the time we got divorced (she changed teams, if you get my gist), she was so damaged by her own issues that she easily agreed to let me have custody of the kids (she said an old Indian chief told her to do so on one of her many retreats), while she walked away with little more than a used Volvo station wagon and half of a considerable tax bill.

As newlyweds in the seventies, though, we were off to Scotland, where I had scored a St. Andrew's Fellowship to study for my master's at one of the four great Scottish "ancients," the University of Aberdeen.

If you've seen the movie *Eye of the Needle*, then you have some sense of the austere granite outcroppings and craggy cliffs that face the chilly North Sea all around Aberdeen, but my own experience was rather different, as though all that dramatic backdrop were taken from a Tolkien fairy tale in which I was the main character. We lived in the Earl of Marischal's castle on a tony street called Rubislaw Den North, which I raced up and down in my brand-new red convertible Triumph. The university was very international and very collegial, as only the bastions of the British Empire can be, and as the sole American, I was surprised how easily I fit in. I played squash every day, had many sherries, played golf on Fridays at the Royal Old Aberdeen Golf Club (Balgonie to the locals), Hazelhead Club, Philadelphia Society, or Yale Club and still managed to write my MLitt thesis in just one year. It was in Aberdeen that I developed a love of single-malt scotch; a fondness for tweed suits and cashmere sweaters, haggis and mince and tatties as well; and a feeling that somehow the "children of the mist" were indeed my own people, as my grandfather had tried to tell me.

And I loved their ancient system of study, reading hundreds of books in tutorial sessions and then ending with a single all-day examination in which you filled a dozen blue books with what you had synthesized. My degree, with "honours" (yes, that is their spelling—it's their language after all) was in "PPE," which, in British academic parlance, stands for Politics, Philosophy and Economics (*The Moderns*).

It was one of those experiences that shape you for life, so that years later I would return to serve as president of the Ancient Scottish Universities Trust. (The other "ancients" are St. Andrew's, Glasgow, and Edinburgh.) Even though these institutions date back to the year 1413 and founded such things as law, science, medicine, and economics, they—shockingly—had no endowments at all, so my charge was to bring them into the twenty-first century financially. Even today the University of Aberdeen has only $45 million set aside for endowment, or, to put that in perspective, one-tenth of 1 percent of Harvard's. Nevertheless, we did what we could, and in 2008 I was rewarded with an honorary LLD, or doctorate of laws, for my "contribution to civil society" from Aberdeen. (I later got three more honorary doctorates in humane letters, science, and divinity.) My legal friends tell me that I am now fully qualified to sit on the Supreme Court. They didn't specify where this court reigns, however, or what it exercises supremacy over, and I'm afraid to ask.

Given my growing addiction to all things cerebral, especially when offered on a campus, it was all but inevitable that I would go on to get my terminal degree—PhD, sometimes referred to as Piled higher and Deeper. I think I knew even in high school that I wouldn't rest until I had it. So when I started casting about for doctoral programs, of course I threw out feelers to the Ivy League. Harvard would accept me into their doctoral program in politics and economics, but I would have to work off the tuition as a lowly teaching assistant on a brutal schedule that would eat up the majority of my study time. But out of the blue came a lightning bolt from Canada: the University of Toronto was offering something called the Hart House Open Fellowship, which paid tuition and all expenses. plus a ten-thousand-dollar stipend and no teaching at all. I decided to take the money since, after all, here was another part of the British Empire I had yet to explore.

Both the University of Toronto and the city of Toronto itself are, it turned out, neglected North American treasures. The city is one of the most cosmopolitan in the world, with a feeling of modernity in design, culture, and outlook, and the university—breeding ground for such forward-thinking intellectuals as Marshall McLuhan, Northrop Frye, and, going back a generation, the inventors of the electron microscope—would certainly be counted among the most prestigious in America were it located forty miles to the south on the opposite bank of Lake Ontario. As it is, the university settles for being the best in Canada by almost every criterion, and it thrives right in the heart of the huge bustling city of some five million people, like a traditional European university.

Toronto is New York or Chicago given its Great Lakes setting, without the grit and without the crime. We lived in Rosedale, the "old money" neighborhood just north of downtown, so I could not only walk to the massive Robarts Library—"Fort Book," we called it—where I generally worked from eight in the morning till six in the evening, six days a week, but also to the grandly named Institute for Christian Studies on College Street, where all my latest enthusiasms were stoked by a single professor, Bernie Zylstra, who gave electrifying lectures and seminars. Tall, thin, angular, with piercing eyes, he liked to take off his glasses to make a point, and all his points were like lances through the brain. I was not the only Zylstra acolyte, of course. Bernie was urbane, witty, brilliant, and, more important for my purposes, an intellectual Doberman pinscher. He had studied intensely as the best student of Herman Dooyeweerd, the Dutch authority of jurisprudence and author of the systematic and influential *New Critique of Theoretical Thought.* I had been a fan of Dutch critical thinking ever since my brief exposure to the Free University of Amsterdam, and it gave me a perverse pleasure to learn how to tear down just about any and every argument. I put this new enthusiasm to use during seminars with the famous Straussian, Allan Bloom (author of *The Closing of the American Mind,* who thought himself second only to God; he lectured to the whiteboard, not to the class, and reserved the highest grade for himself—so he said); Leftist Christian Bay; Neo-Marxists; and any other world-class mind I could ferret out of the university faculty directory, and I was treated well by everyone, partly because I had a graduate degree from a British university and Canadians venerate everything British, including the Queen.

I finished my entire doctoral program in an unprecedented less than three years, but it was no picnic. Oral exams, unfortunately, are oral, and I was not as facile with those as I had been with the Aberdeen blue-book system, including the German language. I was also introduced for the first time to the jungle of academic politics. I wanted Bernie Zylstra to be the core of my thesis committee, but since my area of specialization was political economy, I also had to please an econometrician, an industrial economist, a development economist, a Straussian political philosopher, a behavioralist, a European political scientist, and a Marxist (fortunately a soft, polite one). This hornet's nest can best be summed up in a single sentence uttered by the Straussian on the committee, Clifford Orwin: "I suffered—you, too, shall suffer."

One moment in an academic life that you never forget is the day you defend your dissertation. Mine was tough, interdisciplinary, and deemed original enough to be presented to the academic inquisitors who specialize in hard questions, brutal interrogations, and the humiliation of the unprepared. The worst part of all comes after it's over, when you sit outside the examination room, waiting for the result. It seemed like an eternity, but they told me later the committee only deliberated for fifteen minutes. The vote was unanimous and I was taken to the Faculty Club—their inner sanctum, so to speak—for a celebratory drink. I felt exhilarated by that even more than by the publication of the dissertation a year later under the rather needlessly erudite title *Beyond Reductionism*.

I'm sure if they had a degree beyond PhD, I would have gone for it, but after you've won the Super Bowl of the intelligentsia, your next question is likely to be, "What do I do now?"

In my case, I made the gigantic mistake of going backwards. I returned to Gordon College to teach. It's hard to sort out my reasons for this so many years later, but I think it was partly out of my friendship with my old professors, partly out of gratitude, and partly out of a desire to make the place better. At any rate, I plunged in with my usual enthusiasm, trying to develop new courses, make the curriculum more interdisciplinary, and pioneer programs such as a convocation of notable speakers and a hands-on educational seminar in the microstates of the Caribbean. Since I was so young, the students were easy to talk to, some fewer than three years younger than me, and two of them—Geoff Rendall and Ron Mahurin—become lifelong friends.

Once again I had set out to find Cardinal Newman's ideal university, this time working from the inside to enable it, but at every turn I was shot down by an administration full of higher-education drones. One of them was named President Dick Gross, so, of course, we sophomorically referred to him as Gross Dick. Another nemesis of progress was a dean who had attended a conservative Baptist seminary and had some kind of degree in bean-counting, so for him we were fond of quoting Harold Ockenga, the classicist and theologian who had been chancellor of Gordon in an earlier, better era: "Christian shoddy is still shoddy." Sadly, that point was too often proven to be the norm at Gordon.

I really started running into trouble with my choice of convocation speakers. They included a past head of the CIA, the noted liberal church historian Martin Marty from the University of Chicago, and most egregious sin of all, Cardinal Medeiros of the Boston Roman Catholic Archdiocese. Odd as it may seem now, I was a rabble-rouser at Gordon. They didn't like the courses I wanted to add. They didn't want to give more scholarships to Third World students, a suggestion I made in order to internationalize the student body and add color to it. But what brought everything to a boil was not even so much the content of what I was doing but the form of it. The ineffectual dean finally summoned me to his grand, many-mirrored office one day and gave me a stern warning. "You don't get it," he said. "Either you teach or you do research. Not both. We can't afford research here."

What he was referring to is the Oak Ridge National Research Laboratory grant I'd been awarded the year before, along with a grant from the University of the West Indies. I had also been invited to lecture at the Free University of Amsterdam during their one hundredth anniversary celebration, and I had been publishing like crazy, notably for the Stanford Hoover Institution's Yearbook of International

Communist Affairs. I was a regular book reviewer for the *Christian Century*, a respected magazine (but not at Gordon), and in the summer of 1979 I had been part of the German Academic Exchange (DAAD auf Deutsch) Service's program for scholars, studying economics and law at the Christian Albrecht Universitat in Kiel. The opportunities to do research just kept on coming, and I just kept on accepting. I received a sizable grant from the Center for Energy and Environment of the Organization of American States. I was chosen as a National Endowment for the Humanities scholar, and part of that honor was the chance to study under the famous foundationalist philosopher Alvin Plantinga, but I deferred that for a year to sort of smooth things over with the decidedly uncooperative administration. I was deferring other things as well after being warned to stop doing research. In fact, I may be the first academic who, far from fearing the "publish or perish" culture, was introduced to the concept of "publish and perish."

When I was chosen by the US State Department for a coveted scholar-diplomat position, I could see the divorce from Gordon coming. I was a smart-aleck twenty-eight-year-old who thought he knew all the answers because he'd read all the "great books" and memorized the *Synopticon*. I could go places. I could do things. And Gordon, I was realizing, was not a place where people did things. In a very short period of time I'd been at a university that sacrificed teaching on the altar of research—the University of Toronto had become narrow, fragmented, divisive, and full of individual grant-seekers who had no ties to the larger community of scholars—and, conversely, a college that sacrificed research on the altar of teaching. It was time to move on and see what could be done in the *real* world.

I have taught at five colleges and universities and lectured at dozens and dozens more—including the bilingual Glendon College in Toronto—as well as serving on the boards of four others, and everywhere I have found, well, mediocrity. Heck, I now have four honorary doctorates, including one in divinity! I was made a fellow at Wolfson College at Oxford University. I've also taught at places such as Yale

Divinity School, where you might expect some divine behavior. During my years presiding over the Scottish Universities Trust, I wanted to believe places that are six hundred years old and steeped in tradition might have gotten it right. But no.

Neither the divines, nor the ancients, nor the moderns, nor the liberal arts schools care much anymore about the defining features of a university. In fact, during the time I was serving as a trustee on the Yale board of directors, the chapel steeple gave way and crashed, upsetting the usual calm of the lovely seventeenth-century quadrangle. I thought it must be either a sign from on high or an admission that the place had rotted so completely that the structures themselves were collapsing. But alas, the event passed mostly unremarked, a fitting metaphor for the billion-dollar university in modern society: rich on the outside, crumbling from within. What Yale lacked was a soul. The ancients in Scotland were not much better and, in fact, after six centuries of state tutelage and dependency, had ended up all but bankrupt. Each suffers from disrepair physically and, even more so, academically.

It's certainly not news that universities can be stale places, in spite of the social ties that are formed there and often last a lifetime. In terms of productivity and real learning, the Western university is highly over-priced and equally overvalued. Adam Smith said the same thing some two and a half centuries ago when describing the ancient British system of universities. The greatest innovative ideas and initiatives are typically made outside universities. He wrote, "The greater part of universities have not even been very forward to adopt those improvements . . . Several of those learned societies have chosen to remain, for a long time, the sanctuaries in which exploded systems and obsolete prejudices found shelter and protection after they had been hunted out of every other corner of the world. In general the richest and best-endowed universities have been the slowest in adopting those improvements. The endowments have diminished the necessity of application in the teachers. Their subsistence is derived from a fund altogether independent of their success and reputation in their particular professions. In the University of Oxford the greatest part of the public professors has for some many years given up altogether even the pretense of teaching."[1]

Fortunately, I had some high-level political relationships and had gotten to know some well-placed people at the State Department from my time there. I had written a research paper on bauxite and Jamaica that got published under the Center for National Security and the NSIC, a think tank with close ties to many appointees in the new, conservative administration. With a few phone calls and just one interview, I had a job offer at triple my measly assistant professor's pay and a thousand times the prestige in Washington, DC. I bought some striped suits, shaved, and made my way to Foggy Bottom. We moved at Thanksgiving break of the first Reagan term into a classic old stone house in the Somerset area of Chevy Chase, Maryland, on Stratford Road. I never looked back and immediately declared myself a "recovering" academic. I had jettisoned the sterility of the ivy walls for the political intrigue and action of the most powerful country on the face of the earth.

Some things never change. Which leads to my next point about enterprise: the basis of all achievement is education, and the basis of all folly . . . is education.

MY THIRTEEN FAVORITE BIOGRAPHIES

1. *Theodore Rex* by Edmund Morris. Read the entire trilogy or listen to them as books on tape. They are spellbinding and historically brilliant. These are the epitome of good biographical writing!

2. *Faithful Witness* by Timothy George, the story of the famous missionary William Carey in India.

3. *Witness to Hope: The Biography of Pope John Paul II* by George Weigel. This is a gripping story of the Polish pope who, in a troika of Margaret Thatcher and Ronnie Reagan, brought down the evil Soviet Empire.

4. *Augustine of Hippo* by Peter Brown, the best history of the renowned saint.

5. *Confessions* by St. Augustine, the saint's own words about his transformed, changed life, how, and why, with grainy details.

6. *Jonathan Edwards: A Life* by George Marsden, a masterful study of the sermons and the person.

7. *Babe Ruth: Launching the Legend* by Jim Reisler. Babe Ruth was the sports hero embodied and an idol of the American century.

8. *Churchill: A Life* by Martin Gilbert, the best single volume on the leader of the English-speaking peoples and the reason Nazism was defeated.

9. *Mornings on Horseback: The Story of an Extraordinary Family, a Vanished Way of Life and the Unique Child Who Became Theodore Roosevelt* by David McCullough, a delightful tale that sets the stage for greatness to come. We also remember the author's voice from all those PBS documentaries.

10. *The Life of John Calvin* by Théodore de Bèze, the story of a man so misunderstood but who was so brilliant and formative for "moderns."

11. *Lewis and Clark: Partners in Discovery* by John Bakeless. What better saga than one about discovering the wild, untamed American West?

12. *C. S. Lewis Through the Shadowlands: The Story of His Life with Joy Davidman*, by Brian Sibley. We all grew up reading the Narnia tales, and this is about the life of the Oxbridge don who penned them, and his encounter with Christ.

13. *Benjamin Franklin: An American Life* by Walter Isaacson, the best bio on the quintessential American, founder, and inventor.

5

THE STATE DEPARTMENT VS. THE SENATE COMMITTEE ON FOREIGN RELATIONS: FOGGY BOTTOM AGAINST THE HILL

Blessed is the nation whose God is the LORD, the people whom he has chosen as his heritage!

—PSALM 33:12 ESV

It was heady business for a twenty-something-year-old to walk through the secure doors and turnstiles at the State Department, aka Foggy Bottom, because it was built on a swamp. After receiving my top secret and code word clearances, which included a battery of tests and a polygraph (no, I did not have sex with boys), I was ushered into the supersecret Bureau of Intelligence and Research on the eighth floor of the old building at Twenty-First and C Street Northwest. Everything was secure with cipher locks, and we worked the first few hours of the day in a locked vault next to the op center, scanning the reports from the NSA and NPIC and reading the CIA's *National Intelligence Daily* report (NID) before devouring all the open sources, daily newspapers, and relevant journal articles.

Having an UMBRA clearance (I am not supposed to divulge that term; sorry, I forgot) meant we could not only see everything in the entire US national security apparatus, human and signals intelligence, but that we also produced some of our own. The good brains at INR wrote what was called "the Book" for the Secretary of State, as well as longer reports. We also debated National Intelligence Estimates with other member agencies in "the community." The Book consisted of many short, five- or six-sentence arguments and analyses on current events and a few longer one- to two-pagers, back of the books, as they were known, on longer-range subjects and trends. The writing style demanded objectivity and conciseness. But it demanded insight and judgment as well.

My turf as a senior international economist was "North-South" issues and commodities-related matters. I had no specific country coverage, which allowed me to be global in scope. I followed the UN and wrote papers on everything from the tropical timber accords to the Lomé trade talks. If there was an issue involving a commodity, its nationalization or a shortage, I needed to know about it. General Haig was in charge—at least he thought so—but he had little appetite for economics. It was a good fortune when George Shultz arrived on the scene. He had a PhD in labor economics and often wrote notes back to us asking a question or for more detailed information. He also had the Princeton Tiger tattooed on his arse, as I found out much later at the Bohemian Grove. In time, I was asked to brief the head of AID, Peter McPherson, and Ken Dam, the deputy secretary. I was on a first-name basis with Bob Hormats, the assistant secretary for business affairs, and especially with Senator Helm's nefarious protégé, Richard McCormack, the under secretary for economic affairs.

I was asked to work with the policy planning staff who had direct access to the policymakers and to help write some of the famous "global baloney" (our name for them) speeches for Shultz himself, which meant

I got to have an occasional lunch on the top floor rather than in the cafeteria. I oversaw some external research with university types and worked with the big econometrics firms on projections. The Agency, particularly its National Intelligence Council, was headed by a person I knew and admired, Hal Ford, so I got over there regularly to debate the estimates and do roundtables. I even went to New York a few times and sat in the US seat at UN headquarters in the General Assembly representing the United States (yes, the proverbial good guys).

I was as a former academic on good terms with the (pretty) women in public affairs, who were nice and good to know. They made me a regular speaker for them at spots around the county from foreign affairs councils to universities. I was recommended as an *Am-Part* (the American Participant Program was the VIP Cadillac of American foreign policy, paid for by USIA) to give talks to important audiences around the world. I did so well I got invited back to seven trips stretching from Hong Kong and the Philippines in Asia to Kenya, Egypt, and Mauritius in Africa to the Netherlands and Germany in Europe. It was a good gig if you could get it, and you were highly rewarded, besides the travel. I was told only Jeane Kirkpatrick did more of these speeches than yours truly. I also was selected into the management development program for promising newbies and took tons of courses at the Foreign Service Institute in Arlington across the river. It got me out of the daily grind. The one place we were not permitted was the Hill. The executive branch bureaucracy and the legislative branch were *not* supposed to interact. In fact, the only people who went up there were sent there to give testimony or briefings, and they were told to be free of politics.

The power of the bureaucracy was notorious, and I encountered it in a hundred different and often silly and pesky forms. From permissions to clearances to pecking order and back, I discovered the nature and extent of the beast. My favorite stories involved a long global study on the emergence of steel mills around the world. The capacity and output numbers and projections were valuable to negotiations and trade. It took me three months and fifty-two separate clearances in the whole of Foggy Bottom before we could publish that report. Lesson learned. The second was per diem, a big category for bureaucrats—how much money you got a day in a city or foreign capital. I got the stipend and on return had not spent half of it. When I tried to give it back, I was angrily reprimanded. That office told me, "We don't care if you have to spend it on whores; just don't ever bring it back here." I never had whores, but I bought more gifts and ate better on future trips. My sons had a set of T-shirts from the most exotic places on earth, from Austria to Zimbabwe.

I had been casually introduced on coming to DC to a somewhat underground, nebulous group that ran something called "the Fellowship." Its untitled leader, Doug Coe, was an Oregonian with wavy, black hair and all the traits of a really good kind of salesman, and there were a bunch of former this-and-thats involved as well.

They put on a huge spectacle called the National Prayer Breakfast, a large event in civil religion that it turns out is not run by Congress at all even though it appears to be. We went to All Saints Episcopal Church on Chevy Chase Circle, and a few prominent politicos and State Department people went there as well. I was asked to colead the adult Sunday school forum, which largely consisted of reviewing various books. My cohost was Priscilla Reining, a very well-respected, petite-brainy, and published anthropologist who worked for *Science* magazine. I got to meet a lot of people there. Did I mention that the Fellowship was very connected politically, too? I was invited to join a small group that met every Thursday morning for coffee, prayer, and support. I stayed with that group of men my entire period in the city. It included the likes of a former presidential chief of staff; a leading publisher; the managing director of Jones-Day, the largest law firm; an under secretary of defense; a top litigator; and a few other random souls, even the South African ambassador for a period.

I was simultaneously drawn into a somewhat secretive group of "believers" at the State Department itself that met weekly for lunch in the office of the assistant secretary for population, refugees, and migration,

Gene Dewey. That group talked and prayed and helped each other find a path in the body of the wicked beast. It had senior personnel people, a few ambassadors, (Agency for International Development (AID) types, and some political appointees. One was Tom Nassif, a California operative close to President Reagan himself. He later became ambassador to Morocco and got me invited out there to give some speeches on US policy, and I got to stay at his residence Americano. Heck, we even played golf on the King's private golf course, Dar Es Salam Royal, and visited ancient Fez as well as modern Casablanca—all on the US nickel.

Don Kruse, another senior Pol-Mil guy in the group and a Philadelphia Presbyterian, got me invited later to CincPac headquarters in Naples, where he was a political-military attaché. That worked out well, as I was connecting from an Am-Part trip to Egypt. The only thing that went wrong was security. I had a DIP passport, but I was later very disturbed to learn that the very next flight was hijacked and all the passengers on Egypt Air were killed when the plane was stormed by troops after being hijacked.

I got to fly on nearly every third world airline in the world—and most were unsafe, decrepit leftovers from an earlier age of aviation. Air India was bad, but PIA (Pakistan International Airlines) stood for "planes intended to arrive." The Bulgarian airline, if you can call it that, consisted of Soviet Tupolev aircraft without proper compression.

As a functioning part of the vast "Fellowship" social network, I was able to travel to a number of foreign countries to meet leaders under the auspices of faithful friendliness. One trip involved ten days on literally every island in the Caribbean Sea. I got a great tan, to boot!

Bob Hamrin, my good friend and an economist from the Joint Economic Committee, and I started a once-a-month economists gathering for dinner, and it grew to some thirty to forty people from every agency, the World Bank and IMF, and all the trade associations that lobby and conduct business in our nation's capital. As a result of these contacts, I was introduced to Sen. Paul Tribble (R-VA) and Sen. Dick Lugar (R-IN), both of whom worked on the Senate Foreign Relations

Committee. Both had strong religious faith. It was arranged that I receive a yearlong Pearson Fellowship from my job at State to go up to the Hill and work with them on the committee. The department didn't really like it, but there wasn't much they could say or do. It was a done deal. That year turned into two, and I had to leave State and became a credentialed Hill staffer. I had traded teams, and since I knew how both worked, I could be specifically observant and demanding for my new team, the *Pols*.

Politicians don't much care for federal bureaucrats. They are suspicious of their loyalty and likely realize they have a tendency to outlive them. A great cartoon in the *New Yorker* depicted a State Department bureau chief pulling out one drawer of a file cabinet saying, "Democrats in," while closing the other saying, "Republicans out." The bureaucracy truly has only one objective, maintaining or, I would say, growing itself and its budget. This often clashes head-on with Congress, which has a radically different objective: winning elections and grabbing power, especially for your home district, in the form of pork and earmarks.

At age thirty-one, I was, I used to joke and say, the foreign minister of Virginia, although I never lived there. The committee had a few historical powers that included guiding foreign policy, appointing ambassadors, and holding hearings. I wrote and gave speeches for the senators, and most important, briefed them and whispered in their ears when the committee met or they went to the floor of the Senate to make a speech or cast a vote. The committee staff was a group of super smart and wily political sorts who were quite ideological and crafty in the PR sense.

Sen. Jesse Helms had made a deal with Lugar to be chairman of agriculture in exchange for Lugar getting foreign relations. But this meant Helms was particularly powerful. In fact, I have never seen someone wield so much *negative power,* and so well. He was a master of parliamentary rules and procedures (putting holds on procedural matters) and had some very talented people, like Christopher Manion, Bill Triplett, and Debby DeMoss, among others, working for him. The director of the staff was Jeff Bergner, a smooth and likable former academic in foreign policy. The staff each had their areas of competence, and they divided along political lines, as you would expect. Mitch Daniels (later governor of Indiana) was Lugar's chief of staff, so he had some command over the whole apparatus. He's a talented guy President Bush later called "our man Mitch."

I was very good at writing questions that would elicit either controversial responses or embarrass the person giving testimony, "When did you stop beating your wife?" kinds of questions. I also had the juice on the State Department from the inside, which was particularly evident when it came to passing on the nominations of senior career diplomats and political appointees to be ambassadors. I still recall working behind the scenes with Senator Helm's people, who could be nasty, to question and then question harder a certain former head of my old bureau, INR, to be ambassador to an unnamed Asian country—okay, Indonesia. They kicked him until bloody and even trotted out the commie card, but we got him through—well, with a few blemishes and bruises.

One area the State Department did not care for was religious freedom. They don't have a bureau of religious affairs, and most of the FSOs (foreign service officers, if you didn't know the acronym) hold quite decidedly secular views. Even though they missed the coming of the ayatollahs and the effects of liberation theology in Central America, they were still in denial, wishing the topic would just plain go away.

When Senator Tribble and a bunch of friends from the House, spearheaded by Rep. Frank Wolf, decided to go after the regime in Romania, you'd have thought we had opened a can of worms. I was in the middle, trying to calm down the likes of Frank Wisner, the hothead from State (later ambassador to India and Egypt) who was sent up to the Hill to quash this stuff. "The Wiz," as he was unaffectionately known, walked into a buzz saw, and even though it took years, the stalwarts for freedom of conscience and religion won out, not only with the fall of Romanian-type dictatorial regimes but with the passage of legislation on the reporting of religious freedom. (Truth be known, Paul Marshall of the Hudson Institute and I later wrote the definitive tome on this topic, published as *Religious Freedom Around the World*). That was something worked on for years and years by my friend John Hanford, nephew to Elizabeth Dole, who himself eventually in the Bush administration was named ambassador to the post he had helped to create. He did so under the guidance of Senator Lugar, who was always, in all things, cool, calm, and collected. Many of us joked that when Bush 41 called Dan Quayle to be his running mate, he inadvertently dialed the wrong number, instead wanting to get the senior senator from Indiana.

One of the best parts of being on the Hill was the foreign junket. It turns out that every pariah nation, before the rules changed, had a "fam trip," even some Co-Dels, with Congressmen and women or wives (unnamed guests too), to see firsthand the state of life in their respective countries. Israel had a great and quite biased trip that AIPAC endorsed and funded. It also included all the relevant Christian religious sites and many hours of meetings with Israeli defense experts. The South Africans developed a trip through some fabricated foundation to take us to South Africa and other African countries with a view that apartheid was not all it was cracked up to be. Visiting Mozambique and Angola made South Africa look good by comparison. A bomb went off just down the beach from the ambassador's residence when we were having lunch in Maputo. I liked that visit because I got into a testy debate with a young Marxist foreign minister who really believed in Lenin and Marx (as I did not). He later became President Chissano. When we got home, we x-ed out as much as we could from their foreign assistance budget. We even were flown on a clandestine mission into "Free" Angola to a place in the bush called Jamba, to meet with the legendary General Savimbi, complete with beard and fatigues.

The best trip by far, which I went on twice, was to Taiwan. Flying first-class on China Air, we were catered to like zillionaires, lavished with gifts, and fed so many delectable meals (mostly of unknown origin), complete with goombay toasting to everything and everyone, that it became overindulgent. Peter Kinsler from the Senate Banking Committee was senior to me, so he headed our delegation but often deferred to me to give toasts because I could BS even better than our counterparts. I still have the watch some top admiral gave us as a memento, and cuff links from the king of Sweden, where I was made a two-week bicentennial fellow to study Swedish trade—those "sons of niches." The guys liked the Taiwan trip best for the shopping as much as the gals. Snake Alley was fun and most colorful, and the sight of fresh snake blood is very appealing indeed. We each got measured for multiple custom-made suits and tailored-fitted shirts. I got them to put a Chinese logo script (chop) on all my breast pockets. They said it was my name, but later a native speaker said it meant something to the effect that "Caucasian men do some unkind act to dogs."

I got to go to Haiti with Senator Tribble to try and convince Baby Doc to step down from his criminal and extravagant rule in Haiti. I went to the Philippines and met the lavish Marcos duo. He gave me a box of Tabacalera cigars with my name on each wrapper and a carved box inscribed "T. R. Malloch, Esq." I am not a lawyer, but I accepted them nonetheless; heck, who else was going to smoke them, George Shultz?

So for my country I have: eaten sheep eyeballs, monkey brains, and snake. I have drunk wood grain alcohol (in the Ukraine, where it is administered with a broom to dust yourself off when you get up off the ground); sipped sorghum 100 percent alcohol in Asia; and sampled bee's mead, in Novgorod, Russia (two cups and literally you have no legs—none at all), where because of my family middle name, we were given the keys to the town and the best seats in the best Western restaurant in the ancient walled town. I got my picture on the cover of the *Gulf & Middle East Economist* magazine with some lame quote, but I was wearing a bow tie in the photo and took grief for looking so preppy. I suffered disease in Asia from protozoa in my intestines, jaundice from rat droppings in Latin America, and severe cold, heat, and even extreme bodily danger.

In my official photograph I wore a herringbone three-piece gray suit and held my pipe in my right hand, looking quite debonair and WASP-like. The most remarkable and dangerous place I visited twice was Pakistan. It was way too dangerous even then. Karachi was a teeming poor city with tons of beggars. I did the four major cities tour and met all the political leadership as well as businesspeople. The final stop was Peshawar, in the far northwestern, tribal area. It was notably wild, crazy wild. I felt like Gunga Din. People were riding horses on the main streets, carrying rifles and dressed as if it were 1800, not 1985. On the PIA (planes intended to arrive) flight from Islamabad, some fanatic took out a snake and lit a fire while bowing to the imagined east on his portable prayer rug.

My big assignment was giving a lecture to about three thousand students at the increasingly Islamic university there. The topic was North-South relations. They were not a very friendly bunch and did not much care for my message or slant. The bottom line was not like George Vest's—"We've got it; you want it; and you can go to hell"—but it had a similar thrust, dressed up in pretty economic language and diplomacy. At the dean's house after the speech, the Western-educated faculty were kind and actually quite impressive, most notably when they invited me to recess into a hidden back room to sample some forbidden scotch. They told me about the history of polo, played originally in that area with a sheep's head instead of a ball. They took me up to Afghanistan to see the ravages of war, and I saw the plight of the refugees and the power of the warlords right through the Khyber Pass. We heard gunshots and had to turn back, as I was too ripe a target or prize as a hostage. I bought some nice oriental carpets, including a prayer rug and a silk from Qum, that I still use to this day (not for prayer).

About a week or so after I left, the same students rioted and burned down the USIA offices where I had been housed. I'd like to think I wasn't responsible for the actions, but I need to check the notes from that speech to make perfectly sure.

By the mid-1980s Wall Street was going gangbusters, and the equities and debt markets were very lucrative places to hang out. It seemed everyone was getting their MBA, so many of them were young upstarts who knew less than me and were not nearly as worldly or well traveled.

Besides, the thing that really irked me was that my younger and slightly less studious brother was hired by Lehman Brothers as an investment banker and was making almost three times what I did. I recall conversing with him about my options and career choices. Why not jump to the Street? I had some of what they wanted, and they were hiring. I knew the firms differed considerably, and the white shoe culture at some was vastly different from the rah-rah boiler rooms.

Very few people went between DC and New York, although the Metroliner made the trip in just a few hours. The two centers of political and financial power are (still are) worlds apart, not miles. I made a few inquiries, and it happened that two managing directors at Salomon Brothers, a top-ranked firm, rather liked my résumé and recommendations. They were willing to give me a chance and to make it "worth my while," which meant more than double the pay plus the promise of a sizable bonus, which at that point in time were notoriously generous; well, they were quite ridiculous.

Good-bye, politics; hello, Big Apple. We sold the pretty stone house for a killing and bought a brand-new one, replete with all the latest consumer devices, in Harrison, in Westchester County, where the boys could attend the best Purchase schools. I missed politics, but this was a chance of a lifetime. How many times would I fall prey to that line?

Gordon Gekko was right—or was he? The debate about the value of charity is as old as time itself, and Mandeville wrote about "private vices and public virtues" even before Adam Smith discovered "the invisible hand." Maybe we are not *Homo economicus* after all? Could human nature contain a conscience and work on other than radical self-interest? I would just have to test it and find out.

That was my next lesson. Power corrupts and money even more so, but it is better to have some of each.

MY THIRTEEN FAVORITE MEMENTOS COLLECTED FROM VIPS

1. A hand-carved cigar humidor with "T. R. Malloch, Esq." embossed, full of Philippine *tabacalero*, given by Ferdinand Marcos, in Manila, 1984

2. My Red Star sailing jacket from Leningrad Yacht Club given by Boris Yeltsin during America's Cup Race in San Diego, 1992

3. A gold watch from the head of the Taiwan navy, inscribed in Chinese, given in 1983 in Taipei

4. My own "chop" of Chinese calligraphy, given by President Hu in Beijing during a presidential delegation visit headed by then Secretary of Homeland Security Tom Ridge in 2006

5. The clock from Russian submarine *Hunt for Red October*, given by the Russian ambassador to the SALT talks in Geneva, 1990

6. A Brass sign that reads, "CNN World Economic Development Congress," given by Ted Turner in Washington, DC, in 1992

7. African marble bookends given by President Frederik de Klerk in Pretoria, South Africa, in 1982

8. An African dagger walking stick given by then foreign minister Joachim Chissano in Maputo, Mozambique, in 1984

9. A glass sphere engraved with "World Economic Forum," given in Davos, Switzerland, by Klaus Schwab in 1991

10. A red fox Russian fur hat, presented on the tarmac at Zurich International Airport by Arkady Volsky, head of USSR industry, in 1990.

11. Medal of the Order of St. John, presented on investiture into the Order by Queen Elizabeth, London, England, in 2005

12. An antique book, *L'Annee Pastorale Prosnes*, from the fourteenth century, in French, presented at Fribourg, Switzerland, by Pere Nicolas Buttet, spiritual director and head of Fraternité Eucharistein, in 2009

13. A Scotch silver quaich, presented for my service as president of the Four Ancients University Development Trust in Scotland, in 2006.

6

WALL STREET: GREED IS *VERY* GOOD?

Humble yourselves, therefore, under God's mighty hand, that he may lift you up in due time.

—1 PETER 5:6

I n 1985, its peak year, Salomon Brothers, Inc., brought in $760 million in pretax profits, more than the entire securities industry earned in 1978. Riding the crest was John Gutfreund, the self-acclaimed King of the Street, whose photo adorned all the papers and financial glossies, usually chomping on his prebreakfast cigar.

As CEO, he planned to take Salomon out of its longtime offices at One New York Plaza, in lower Manhattan, and erect what was to have been the city's most glittery new office tower as its headquarters, uptown, on Columbus Circle. John was a real character, bigger than life and full of himself. He would lead by walking around and towered down on the massive trading floor he had built by hollering commands.

I joined Solly (as she was known) in June of that year at the top of its game, as the most successful of all the players in the gilded jungle called Wall Street. It was a rough-and-tumble place, full of itself, as depicted in Michael Lewis's classic humor-laced epic, *Liar's Poker*. Nearly every word in that tome is correct, and I know, as I was in the class entering just before the now-famed author. As a German Jewish, take-no-prisoners, get-the-deal-at-all-costs, rip-off-their-face kind of place, Solly prospered on the debt side of the business. Its traders, from Meriwether to Coates, were legendary, and they would squeeze any market they could make. It eventually got them into trouble with the law and led to the firm's demise and takeover by Citigroup and merger with the lowly retail unit Smith Barney. At Salomon greed was not just good; it was *very* good, to steal a movie line uttered by Michael Douglas.

When I was interviewed by Warren Fosse (head of junk and a smarmy, fat, genius); Ronnie Stuart (head of swaps, a flashy, smart quant); and Deryck Maughan (head of cap markets, a Brit of some distinction), they could choose anyone they wanted. They blackballed nine out of ten people for the crudest of reasons, such as "he parts his hair wrong," or "he has too much of an accent," or "he doesn't play (or more important, win) at 'team' sports."

The trading floor on the forty through forty-second floors was a mad jungle of computer terminals and screens, squawk boxes, and people screaming at each other at the top of their lungs. No one had a private office. Each segment of the business had its own little rabbit warren or nook. I was in capital markets and worked with Stephen Dishart and his boys under the bigwigs on what was then an emerging market, yet undefined as debt for equity, mostly swaps and big foreign country sovereign deals. It later evolved into a fast-paced poker game called "asset trading" of mostly the debt of sovereign countries and Brady bonds or "emerging markets" but at the start it was slower, politically driven, and still being invented. I was an unlikely candidate for this kind of work, as it required a trader's skill mix, not those of an economist or analyst. The thought was that I could travel well in distant places, work with people in Washington, as necessary, and present to corporate clients. You may know parts of this story from my friend Michael Lewis's very accurate spoof, *Liar's Poker*. I was there in the class just before his.

Once I had a new Rolex, I would fit in well. I would also be able to talk shoptalk with their ace economists, John Lipsky (from the IMF and with a lovely handlebar mustache) and the legendary market mover himself, Henry Kaufman. First, I was trained to pass the Series 7 and like exams, which amounted to weeks and weeks of stupid rote memorization. I took the exam one Saturday morning at some poor New York City high school and scored 98, one of the highest scores ever by a Solly employee. The scare was a well-circulated rumor that if you didn't pass, you had to clear out your desk, without severance. You were gone, banished forever. In reality only two words, two motives, were ever operative on the Street. One was *greed*—as in, grab as much as you can, and often it was like drinking from a fire hose. The other was *fear*. Fear is a great motivator, as it vividly illustrates, usually in oft-repeated tales and sagas, what happens if you don't _____ (fill in the blank). Or sometimes what happens if you do _____ (fill in the blank). The effect is the same: action → reaction.

I had never before, oddly, given much thought to corporate culture and the effect that it has on a workforce, interpersonal relations, or the mission. But here it was so shocking that it screamed out at you. Salomon had a distinct rough-and-tumble, working-class, Jewish culture that was summed up in a single word, *traders.*

Solly did not have a huge investment banking division, and what they had focused on M&A and competing with Drexel and Milken on doing junk bonds. Their international side was growing. In equities they had grown a lot and had a bunch of people interested in studying and selling international debt. They had invented, under the perilous Lewie Ranieri (an overweight Italian trader), the mortgage-backed security market and were busy doing the same in interest rate swaps. The view was that they could sell anything from junk bonds to fancy derivatives, that in fact, to quote a standing line, "they could sell nuclear waste to Jane Fonda."

Salomon earned its stripes in government and corporate debt and arbitrage trading for itself. It had a strong sales unit and syndicate desk. Its commercial paper and corporate desks made or broke entire companies. They were active in forex and public/muni finance. The sovereign markets I knew were very respectable but still infantile, as many countries were badly hurt by the Latin American debt crisis and overhang. There were no functioning markets in many parts of the world then—in the Eastern Bloc, China, or the like. But if you could take the debt of a third world country, say, Mexico or the Philippines, and swap it for some equity in that country, say, of interest to a PepsiCo or Unilever, then you could do a deal.

And at Solly they only wanted to hear one word, *Done!* The deals were few and far apart, so I got shipped around to do a number of other clever things. I had a project launched in the notorious training class to set up a South Africa–free Index and fund. After traveling there in the years previous and helping draft the economic sanctions laws, I knew of the political repercussions on that issue. We set up such a fund just in time to catch the business of some cities and states and pension funds that were moving in that enlightened direction. Many people laughed at the idea until it made money. Maughan, the Brit (now a CBE) who was at the top of capital markets, asked me to take a look at how to penetrate China. I did research and presented a path through Taiwan, which I also knew from my visits there. It made sense, and we established an office there that eventually helped with the vast Chinese business down the road. I worked on a kuku trade of a nickel mine in the Philippines. I introduced the firm to Cory Aquino, the opposition leader soon to become president when she spoke in New York. I had known her husband, the assassinated exiled leader. Dick Schmeelk, one of the top lieutenants to Gutfreund, learned of my Dutch connections and took me to the Knickerbocker Club. It is one of the city's oldest and most prestigious men's clubs on East Sixty-Second Street—and is not for Knicks fans. As a result we had a group of Dutch luminaries and CEOs visit the firm for a full day, and it led to real business.

The schmoozing was beyond anything I had ever seen even in the talkfest of Washington. And the f-bomb was so common and repeated that it made for a very creative use of the English language. Seven times in a single sentence was the all-time record, I recall. All of this was grating and ran counter to my background and WASP mores.

The worst things were the hellish commute and the long hours. Every day I got up at 4:30 a.m. to catch an early train to Grand Central from Harrison on the Metro North line. That was not so bad. It was the crowded subway downtown in heat or cold, squashed in, that stunk. But we had to be there well before 7 a.m. and working to be seen and to do business. You rarely got up from your desk all day, except to go to the bathroom. And then someone might stab you in the back (or at Solly, more likely in the front). Lunch was delivered. A notorious account of a trader sucker punching the elevator operator was not untrue. Working until 7, 8, even 9 p.m. was pretty common. Often there was some dinner, client event, heavy drinking, or tickets to a sports event some client wanted to attend. But most of the time you schlepped back uptown to catch a late commuter train back to the burbs.

More than once, I have to admit, I fell asleep and woke up somewhere in Connecticut and had to get off, cross the tracks, and catch a reverse train back to my home station, then drive home. This all grated on my nerves and social habits and affected my marriage and family more than anyone ever is bold enough to admit. Then the next day, you get up, alone and in the dark, and do it all over again. One Sunday afternoon, my oldest son said to me in all truthfulness, "Where have you been, Dad? We never see you anymore. I thought you were on one of those planes again, going to another country." I was not. I slept at home every night. I just never saw him, his mother, or his brother anymore. Then by surprise, we found out that another baby was on the way. Really!

The incident that broke the camel's back occurred in a heated discussion with some lame traders who had caged me into debating them. It wasn't about politics, the Fed, or numbers on a dollar bill. The topic was bonus pay. People would get hundreds of thousands of dollars or more, and it was big-time. The decisions were not totally objective or meritorious but instead were based subjectively on how much people liked you.

One story, which I witnessed, involved an options trader too big for his britches, who thought he earned a huge bonus. It was deserved. Anyway, when he was paid less than he expected, he quit on the spot and told everyone to "f*** off" and that he was the "f*** out of here." Punitively, the firm decided instead not to cash his check at all. My incident turned out to be an odd one for Wall Street; it revolved around charity. These guys taunted me, asking, "How can you give any of your hard earned money away?" What is need anyway? Fosse had seven Ferraris. People could spend more in a day than most people make in a year. One guy owned some two hundred high-end watches. There was a standing game to see who could take the client out to dinner and spend the most money. With the best wine, the tabs were all between three and five thousand dollars. The debate got more and more heated, and they just could not stand it that I both gave to charity (church or relief or whatever) and thought everyone else should. They loathed my ethics, as they had none.

I had been working with some international investors who were planning to buy Wharton Econometrics and later fuse it with a unit of even larger magnitude from Chase Manhattan Bank, Chase Econometrics, thereby creating a consulting firm with reputation capital, tons of clients, and an upside. Privately held, there was a potential opportunity here. I hated what I was doing, the grind, and the loss of a life and the very culture of the firm itself, so I accepted a move back to Washington, DC, to head their national office and all consulting. It was sure to be a cut in pay, but it saved my life, as I had suffered high blood pressure and a liver ailment that dated back to bad rat-infested food I had eaten in one of those many trips abroad—this one to Trinidad and Venezuela. We sold our house for a record profit, thankfully, and now we had three young sons. Oh boy(s)! We moved to the Downs in Annapolis, Maryland, on the Severn River, where we bought a large deckhouse on the water with a boat dock and the biggest pool in the county—thirteen feet deep with a diving board. I could now jump off the deep end and not have to worry about the sharks.

The lesson here is that generosity has its costs, but the meaning of life is all about giving and self-donation.

MY THIRTEEN FAVORITE CARS I HAVE OWNED

I have owned dozens and dozens of cars. It is my "thing"—better than women, I suppose, or so my wife says. I have even owned interests in exotic used car dealers just to satisfy my habit/addiction.

The cars that meant the most:

1. My first car purchased in 1973 in Boston was a 1973 red BMW 2002tii, the cult car and one of the first imported. People would flash the high beams as an elite signal at each other. Bayerische Motoren Werke AG meant something!

2. When I studied in Scotland in 1974–75, I owned a red Triumph Stag hard-top four-speed stick. It was fast and very sexy.

3. In the 1995–97 period, I owned a Mercedes S600 V12, which was previously owned by Puff Daddy, the rap star. Very manly.

4. I also owned a 750 BMW that was owned by Vic Damone, and it had a TV built into the dashboard.

5. When in Geneva, I owed a bunch of cars, all of which I registered as a Dip(lomat) with CD plates (no tickets could be issued). One was a BMW 630 CSi, which went 200 miles per hour, and I did on the Autobahn.

6. The other was a first, a black, two-seat, BMW Z1, which was a roller skate with a large engine. I could not bring it back to the United States, as it did not pass safety standards. All accidents ended in fatality.

7. A 2006 blue Corvette that went 190 miles per hour. Really! We used to drive it at that speed at the track.

8. 2004 and 2005 Mercedes Benz G Wagons. These are the ultimate professional athlete mobiles. You can mount guns on the top.

9. My 2009 Lexus 460 L (extra long wheel base), which felt like a limo and was ultrasmooth driving.

10. My 2003 BMW Z3. More tickets per capita than any other car! The police just issue them on sight.

11. My 2006 Bentley (very 007!) in British racing green and ivory leather seats with green trim.

12. My 1976 Saab EMS. Graduate school model. Broke down every week.

13. My 2004 white supercharged Porsche Cayenne, a very fast SUV—for my wife to pick up the groceries!

7

ECONOMETRICS CONSULTING: WHICH SIGN DID YOU WANT?

A false balance is an abomination to the LORD, but a just weight is his delight.

—PROVERBS 11:1 ESV

According to the now-definitive source *Wikipedia*, "econometrics" is concerned with the tasks of developing and applying quantitative or statistical methods to the study and elucidation of economic principles. Econometrics combines economic theory with statistics to analyze and test economic relationships. Theoretical econometrics considers questions about the statistical properties of estimators and tests, while applied econometrics is concerned with the application of econometric methods to assess economic theories. Got all that? Although the first known use of the term *econometrics* was by a guy named Ciompa in 1910, Norwegian economist Ragnar Frisch is given credit for coining the term that is used today. There will be a test on all these facts.

Although many econometric methods represent applications of standard statistical models, there are some special features of economic data that distinguish econometrics from other branches of statistics. Economic data are generally observational, rather than being derived from controlled experiments. Because the individual units in an economy interact with each other, the observed data tend to reflect complex economic equilibrium conditions rather than simple behavioral relationships based on preferences or technology. Consequently, the field of econometrics has developed methods for identification and estimation of simultaneous equation models.

You understand that and don't need to see the equations, right? Lawrence Klein, the UPenn professor who founded Wharton Econometric Forecasting Associates (WEFA) and won the Nobel Prize for Economics in the process (he was also a huge Phillies fan) elaborated a six-thousand-equation world model that we could tweak to give us the answer to just about anything. It took hours just to run one iteration. We had models of this and models of that. Regional, US, international, every country that matters, Europe, the OECD, and Japan—you name it. Industry-specific models, sure. Klein was a jovial, truly fun-loving guy who just happened to be economically brilliant.

It was like the old fashioned Magic 8 Ball. You ask the question; the model provides the answer. It is amazing how many sophisticated people like black-box solutions. If it had economic activity, we could model it. Sure. We also had some of the best economists in the world. These were not university types, given to pontification. No, they were slick, fast-talkers who could snow people and sell projects. George Schink (a rotund guy with wire-framed glasses and a belly laugh) was Klein's best student, and he could out-econometric anyone. Jerry Godshaw (a kind of expert from Syracuse) was so good he spent all his time in courthouses, giving expert witness for big companies fighting lawsuits. The main line of business was standard forecasts and write-ups sold generally by region, with or without all the backup data. Once you had done one forecast, the margins on everything else you sold were enormous. It was a cash nexus.

If a client wanted a *special* study or model run using some proprietary data or some new assumptions, well, we could do it, but it cost.

It cost a lot because you got not just some fancy pie charts and wordy statement of analysis. You got the reputation of *Wharton*, and all that cache was included in the price, plus some fancy lunches and dinners.

The bizarre thing about econometric modeling, truth be told, is you get out what you put in. If you want to get a different answer, an expert knows how to fix that. It's not rigged just a bit, I hate to say, subjective. We always had baseline and high and low alternatives to cover our butts. If you want it to be x, we can get x or $x1$ . . . So, if the Beer and Wine Institute wants a slightly different elasticity on taxing alcoholic beverages, it can be done. If the Commerce Department doesn't like the output from the copper model, we can change a few variables so they get closer to what they were looking for. You could always increase the size of the sample or change the all-important time series to a period that better fit your desired outcome. Economists are scientists. Right. They don't lie. Figures lie; liars don't figure. Or is it the other way around?

Wharton had every major corporation and the entire government as clients. The DCAA (that's the Defense Department's Contract Audits Agency, for those of you who don't do the Washington acronym game) even used our stuff to audit defense contracts, and another agency used our outputs to set the all-important per diems in every city in the world, as well as cost-of-living increases. We gave congressional testimony, but mostly we were hired guns in suits. We did expert witness in court cases, and worked extensively with the likes of the Tobacco Institute to show smoking was not so bad, maybe bad, but not *so* bad. We did the country models for AID (Agency for International Development) and the World Bank. Our fingerprints—well, model sims—were everywhere.

Running the national office with a large sales force and all the economists sitting up in Philadelphia—actually, Bala Cynwyd after the merger—meant I was at the crossroads of about half of all our business, and I was paid a base and an incentive to manage and grow that business. I was the consulting economist talking to the chief economists. They all had budgets, and in the government if you didn't spend it you couldn't get more the next year. That's the nature of a bureaucratic system. Use it or lose it.

My favorite story relates to an idea I had that materialized big-time. The Council on Competitiveness, where I knew the then president, Alan Magazine, needed a single figure or index to vividly demonstrate where the United States stood in terms of economic competitiveness. I showed them not only how we could build such an index, publicize it with their name and our credible logo, but also maintain it over time, crunch all the numbers, and then work with their chief consultant, the very large-egoed strategist Michael Porter, from Harvard Business School (his ego fills more than one room, and he is the only academic to have his own building, replete with a waiting room with what may be the largest Oriental rug in the Western world) to tell the story. It was a huge contract and it worked, and continues to this very day.

When two companies (Chase and Wharton in this case) merge, it is not always pretty. That is truer when one comes out of a university-style culture and the other was a division, indeed, a profit center of a money-center bank. This marriage was not made in heaven. First of all they fought over who the chief economist would be. Wharton had likable Nariman Behravesh, a competent and well-presented Iranian; while Chase brought the rock star Larry Chimerine. Chase won. The new owners were Lebanese bankers and Italian venture players who knew something about consulting but nothing about merger strategy or implementation. Everything got thrown together. Where there were duplicates, someone inevitably suffered injury. I was lucky to have been involved up front and brought in to run the Washington show, which, when combined, was quite large. But I too suffered personnel issues, with egos hurt, turf wars, and an attractive, busty blonde pushing out a crude, ugly older guy for "territory." I brought a new guy down from Philly to run some of the government accounts after an old, crusty, Jewish guy retired, and he did particularly well and had the good sense to take me to nice lunches a lot. There are plenty of good restaurants in DC, with all the lobbying that goes on there. I even had to deal with the long illness and death of one employee from AIDS. I liked management and leading the effort and digging up, and selling new leads.

Except for the hour-long commute in heavy traffic on Route 50 going into and out of downtown DC in rush hour, the job fit. Annapolis was a nice yet quaint, small colonial city on the bay. My parents decided to move down to the Eastern Shore in retirement and get a sailboat and spend time with their grandchildren. We had lots of friends, socially, at the yacht club, in the neighborhood made up of similar executive families, and on the swim team, Little League, soccer team, and basketball team, which I coached. The Episcopal Church on the circle, St. Anne's, was historic and adequately WASP. The Rector had two sons the same ages as my sons. All was well. Life was good. We had a boat, ate lots of steamed crabs, vacationed, and kept plugged in to all the old Washington networks. Living in Annapolis, working in DC, and going to Philadelphia and New York by fast train were appealing and sort of well balanced.

One day I got a call at work from an old friend who had been in a carpool with me at the State Department. He was now assigned to Geneva, Switzerland, as econ officer and I hadn't heard from jovial Bernie for a few years. He asked me to have lunch with him back at the State Department the next day. It was hush-hush. I said, fine. The next day he relayed to me in *confidence* that my name had been brought forward for the top American post in the United Nations Europe, at the Geneva office. It was a D-2 post that was ambassadorial in rank. They wanted a person with economics and good political sensitivities who could serve as deputy to the executive secretary and run the place as a sort of COO, yet be respected by diplomats and professionals alike. They wanted an American they knew and could work with, someone they could *trust*. My name, he said, was one of five; they were not ranked, but the other four were much older, senior people, all who had previously served as ambassadors.

Umm, it is amazing how quickly the cart can be overturned. Just when things appear to be going well, something flies smack into your windshield. Now, I could have said, "That's nice. What's for dessert?" But oh no, not me. I am smitten by the political bug and was, at a younger age, overly opportunistic. It's in my genes. Advancement. A competition. Besides, the fact that my competitors were all old ambassadors set me off. Good company. *I probably won't get this anyway*, I thought. *Who knows? Who has the better credentials? Set of contacts? Rabbis?*

After doing some research, talking to old friends in IO, the Bureau of International Organizations at State, who oversee this stuff, I decided to go for it, to give it the old college try. I had nothing to lose.

I got a game plan together. Besides reaching out to my allies at State, I went back to the Hill. I got Senator Trible, Senator Lugar, and Senator Dole to write letters—not just sweet letters, but hard-core, "he is the best person in the world" letters—to the White House, which, in the end, decided. I also got my political pals in the White House to keep me abreast and to push my name as the most qualified. It was a stretch. After three months or so, IO (the bureau at State) got the point. I had to be a real contender, but some of the other candidates were their life-long buddies—real ambassadors. In the White House one good friend went to bat with President Reagan for me, and we won out. The US government candidate was Theodore Roosevelt Malloch.

The odd thing about this appointment was that the UN itself had a veto power. The position was an agreed top American spot. It was set up that way in 1947 when the UN was created. The incumbent had been there for decades and came out of State. The first person to hold the position ran the Marshall Plan in Europe after World War II. The executive secretary was always from a neutral country (it was the Cold War, remember). In this case it was Gerald Hinteregger; he was Austrian. He had been head of the Austrian Foreign Service diplomatic corps and an ambassador to the USSR. He spoke seven languages, and after being part of Hitler Youth, he was given a scholarship to attend an American university. It was the University of Mississippi in 1947, deep in the segregated South, where he did Faulkner studies. Hinteregger the ex-Nazi (according to the dossier) was in the Waldheim tradition, prim and proper, with something to hide but generally a nice old man.

The UN flew me over to Geneva in early May to have a daylong meeting with Herr Hinteregger. The discussions were pleasant and turned around economic analysis, management, and the UN. He was grandfatherly and genuinely seemed to like me. We spoke some German, which pleased him greatly, as it is not an official language of the UN (a defeated power). He didn't introduce me to anyone else. I thought that strange, but the veto was his and the UN secretary general's. I left on a Friday morning and drove up to Vevey, the chocolate town, then down by the Lac Léman to Montreux, where the jazz festival was being staged. I spent Saturday in Zermatt, taking the train up to see the splendid mountain in all its golden glory. (Who knew that later I would be the only American to be on the board of the Zermatt Summit to "humanize globalization"?) I took the gondola all the way to the peak. The day was sunny, blue, and crystal clear. At the highest station I looked down over all the Alps and decided this would really be a great assignment. I really wanted to do this. One of my friends from the network in DC, Gene Dewey (who ran all the helicopters for Colin Powell in Vietnam), was the number two at the UN High Commission for Refugees. I spent a night with him and his wife in old town Geneva before leaving. I think we ate fondue. He said he could informally talk to Hinteregger for me to put in a good word. I thanked him profusely.

When Hinteregger came to DC the next month on business, he asked to see me in private. We met in a basement conference room at State. He said to me, "I want you to join the UN and be my deputy, but the people in UN New York are giving me grief over it." My experience was too thin, my French too weak, and some of the other candidates had been rather senior diplomats, serving multiple times as ambassadors. I said I understood and gave him the three letters of reference from the US senators. He said he had never seen them before. That surprised me. Impressed, he said he would see what he could do. He wanted me over these others, I think, because he saw the potential for a close relationship, based in trust, and for my economic judgment/expertise. Oddly, the Wharton thing, its reputation capital, impressed him the most, although he could not tell micro- from macroeconomics.

I decided one last push was required. I remembered that Hugh Montgomery, one of my old bosses at INR (and a real cloak-and-dagger man going back to the OSS days) was now an ambassador at the UN in New York. I called him up, reintroduced myself, and because of the INR imprimatur, he said he had an idea. I didn't ask for details.

Hugh made an appointment with the UN secretary general, Javier Pérez de Cuéllar, and marched in there and made a demarche that I be selected right away, then and there. Hugh is a convincing guy, a former OSS operative who walks with a limp but is most convincing, and he was the archenemy of the Soviets. Who knows what he said or threatened? Anyway, it worked.

Within a week I was offered and accepted the top US position in Geneva. I was invited back to the White House and ushered into the Oval Office to shake hands with President Ronald Reagan himself. He gave me a pair of presidential cuff links, which I wear with pride to this very day, and he said to me, "Give 'em heck, Ted."

At age thirty-five, I was about to make a major move into my new suite of offices in the old, historic *Palais des Nations*, where the League of Nations was formerly housed. Oddly enough, my view out over the lake and the Jet d'Eau fountain was exactly the spot where my college adviser, Bill Harper, and I took a memorable photograph making the *V* sign some sixteen years earlier. My colleagues at work gave me a boisterous send-off party, and I left for Europe in late July, and my family joined me later in November. We were packing boxes once again, but this time the UN paid for it, given my newfound diplomatic status.

Qu'est-ce que l'acier!

The lesson is the proverbial—never burn a bridge; a friend in deed is a friend in fact.

MT THIRTEEN FAVORITE BUSINESS STRATEGIES

1. Get the Value Proposition Right

    A value proposition (VP) is a statement that clearly identifies what advantages a customer will receive by purchasing a particular product or service. Every business needs a sound one.

2. Pay Attention to Your Customer

    Management guru Peter Drucker argued that leaders fail to make their customers the primary focus of their attention. The key step is to figure out what it is that your customer values most.

3. Grow the Core Business

    Grow the core stands conventional wisdom about business growth on its head and provides a proven formula for growing a business focusing on the basics.

4. Build Organizational Capacities

    Monitoring and evaluating capacity building strategies strengthens the abilities of individuals, organizations, and systems to perform core functions.

5. Do Performance Metrics

    Performance measurement is a fundamental building block of total quality management (TQM). You get what you measure.

6. Fast Forward into Future Scenarios

    Scenarios do not predict the future; they are tools to explore different ways the future might unfold so that organizations may form shared vision and develop coping mechanisms while looming mitigating risks.

7. Compete Globally (Porter's 5 Forces)

   1. Competitive Rivalry; 2. Threat of New Entrants; 3. Threat of Substitutes; 4. Bargaining Power of Buyers; and, 5. Bargaining Power of Suppliers.

8. Be Prudent and Use Enterprise-wide Risk Management (ERM)

   ERM is the process of planning, organizing, leading, and controlling the activities of an organization in order to minimize the effects of risk on an organization's capital and earnings.

9. Conduct Corporate Governance and Ethics Audits

   Corporate governance is the way a corporation polices itself. In short, it is a method of governing the company. It increases the accountability of a company and can avoid massive disasters before they occur.

10. Be Purpose Driven

    Companies that practice "conscious capitalism" benefit from putting their employees first. This is a stakeholder model of business in society.

11. Know Your Core Competency

    The combination of pooled knowledge and technical capacities allow a business to be competitive in the marketplace.

12. Strengthen Leadership Practices

    Model the way; inspire shared vision; challenge processes; enable others to act; and encourage the heart.

13. Culture Trumps Strategy

    Ultimately, beliefs and behaviors determine how a company's employees and management interact and handle any and all outside business transactions.

8

THE UNITED NATIONS: ALWAYS FINDING A
LOWEST COMMON DENOMINATOR

Let your light so shine before men, that they may see your good works, and glorify your Father, which is in heaven.

—MATTHEW 5:16 KJV

In the summer of 1988, the Cold War was heated up. The Americans and the Soviets were lodged in a battle for supremacy. Reagan was in the last year of his presidency, and George H. Bush was running to extend the Republican streak. It was a real war, but by other than military means. Geneva had become a center of the battle.

With all the UN activities and specialized agencies there, the private banking, the international corporations and scientific activity (CERN, IBM, DEC), it was at ground zero. As the nexus of espionage, of listening and intrigue, Geneva had two sides. One was what the tourists and the Swiss wanted you to see. The snowcapped peaks and Mont Blanc framed the cheese, chocolate, clocks, and fondue. The history of the Reformation hung neatly on the wall in the park. Everything, every iota, was ideal, and the trains ran on time. The Swiss themselves may have been aloof and distant or anal (take your choice; I have my theories) but everything appeared picture-perfect.

The other side of the coin was not so apparent and in fact quite hidden from the casual observer. Switzerland was neutral, not on our side or the Soviets' side, and not part of Europe. They worshipped the Swiss franc alone. They were just a convenient country of fewer than 6 million peasant farmers and cows and a few bankers in the middle of Europe. They had done no wrong and banked whoever came to them seeking secrecy and a numbered account. If it was a Russian industrialist, Arab sheikh, Latin or African dictator, zillionaire, it mattered less than their net worth. It didn't matter who you were; what counted was your flow of funds. You bought your Rolex, Breitling, or Omega, had a glass of that pissy Swiss white wine, and everything was taken care of; and no report was made or record kept. There were people from every country, many of great wealth, and the ever-growing diplomatic community.

The host of international organizations: UN, ILO, WHO, GATT, HCR, ISO, etc., etc., all had their esteemed bureaucrats that they called in the French tongue *functionaires*. I had more than two thousand of them reporting through me, doing everything from statistics to translation to development and relief. After five years working in the UN system, those so-called "professionals" were made permanent employees, which essentially meant you could not fire them, even "for cause"—well, maybe murder. It also meant they stopped working in the sixth year. All the work was essentially done by about 10 percent of the workforce. Many were what we called "free riders" or "passengers," baggage, along for the ride. And many of these were, in reality, spies!

How many nations are there in the world? The number keeps going up. Which ones are the loudest and most demanding? Well, the UN is not only full of those same countries, but it is housed with their nationals, as employees. You think when you go to work for the UN you become an international civil servant. Sure, on the outside. But on the inside you still belong somewhere. In the case of the Eastern and

Soviet employees—and there were many, and almost none were qualified for the jobs they held—all of the salary went to the mission, and only a portion was given to the person. Where did their real loyalties actually lie?

I got my Laissez-Passer, the powerful, UN, light-blue passport, which let you travel anywhere unobstructed. As I settled in and found a pleasant and suitably large house with a pool, a sauna, and a wine room that doubled as a bomb shelter (all subsidized by the UN) for my family in Canton de Vaud, near the forest, in a small village called Chavannes des Bois on the French border, whose claim to fame was a restaurant that served wild game, people were watching. Indeed, they were watching and waiting to see who I was and how I behaved. In the first year we discovered our home was bugged, my office was bugged, and my car was even bugged. I don't think Tanganyika was doing it.

My equal as deputy, the Soviet appointee, was the formidable nemesis Igor Ornatski. Igor had a bit of a reputation: as a bad boy. He was a full general in the Soviet GRU. His ties to the KGB were legion, and he had worked in the UN and in Geneva before. His direct tie to the Soviet mission was no secret. He could pound his fist on the table and scare just about anyone. He was wily and smart in a sinister way, and had many contacts and underlings that would do his bidding for him. He had a sway over Hinteregger that the old man did not like. The Soviets knew how to maneuver and manipulate, and they executed particularly well against Austrians who had been compromised. Ornatski had a beautiful Russian secretary, whom I am told he used to deploy to entrap people, mostly in the sack. Hinteregger was so afraid of Ornatski that he often tried to get things done behind his back or in his absence. Ornatski was restricted from travel, so he loved to be sent on missions or to some conference, always in places like Italy or Turkey. He didn't drink, which seemed odd for a Russian; in reality he was from Minsk, in Byelorussia. When Hinteregger was gone or on vacation back in Vienna, Ornatski was particularly devious and tried to ram things through.

In my third month in Geneva, with my CD plates on both cars

At three months old with my dear mother, Dorothy, in
Rittenhouse Square, Philadelphia, October 1952

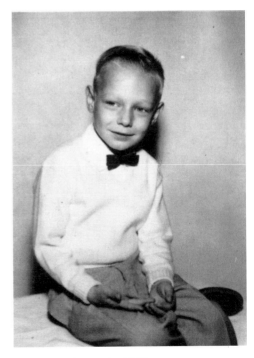

Teddy Malloch, age six, 1958

My official US State Department photo,
1982

With Lord Wilson (right), University of Aberdeen,
Scotland, after receiving an honorary LLD Degree for
"my contribution to civil society," 2008

"Sir Ted" in Palm Beach Florida, 2008

In Oman during a governmental meeting in the Gulf, 2015

At Exeter Cathedral, Great Britain, 2010

In Tamil Nadu, India, with my honor/body guards

The Malloch Clan at my parents fiftieth anniversary in 2000 at Blackbeard's Bluff Estate, Queenstown, Maryland

My wedding to Beth Ellen Miller at Pintail Point Farm, Maryland, July 23, 1994

Wearing my MacGregor tartan kilt at Christmas, 2003

Research Professor, Yale University, 2012

Giving the leadership lecture to five thousand cadets at the US Military Academy, West Point, New York, 2012

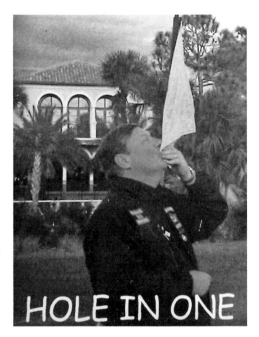

My "Hole in One," 7th Hole, Par 3, The Bear's
Club, Jupiter, Florida, 2012

Me and The Donald

(one was the fastest BMW ever made) and a sense of belonging—the economists in Trade and General Analysis and Statistics liked me and saw me as one of their own, since I had a degree and had to approve their output—I was about to be challenged. Ornatski struck, and we—that is, the CIA chief of station, whom I talked with regularly—believed it was indeed a larger Soviet plot or test.

The annual *Economic Survey* had just been released, and there was excitement from a job well done and the publication of what at that time were the best and only statistics and good analysis on economic production and output in the Eastern Bloc. Those countries cooperated with the UN, no one else. A big party was planned upstairs in the GAAD offices, hosted by their chief economist, a Serb, proudly Yugoslavian, named Sasha Vasic. He was inferior and knew it, but needed my approval to publish anything. The alcohol-prone (a big problem in the UN) who ran our department of public affairs, a German named Hans Lassen, also reported to me, and everyone wanted good press. The party went late, and there was plenty of booze, beer, and vodka (the Russians were there, after all). I left early, sneaking out through a side door, and went back to my office on the third floor to put things away and pack up my briefcase to go home. My secretary, a craggy old Belgian woman, Marisha, who guarded my premises like a Rottweiler, had already left, so I was there in a suite of offices and her antechamber, alone. Then a large, very intoxicated goon, a Soviet who was at the party, burst through both sets of doors and confronted me eyeball to eyeball. He made all kinds of disgusting gestures, moving his arms and giving me the finger. He didn't have a weapon and he didn't take a swing, but he said in perfect English some things that were most provocative. He said my mother should have had an abortion, that I was scum, and that America was a weak prick of a nation. He said I would die, but it didn't matter anyway. I pushed him aside and departed the office with some fear and trembling, wondering what this was all about and who was behind such insults and provocations.

Early the next morning, I sat alone with Herr Hinteregger and relayed the story. He wanted me to keep quiet about it and let it blow over as a bad incident. My next visit was with the US ambassador and the CIA folks. Reading over the account we concluded it was a direct Soviet attack to challenge me early on to see what I would do or if I would perhaps hit him and thereby create an incident of joint responsibility.

I went back to Hinteregger and said this was what it was and I was not going to stand for it. I said if the person was not removed and returned to his home country, the USSR in this case, I would make it public and would be backed up by the American ambassador. The problem was this was no ordinary Soviet citizen. The culprit had been at the UN for three years, was a drunk without doubt, but he was a KGB operative, and more important, was the son of a highly decorated retired Soviet army general who ran the tank corps in all their victorious battles during the Great Patriotic War. We stood our ground with a nervousness and bated breath. In two days he had cleared out and was sent back to the USSR, but unlike the Beatles song, I don't think he found himself very *lucky*.

I was invited to the Soviet mission, a huge concrete monstrosity with tons of checkpoints and security, a few weeks later for a diplomatic reception. I decided to go on principle. When I arrived, they certainly knew who I was, and I am told my entire family history, middle name, pictures, and all my credentials were in their dossier. The fat Soviet ambassador greeted me formally in the reception line, which was customary. He was wearing a full military uniform and hat with about one hundred medals stuck prominently on his chest. He said to me, "We know who you are, Dr. Malloch. INR produces the best, and strength begets strength." It was a provocation, and they never expected what we dished out in return. I now had "big balls" and fortitude in the eyes of the Soviets.

They had far overestimated INR, which they thought, since it was in the State Department, made it the pinnacle of the whole US intelligence community. Ornatski and his ilk respected me from then on. I didn't take crap! It's remarkable how that story circulated, and so quickly, throughout the entire UN. It also, I believe, had an effect on my relationship with Hinteregger. He became more fatherly to me and showed an unusual affection. In fact, around the UN I was called behind my back "Son of Hinteregger" (at least it wasn't "son of something else") and people came to and through me to get all kinds of things, from promotions, to stipends, to permissions for this and that, vacations and travel, you name it. Even the grumpy commission secretary, who did all the donkeywork and passed paper, Brian Duke, a Brit and lame administrator, was envious.

My three and a half years in Geneva passed quickly and involved a significant amount of travel. I went back to New York and DC eighteen times and represented UN Europe in ABCQ budget meetings, in the Fifth Committee, and on a number of special assignments and missions, including a few headed by UNDP, where I was the expert. I was in charge of the work plan, which meant all the divisions and their workers had a hand or probably two in it. I had about ten inches of cables to read every morning on arrival, and since I had passed the Evelyn Wood Speed Reading course in tenth grade, I was done far before my rival, Ornatski.

It was a large, $230 million budget and a multilateral institution with about two thousand employees. Some of the people were good; most were mediocre or far worse. Joe Smolek, a University of Chicago economist, stood out, as did Paul Rayment, who had studied at Oxford. Norman Scott was from Orkney and had a full beard and was a raconteur of the first rank. The Spaniard who ran environmental programs was competent and hired mostly good people. But the bad ones, like Boiko, a Ukrainian, who ran science and technology, were a joke. The statistics division had an East German who was right out of Stalag 13—I mean, the Stasi. And Denti, an Italian who ran transport and had a huge plate of responsibility (they did the IRR), was corrupt.

One of the responsibilities I had was bringing the UN Europe into the late twentieth century, as there was poor infrastructure and few computers. I arranged for the first LAN and wanted to buy Dells, but the UN was afraid if it didn't buy IBM. So we went with IBM and got half the number of computers. Wise decision. A somewhat lazy Italian ran computing and had more excuses than Job. We did have a strong tie to the private sector through the EDIFACT system, which was invented and standardized there. It was the precursor to electronic trade. Companies cared more about it than countries, so I personally made sure that it got all the resources they wanted and needed.

One of my first assignments was literally to do a PR annual report. Amazingly, none had ever been done. I got everyone to cooperate. I edited it heavily, spruced it up, and had tons of pictures taken and graphs added. I went to the UN printers personally and told them I wanted it done in glossy paper with a shiny silver cover and a cutout with the hemisphere showing through. On the second page was a lovely photo of Hinteregger smiling and a nice greeting with his signature. People were shocked when it arrived and all the copies were gone in a fortnight, so many more had to be ordered. The employees themselves were taking them home as bragging rights since never before had anyone taken the time and effort to showcase what they were actually doing. Hinteregger was so proud he gave them out to every single visitor who entered through his wooden office doors.

Another idea I had panned out even better. The UN system issues stamps and sells them mostly as collector's items. Some of them are historic or celebratory; others, commemorative. I had a friend, a Chilean aristocrat, who was quite flamboyant, who ran that office in Europe. I convinced him that we could get an artist to render three Audubon-quality paintings of the endangered species of the three European habitats: Alpine, Woodlands, and Mediterranean. He had to sell it in New York, so I went there with him and convinced the old lady that ran the office with some charm. When the paintings were done, they were astounding. The species corresponded with the Red Book list that our environment division kept. We had a big wine and cheese party to celebrate the first issue of the three-stamp set. Within two weeks it was the biggest-selling stamp in the history of the UN. It completely sold out.

There were some perks that came with the position. These included the big office, new furniture, assistants, and the duty-free liquor, petrol, and subsidies for everything from housing to auto to education. Did I mention my salary was tax-free? My sons went to the bilingual College du Léman, a very international academy near our house, and it too was paid for. They most enjoyed Wednesdays, when the entire school would go skiing. My head of finance and budget was a very friendly Filipino, named Perry Libre. He made everything easy and helped me learn the ropes in the caverns of the UN. I often went to New York with him for meetings and work sessions. I was once tasked with organizing a training session for all senior officials. I got two leading MIT Sloan School profs to run it, and it went off very well. The head of UN personnel at that time was a beaming Ghanaian named Kofi Annan, who years later ascended to the top spot. He smiled a lot and tried to befriend everyone.

Aside from managing the flow of work, most of which was either duplicative or second-rate, I attended, often as the chair, international meetings and UN conferences. One involved a week's stay at a retreat of the dictator of Bulgaria, Zukof; another took me to Brussels to lock horns with the increasingly powerful European Union, who thought themselves all-important. I went to the United States to keep the State Department happy and informed and brought Hinteregger more than once. He had never met the secretary of state and wanted to, but the protocol didn't allow it. So I pulled an end run, going through my friend Bob Kimmitt, who at that point was under secretary for political affairs. We set the meeting up with him and Bob walked us in to meet James Baker. Mission accomplished. Hinteregger was ecstatic and bragged all over the place.

One of my missions involved going to the three Eastern European countries, Hungary, Poland, and then Czechoslovakia to help and assist and advise them in what they called their "economic reforms." All were socialist and under the foot of the Soviet empire but in their own ways were trying to get free. The economic sector was a place they sought to transform or liberalize. The radical economists we met with, besides the old-line bureaucrats, all in time became prominent people. One was made finance minister, Balcerowicz; another, head of privatization; still another, Klaus, prime minister; and another, head of the central bank. They were our drinking buddies. And we got on like gangbusters. In fact, we did so well that the West Germans paid for a private conference with them and our staff at a CDU/CSU retreat, some castle in Bavaria. The talking and drinking went on late into the night, as there was so much to reform.

In 1990 the world was focusing on the state of the environment, and the UN conference on Sustainable Development was staged for a month in June, in Bergen, Norway. I was there for the duration, representing the UN Europe, since we organized the meeting. It was endless meetings and speeches by minister after minister. Every night offered another special reception. We consumed so much salmon you could start a supermarket. On the weekends the Norwegians took us on grand tours to fjords and to festivals, on train rides, and up to the Arctic Circle. It is a beautiful country in spring. One evening we were escorted on a few large tour buses, mostly minister-level delegates, to a recital of Grieg's music and wine and cheese. When we returned to our five-star hotel, there was a huge demonstration going on with green activists and signs and dead animal blood. They rushed our bus and chanted louder and louder, "No more meeting, no more eating." I didn't care for their politics or tactics, but I couldn't agree more with their suggestion. The next day, we learned that the police had killed one of the protestors in the incident.

The finest tour we made was to Canada, of all places. I went with Hinteregger, and the Canadians treated the UN like royalty. Their counselor in Geneva was John Sloan, a Stanford grad with a good head on his shoulders. His wife, a Quebecker, and he had become good friends. He organized a super time, with content, state dinners, and tours that were second to none. And all this in boring Ottawa. The trip to Toronto was very special for me, as they organized a panel and a dinner at Hart House, where I had studied years ago. It was full of fond memories, class, and distinction. I always found the Canadians first-rate, serious players in the international arena, who carried far more than their weight. I was honored to be considered by them an honorary Canadian, although I didn't wear the maple leaf in public and didn't mumble *eh?* nearly enough.

The United Nations, when all is said and done, is an institution whose time has passed and it has worn out its usefulness. It has too many meetings and conferences that have no result and produce little of value. UNCTAD is a conference of developing countries that has gone on for more than forty years, but it does get all those third world elites to Geneva, by the lake, every summer—and on stipend. Most of what the UN does, other organizations do better. Except for the Security Council, there is little that is life-and-death and much that is just make-work and patronage. Sure, I became rather adept at diplomatic receptions, as I went to them five nights a week at embassies. The wine and cheese and hors d'oeuvres were delightful, and the chatter, bland and deceitful. But someone had to do it. As Henry Wooton confessed in 1604, "An ambassador is an honest gentleman sent to lie abroad for the good of his country." When I came back to the United States after my stint, I wrote a deeply personal and factual account with recommendations on what we, the United States, should do at the UN for the secretary of state. My conclusion was not reform. I said we should drop out and form an organ for democratic countries fitted as a forum for the needs of the next century. We should also in any case stop paying so much for so little. I never got a response.

When the Berlin Wall came down, I was at a CSCE conference for two weeks in Bonn, West Germany, on the future of European cooperation. Timely subject. Mr. Gorbachev did not tear down that wall, as Reagan had demanded, but the people disassembled it piece by bloody piece. When they let those first Hungarians through, no one guessed it would peacefully end the way it did. *Elation* was the only word to describe the atmosphere. And disbelief. And just days later our group of diplomats was flown over to see the results—on the Concorde, nonetheless. I got my souvenir piece of cement from that twenty-six-year-old tragic relic that separated us from them. The other countries fell like dominoes soon thereafter, and eventually the big prize, the evil empire itself, collapsed. I knew the state of its economy and society, as I had been there so many times, but who thought this could happen, and on my watch?

With the collapse of a union that it turns out was neither a union nor really all that Soviet, and the dismantling of all those Lenin statues, I felt a sense of accomplishment. Not only had we won, but I was there. I had a first row seat and participated in some (small-large) way in the battle that defined our lifetime. The pundits and intelligence agencies around the world did not see it coming, nor, honestly, did I. Certainly Ornatski did not, and he was forlorn for weeks and thought only about his coming retirement in Minsk on a large UN stipend, of course. Everything we had fought for in my generation came to a halt, and the Giants were now but one. The United States was the sole superpower even if the world was still a messy place.

One Saturday evening, Rick Burt, our slick ambassador to the Geneva SALT talks with the Russians and an old friend from his days as a *New York Times* reporter with his then wife, Gahl Hodges (Nancy Reagan's former chief of staff), invited me to a special first screening of the soon-to-be-released movie *The Hunt for Red October*. It was a thriller about the mutiny of a Soviet submarine and its brave crew. It starred Sean Connery (with a good Russian accent, to boot). The great thing about that private showing and reception was that our guests were real-life commies, the Russian dips themselves. And now that world was rapidly coming to a close.

While I was in Geneva early on, I was introduced to a mad professor named Klaus Schwab, who ran a meeting and organization called the World Economic Forum. They met in Davos. It was a chartered Swiss foundation and was gaining worldwide recognition as a convening place (hub) for world leaders and business executives. Schwab pursued and snared me and brought me into his doings.

The lesson obviously is it takes having—*courage*—to take on any situation, person, or set of circumstances, especially a bully.

THIRTEEN FAVORITE PLACES I HAVE LIVED

1. Rittenhouse Square, Philadelphia, the Waspy center city in Philadelphia's best neighborhood

2. The Main Line, Pennsylvania, where all the WASPs reside in order to fly the travails and violence in the big, dirty city

3. Wenham, Massachusetts, a Waspy North Shore college town and very horsy

4. Rubislaw Den, Aberdeen, Scotland, the coveted rich zone in the oil city, complete with its own den for walking in the Granite City

5. Rosedale, Toronto, the moneyed inner-city spot for Canadian WASPs

6. Beverly Farms, Massachusetts, the farms with a Boston accent (pronounced *fams*) after which they named Beverly Hills when the rich moved west, tight on West Beach and the Atlantic coast.

7. Chevy Chase, Maryland, the old WASP suburb, close in to Washington, DC

8. Harrison, New York, in Waspy Westchester County, full of Wall Streeters

9. Annapolis, Maryland, the sailing capital of the world, and of course, home to the US Naval Academy

10. Geneva, Switzerland, international city and the home of Calvin(ism)

11. Queenstown, Maryland, hard on the eastern shore and looking out onto the Chesapeake Bay across to Fort McHenry, of fame in our national anthem.

12. Jupiter, Florida, a seventeen-mile coast on the turquoise blue sea, with more WASP wealth then heaven

13. Madison and Farmington, Connecticut, Waspy shore towns outside of dirty and dilapadated New Haven on the gold coast

9

DAVOS: PEERING BEHIND THE ELITE CURIOSITY CURTAIN

For the kingdom of God is not in word, but in power.

—1 CORINTHIANS 4:20 KJV

Thomas Mann, the German Nobel laureate and author of *The Magic Mountain*, made Davos famous for its mystical and curative powers. For him, it was a sanatorium to overcome the disease and psychological stress and damage inflicted by modern life. In some ways it remains so. These are my personal impressions as a former executive board member of the inside, albeit a snapshot in time. Davos is many things to many people but it remains a curiosity. It was also according to many accounts the place Bill Clinton got the bug and started his own Clinton Global Initiative—seeing gold in them hills.

Today Davos is synonymous with a different kind of cult. It is the cult of business celebrity; elites from every avenue of life, every industry, every country, leaders and wannabes, will do anything to be seen there, especially during the last week of January, when the World Economic

Forum conducts its annual meeting.

They pay over seventy thousand dollars just to be invited or over a million to be members according to the *Guardian*. It has become the hub of political, economic, cultural, and every other kind of power imagined by postmodern man. In fact, it is about the emergence of what the ringmaster at Davos calls "Davos-Man,"(he actually borrowed the phrase from the late Harvard professor Samuel Huntington) a kind of übermensch that can transform the world. Nietzsche would be proud.

This wasn't always the case. After World War II the German part of Switzerland in the far eastern part of the land and up in the rugged mountains was underdeveloped. Skiing, new hotels, and better train service brought in more tourists, but it wasn't until a half nutty, half brilliant professor of business policy brought his European Management Forum there in 1971 that it started to take off.

In its own words the WEF is on a mission: the World Economic Forum is an independent international organization committed to improving the state of the world by engaging leaders in partnerships to shape global, regional, and industry agendas. Over the course of its history, the World Economic Forum has achieved a limited record of accomplishment in advancing progress on some key issues of global concern. It has also placed itself as the epicenter of New Age *globalism*—a new ideology. Globalism is not the same as the gradual process of globalization, which sees countries involved in more and more trade and investment across borders. Globalism is a movement to and a belief in one world government.

The WEF logo itself puts the organization in the center of the globe's sphere; and Herr Professor Dr. Schwab is the "Wizard" of this "Oz" behind the curtain who makes the whole thing run—just as in the movie.

Every year now, for decades, high in the wintry alpine resort of Davos-Klosters, Switzerland, the world's elite convenes under the auspices of the World Economic Forum. They have what is termed "convening power." It's all over the news. But not much is really known about the organization—the convener. Everyone sips schnapps and talks about the future of the globe under the banner "Rethink, Redesign, Rebuild." The *Re-* word is always the operative phrase! Be sure to use it in every sentence and you can pass Go.

True, Davos can be cynical and trite, and the best thing to be said for it is perhaps as I said in the *Weekly Standard*, that it does not believe the answer to the world's problems is more Marx. But they come close. Davos phrases abound: Rethink economics, redesign governance, put (European) socialist values back in business, promote financial literacy, the future of this and that, risk abatement, go on and on . . . Frankly, while the WEF is full of suggestions, most of them are half-baked.

Here is a sample insight from Davos: "At times of panic credit markets have a tendency to freeze." Here is another: "The bubble forms when expectations exceed reality." Cue the applause from the civics class.

The WEF applauded the public rescue of banking and government-inspired guarantees (bailouts), and their mantra has been "print more money" and, when in doubt, "strengthen regulatory measures." We also need much more "coordination" to defeat systemic risk, according to the Davos line. Did Keynes really get it right? Is Big Government good government? Do markets always fail when left to their own devices? These questions are verboten in Davos—for the hallmark of all believers here gathered is that government is the solution—perhaps assisted by some special council, formed of course by "FOK"—friends of Klaus (Schwab).

Davos wants to tame the "animal spirits" of the market, which are not good and must be tamed. Their authority on this is none less than the turncoat, George Soros, a former robber baron and greenmailer who saw the light. Radical stakeholder capitalism enters left stage, with improved statistics, and a Nicolas Sarkozy–style Commission on Measurement of Economic Performance and Social Progress. We can change accounting as we know it and have a perfect "global solution"—a super–International Monetary Fund. At Davos it is always a GLOBALIST solution. Besides dumping the dollar, the world must also have "international consensus" since the United States has been so naughty and learning to share power and give up control can be difficult. But it is necessary.

For Davos-Man (and occasionally now a woman or two), an all-powerful global central bank will run money, ignoring notions of national interest; but like gun ownership, the spread of capital will also need to be controlled. We will also need a Tobin carbon tax collected by the UN. Bill Gates' version of "creative capitalism" flies well here, and he goes to Davos every year—where he preaches that we must all "give back" and invest entirely on a social basis. His zeal is perennially featured these days, now that he's retired from bad old Microsoft.

Ironically, in the end at Davos—powerful and lucre filled as it is—*money* is the great taboo; it's what leads to subprime lending and to bad capitalism. Realizing that the love of money is the "root of all evil," a "competent global economic citizenry" must fight the inherent flaws of capitalism. If we don't fight capitalism, we are warned, we could end up with Chinese-style authoritarianism.

At Davos, it's repeatedly said, we can't do "business as usual" any longer, and most certainly America, who started all this money madness and interventionism, cannot dictate since the United States is no longer a "hegemon." A thin veil of anti-Americanism lurks behind a lot of the content at Davos. It is a cabal of multilateralism with an impresario professor as its progenitor.

It's interesting to note that, through all the sermonizing and flagellation at Davos, short shrift is given to the classical virtues and religion. Instead, the underlying *credo* here is the need for more confidence in global government, since finance is an imperfect tool for managing risk in an uncertain world.

I went to Davos as a special guest of Herr Dr. Schwab (K-man to his friends) for the first time in 1988. It was fascinating and certainly involved many leaders and business types, mostly from Europe and especially the Third World. Some were on the make and others on the take.

Throughout 1989 Schwab courted me, had me to dinner over and over, invited me to meetings, and pressed me to give him advice on how to stretch the goals and involve both more CEOs and particularly top Americans from all walks, across all sectors and in every major industry group. In his thick, German accent he would say, "Vell, Ted, kunt vie change die velt?" He wouldn't stop and at one point stuck his lieutenants on me as well. One was an attractive woman with long, dark hair, an American named Gail Bidwell. She was good looking and bright, and she and her German counterpart, who was ill with cancer, both kept calling on me in my office at the UN. Schwab had Lester Thurow (economists refer to him as "less than thorough" for his popularizing tendencies) over from MIT. He invited me to lunch. The minister of finance was in from Pakistan; could I spare time for "an interesting" dinner? The head of the central bank of XYZ was here; could I convene in a few hours? No end.

By 1990 he had asked me to serve on some loony council and to help prepare the agenda for the next annual meeting. What were the "veally big questions, *mit ein* Q" going to be? He asked in his dreary, thick accent.

His staff was mostly low-level flunkies and hangers-on, very young, no higher degrees, just yes-men and plenty of women (many were sexy who were randy with the professor, I later discovered), as well. They reported directly to the Wizard of Oz, as we referred to him behind his back. I was pitching in, adding key names, and eventually they asked me to moderate some sessions at the big confab.

Hinteregger and others were slightly jealous, as they were not invited. The head of the UN was there, and increasingly more and better CEOs were attending. With my invitations we got some of the top Americans to join the ranks. Even Coca-Cola came, and they brought so much Coke with them it could have filled entire lakes with that fizz.

Schwab also had an in-house rag, a glossy vanity magazine with lots of pictures of leaders at his meetings and articles by those same leaders. It had a goofy look and name: *World Link*. The idea was to link world leaders permanently. He also devised a failed electronic system to do the same that was well before its time. He called that *Welkom*. Way too Germanic, I thought. Schwab got me to write a few pieces for his publication, on the US economy and on reform in Eastern Europe, and published them with my picture. It was all rather flattering.

The organization was, however, far too Eurocentric, and he knew it and wanted to break out and step up. He knew of my background, history, and work in academe, industry, on Wall Street, in politics, and as a diplomat. He wanted my help and convinced me that we could work together. Pronounce that in German three times!

When we talked privately, Schwab said we were both "thinkers and doers." He liked to ask that trick question of people: which are you, a thinker or a doer? Pick one and you were wrong. Now, I was warned that Schwab used people, ran through directors like water, and was a first-class name-dropper. Some said there was no substance in his doings, just frills, a media fest. He was a pompous windbag to some. In checking him out I found out some things I didn't like. He was a German (born in Ravensburg, 1938 where Hitler had come to power), not Swiss, reportedly with strong ties to those who fled to Switzerland. Like Waldheim, he had Nazi-youth in his résumé and tried to hide it. Davos has always been known as a place for the rich and the sick; that much is well established. Not much has changed!

Less well known, the Nazi Party in Switzerland was headquartered there. In 1936 a famous assassination of Wilhelm Gustloff, the top Nazi in all of Switzerland by a Yugoslavian Jew named, David Frankfurter was in all the international headlines and made the Nazis machine irate. The Nazi connection in Davos is noteworthy given the now established Swiss complicity in the German war effort, hidden accounts, stolen goods, holocaust victims and the anti-Zionism that continues to this day. The World Economic Forum even in recent years has itself called for the boycott of Israel (before it retracted it). Schwab was in total cahoots with the Swiss government. In fact, the Swiss Federal Council paid many of his bills.

Why? Because the WEF strategy was to get people to Switzerland to invest there, to bank there, and to use its central location and supposed neutrality. It was all a clever public relations tool or ploy for the Swiss.

Schwab lacked good American connections and didn't sell particularly well in the CEO corner offices with his thick accent, professorial look, and all this mystical (we called it Davosian) talk about a better world and partnerships for this and that, which sounded like and were mostly "you give us money and we make you a member; more money and you can be a higher-order member; more yet, and you're on some board." He was, simply put, what some people call, an old-fashioned snake oil salesman. But the companies were buying: from Arthur Andersen to A. T. Kearney to Booz Allen Hamilton and hundreds more. The membership consisted of more than 1,001 companies; some were only midsized but from all over the world. He sold memberships as a way for them to meet other members. Clever. Too clever? He took some hits as a grandstander and then many more from the anti-globalists on the left and right. Protests mounted in the tiny ski village, and he had to get the Swiss troops to guard everything.

At a certain point at Christmas 1990, Schwab had me to dinner at his own house in Cologny with his wife and children. It was one of those Swiss chalets on the lakeside, quite large and immaculate. He asked me at dinner if I would consider some arrangement whereby I could join him and go onto the executive board full-time. Money was no problem; he said they would match what I was being paid, although that amount was the highest paid to any employee, so I should keep it quiet. I would get six weeks' vacation, home leave, and could travel anywhere in the world I needed to go. The offer was interesting, but I had a job, and the term was set. I said I'd think about it and wanted to work with him in some fashion. Klaus is a hard person to say no to, as he is so fawning. He also makes it appear that the noble mission to save the world that he has created is, well, missionary work.

I had to tell Hinteregger, and I knew it would break his heart. So we worked a deal out whereby I could spend a portion of my time working on WEF affairs and gradually shift over. By end of the following year, I would switch teams and play for Schwab and the Davosians and appease the gods of business. Schwab meantime had to do some fast moves to get me a Swiss work visa and to tell the UN he would not poach any more people. He also went to his Geneva bankers and arranged for me to not only get a mortgage but to get the right to buy a house in the Canton de Geneva. These were not small things. The WEF as a Swiss Foundation has lots of pull with the cantons, especially where it is based, and in Graubunden, where Davos is situated. It is not a lightweight by any means.

I became not just involved but seminal to the Davos planning and helped set the themes and choose the speakers. Klaus and I made many trips together to the United States and other capitals to get the heads of state and captains of industry on board.

I was brought into the supersecret World Wide Web brainstorming on the future forecasts of the global economy. Those sessions brought together chief economists from leading organizations, banks, and certain economic ministers to spin a story about what lay ahead and where the challenges lie.

At Davos itself, I was a panel moderator of a half dozen sessions and in the big stage held forth as the questioner or respondent on the big economic sessions. My favorite one included the likes of the chairman of the US Fed, the CEO of a global bank, the CEO of Salomon Brothers, my old pal John Gutfreund, the new head of the bank set up for Eastern Europe, a leading French intellectual, the president of the World Bank, and the CEO of Moody's, the rating agency. I beat up on each of them but let John off the hook. I ended by having each of them play the role of one of their counterparts and tell the "honest" truth. It was a hoot and brought the house down in laughter.

I suggested to Klaus that because we had so many bankers from around the world going to Davos, we should create a World Financial Services Forum meeting as a subset. He was afraid of that for some reason, I think because he did not speak "financese." We decided to have a governors meeting with CEOs alone and then on the last day open it up to the entire financial services industry. It succeeded wonderfully and completely sold out. I chaired both sessions and played Phil Donahue at the latter, with a roving mike, sticking it literally in people's faces to get instant responses. Everyone wanted to go to Davos, and this was a new way to include more people, and most critically, collect their lucrative fees. The head of Citibank wondered out loud why nobody had done this before. He knew it was a cash cow.

The two countries that were weakest in representation at Davos were the United States and the USSR (until it broke up in 1992).

I was given a mission. The United States was the easy part. Getting the right people, the stars, the CEOs, and the think tank heads and members of Congress and the administration was just a matter of pecking away and showing them the materials and noting the benefits: personal and institutional. The toughest sell was their most precious commodity—their time itself. But with spouse programs, superb skiing, Audi driving schools, and all the socializing and partying, who wouldn't want to join the world's greatest schmooze fest in an Alpine village? Besides it was tax deductible, and the fees were paid to a foundation!

The most powerful elites in the history of the world all gathered in one place? And that place is Davos? The media certainly ate it up. They enjoyed themselves and the after-hours drinking and dancing more than the participants themselves. They came in droves. It made their job easy having so many world leaders in one small town, captive to give "exclusive" interviews. We let companies break stories there. Countries could do the same, but usually only those who had paid some huge tab to sponsor a reception, a gala (complete with famous rock bands), or initiate some new policy announcing it to the world. Turkey's then prime minister asked to be admitted to the EU one year, which caused quite a stir; they even made peace with the Greeks. The Alpine countries announced an initiative to save the Alps another year. The Aga Kahn announced his new Central Asian University. The West Germans announced the unification there and the bold one-mark policy. It took the roof down. The UN unleashed a program for corporate citizenship there. Every year the UN or World Bank came up with some new, far-fetched proposal. Most of these initiatives lasted about a year, some two, and then fizzled out, soon to be replaced with a new, far more urgent one. They too fizzled in about the life span of a newt.

The other country that was underrepresented was the USSR. They were suspicious of market capitalism and didn't quite know how to use such a forum. But when glasnost hit and the leaders bent to the West, the doors swung wide open.

I was sent to Moscow three times, and twice with the perky Maria Livanos, who was Klaus's go-to girl. A rich, bossy, very organized Greek who lived for the Davos energy boost. She was a real groupie. We talked the Soviets into both sending a high-level delegation with top ministerial leaders to interact at Davos, but also into doing what we called a "country forum" in Moscow that would bring hundreds of investors and their companies to learn more about the opportunities and changes sweeping their country. We said cash in the form of foreign direct investment would flow the next week. They ate it up. We ate too much caviar! I even bought—well, traded—Marlboros for a few extra pounds of the fish eggs to eat at home. A box of cigs would buy anything in the USSR—in those days.

The first Soviet delegation to appear at Davos was in 1990, and I was asked to be their official host. I went to Zurich airport tarmac to greet the Aeroflot flight arrival on a red-carpeted runway. When he stepped off the plane, their delegation head, the all-powerful Arkady Volsky, head of all industry in the USSR, gave me a bear hug and presented me with the most beautiful Russian red fox hat you have ever seen. He greeted me in a dachalike-laced, Russian accent and gave me the typical kiss on both cheeks. With him were twenty-odd CEOs of all the giant Kombines, oil and gas, autos, agriculture, steel, timber, minerals, you name it. A few of their top pro-market economists who spoke good English were also along for the ride and the free show.

The Forum paid their freight completely, and boy could these guys— only one translator female—drink! It was a demanding group, but we bonded and everyone wanted to meet and hear from them. Volsky's sole demand was that they be put up at a good hotel with a swimming pool. He was a daily swimmer. We accommodated. We also organized a giant powwow with a Soviet at each table of eight, and the room was so overflowing that people were gathered around the outer walls. Everyone at Davos wanted to know what the market opening meant for him or her and their corporate interests in a future Russia.

Six months later we put on the show in Moscow, and more than 250 Western business leaders seeking to do business in the new Russia eagerly attended and paid big bucks (ok, Swiss francs) to be there, to have dinner in the Kremlin and to seize the day. Deals were struck and relations enjoined.

At that time many of the pundits wondered about the future of per-estroika and Mr. Gorbachev, our man in Moscow. One of my favorite little stories about one of these visits to Moscow in this time frame, in the dead of frozen winter, was the accommodation we were given. Volsky's people, for safety and effect, in a chauffeured ZIL limousine, met us at the airport. Rushed off to the elite Little Oktoberist hotel, we were greeted like VIP party members of the CCCP.

I don't think any foreign dignitaries had stayed at this small, elite, off-limits Party hotel before. It was posh and filled with goods in a non-Soviet sort of way, but it was meant for upper-echelon apparatchiks from the *nomenklatura*. After a late dinner and the obligatory Stoli, I checked in for the night. At about 2 a.m. my phone rang and I awoke from a deep sleep. I couldn't figure who would be calling me at such an hour. It was a soft woman's voice, and she said with a delicate Russian accent, "Do you vant *kompanie*?" My brain lit up and I shot back and spontaneously answered, "No, and I don't want photos, either" and hung up. They were still the same old Soviet Union.

At lunch the next day, I had a reserved table arranged with Boris Fyodorov, who had a Western education from, of all places, the University of Glasgow (Adam's Smith birthplace), and he had just become head of the central bank. He was polite, had good questions, and seemed somewhat embarrassed.

We had caviar, the best from the Caspian Sea, the finest Soviet champagne, and Georgian red wine. We had three delightful courses of fish, beef, and pork with roasted fresh potatoes and many vegetables. Dessert was a fine chocolate torte, served with strong coffee. It was the best meal I had ever had in the Soviet days. When the bill came, he took it after I pleaded to pick it up. The cost was seventy-eight rubles. The exchange rate may have been one to one officially, but we got ours for exactly seventy-eight to one. The elegant lunch cost all of one dollar. How long could this last? I wondered. Was the USSR ready to implode?

Behind the scenes at Davos and in the various country capitals, however, real business got done. At Davos and at the country forums around the world, real businesspeople, top execs, paid hard cash not to be photographed or just for bragging rights—well, not entirely; they came and spent money to get access to important people to do deals.

I was involved in dozens of those in Eastern Europe, India, Brazil, and most prominently, in the United States. The US Forum had been poorly attended and deadly dull. It was hard to get top speakers. These things are a dime a dozen in Washington and happen nearly every other week. So we reinvented the US country forum, and I got all of my old pals and their bosses, and their bosses' bosses, to come, if only for a few hours. It had a who's who cast. With these players we were able to bait the hook and pull in all the gullible Europeans and Third Worlders who badly wanted closer access to the real American leaders and powerbrokers. It worked and became another cash cow. We held it at the Willard Hotel and it oozed—power.

Behind closed doors is where all the collusion and cartelization took place, *ha-ha*. At Davos two bankers met from UBS and Swiss Bank Corp, and later you read of a merger. The steel company of Holland sold out to their counterparts in India. Investment dollars flew like sand in the desert wind. The Japanese wanted plants in America; *hello Mr. Governor (you give tax holiday, let's shake on it)*. The Chinese wanted factories, and they lined up from Nortel to Motorola just to shake hands. Big Pharma met and colluded on patents and pricing. Did I see that? I swear the oil companies had a cartel going. And ADM it was said, cooked the price of corn fructose, right there. Want to sell airplanes? Autos? You name it, even armaments. It was a global bazaar of high-altitude wheeling and dealing with high price tags. And Schwab got not just praise but perhaps a cut—or at least more sponsors in the process.

There were closed dinners *only* for Goldman Sachs clients and lunches with Price Waterhouse where the latest and greatest author on some exotic subject held sway. The Business Exchange office had people waiting to get in to make appointments with a potential supplier, vendor, or joint venture partner. There was a fee for that service; did I mention it? You could rent a Soviet reformer or a university president; any and everything was for sale. Jeff Sachs, the notorious then Harvard economist, was there rounding up country clients for his reform and anti-IMF packages. Whenever we heard he had signed someone up, it was time to "short" the countries' debt, as I knew his advice would lead in just one direction—down.

Bono and the movie star set were parading as intellectuals and begging for donations for their favorite causes. Angelina Jolie in a hot tub, some swami in a headdress talking about inner spirituality, and a German theologian talking interfaith dialogue—it was so Davosian.

It was all there like a marketplace, the Agora. Mr. Zia, have you met Mr. Singh? Oh, you two are enemies? Well, not here in Davos. We all get along and do business. Jews and Arabs not allowed to meet? Everyone had a so-called project to sell. No one knows that here. And all the while the cash registers are going *cha-ching* for the impresario, the Wizard of Oz. They were not just stroking his ego and bowing to Swiss acumen but coughing up fees, donating again and again.

There was a lounge in the upper reaches of the huge concrete Congress Hall and a busty Texan, a former Miss Texas, I believe, worked it, serving coffee of every delight and catering to the "needs" (need to ask) of the delegates, as well. Massages, rubdowns, she knew how to please, and the lounge always seemed full for some odd reason, even at eight in the morning.

It was hard to keep going at that pace for days on end. There were partying, receptions, and dancing late at night into the wee hours of the morning. Is that the young Mr. Baja I see dancing with the Swissair stewardess(es)? Did I mention Klaus handpicked the prettiest steward-esses, and they were assigned to Davos as escorts? A lot of older men had that *thank you, madam* look on their faces in the morning briefings. There was considerable one-upmanship, too. Who has the biggest wallet, deal, and penis, kind of talk. Boris Johnson, the mayor of London, later called it, "an orgy of the audacious."

One final tale at Davos involved a former employee journalist, an Irish-American from Chicago, who drank far too much. He also laughed a lot. John had taken a job at the International Labor Organization in Geneva as a press officer after his Davos stint, and he invited me to dinner one night at a less-than-reputable restaurant in Paquis near the red-light district. He had someone I "had" to meet. When I got there, we had drinks at the bar, and he took me to a back room to meet Sergei, a Russian. We broke bread and exchanged pleasantries. Near the end of the meal, he said, "I have an offer for you; would you be willing to work for us in exchange for money? We like your access to people, leaders, and businessmen, and it could be of use to us." I got up and said on leaving, "No thanks, and I don't appreciate such KGB solicitations." John seemed disappointed, as he clearly was on their take.

The two most secret items at the World Economic Forum were the budget and the VIP list and its attachment, noting their "guests," i.e., who they were sleeping with. The budget was not a public document, and it showed the income at well over $100 million. Less than half apparently came from membership fees; and more than half was an outright line item gift from the Swiss federal government, and that didn't even include the vast sums of money that were spent on security, military, and otherwise.

When some protests materialized one year, those costs went through the roof. Best of all was the supersecret list I mentioned above. I once, in jest, joked that I had mistakenly given that list to the press. By leaking it to the equivalent of *People* magazine, the world would know the next day who was in bed with whom, both boys and girls, and notice that many were, well, not exactly married. No one thought it was funny, but of course I was only kidding.

The other favorite story I can personally relate is the battle over pricey real estate. Naturally, the biggest CEOs and heads of states wanted the best rooms. What's new? But there are only so many of them to go around in a small ski village like Davos. Or next-door Klosters, which was viewed as second class. They came at a steep price, and priority went to the loudest complainers. The president of Peru was lodged in prime top-floor space in the best, Hotel Belvedere (and with a mistress, I might add). When the CEO of Salomon Brothers at the time arrived, he had shabby accommodations, unfit for the king of the money game. In a normal diplomatic protocol, a head of state would outrank a CEO, but not at Davos. We kicked the president out of his room with apologies so we could please and satisfy the CEO and his perky wife, Susan. Money talks and power walks. Wicked Solly traders probably shorted Peru's debt the next day just to rub it in.

After Klaus reneged on a firm promise he had made to me, which was to open an office in the United States, I felt I had been let down and lied to and had to leave. My wife of the time said she could no longer live as an expatriate in a foreign land, and if the marriage was to survive, I had to return home. Yes, it was an ultimatum. My middle son, Trevor, somewhat mischievous in nature (but now an accomplished petroleum geologist), decided one afternoon that he had had enough of our Siamese cat, and I caught him trying to force her into the microwave oven. She survived but ran away about a week later and never returned.

There was an analogy to our family situation. So the packers came, and we took Swissair to New York City first-class, along with our Vizsla, named Heidi, who was a gift from the Hungarian ambassador. Heidi was an inbred, like many things in Switzerland, and had a tendency to bite, especially men, and more particularly, black men. After biting three such work people back in Annapolis, the Animal Control people told me she would have to be destroyed if we did not get rid of her. I made a deal with my three sons that we would sell her to a Foreign Service officer and his wife who were being assigned to Ethiopia, of all places, and they would each get one hundred dollars from the transaction. The deal was struck, and Heidi went off to a land of all black people.

We were ready for the next episode in our itinerant but elitist lifestyle, now living on prestigious and Waspy Spa Creek in downtown Annapolis, Maryland, with a boathouse; a Filipino, maid—named Purring, whom we brought back legally from Switzerland; and a wife and mother who was shortly to also leave us. It called into question the whole reason for leaving the good life we had come to know and "suffer" abroad. I suppose nothing lasts forever, as the maxim goes.

The lesson in this power tale is, simply, never trust before you verify. It worked well for the Gipper.

THIRTEEN FAVORITE BOTTLES OF WINE I HAVE DRUNK (SOME AT DAVOS)

1. 1982 Burgundy Gevrey-Chambertin Domaine des Chateau, called "Red Velvet." It was Napoleon's favorite wine.

2. 1961 Bordeaux Petrus. I had this at a party in Palm Beach, and they guzzled many bottles of the expensive stuff, not even appreciating its finer qualities.

3. 1994 Meursault-Genevrieres. What a beautiful white, fresh, floral, delicious wine.

4. 2002 Napa Silver Oak Cab. This is a big Cab from a great region that scores high points on every scale.

5. 1976 Penfolds Grange Hermitage. Well, one Aussie just to mix things up and for that bouquet.

6. 1989 Gewurztraminer SGN Hugel. These wines are distinctive and unique. A regional call. Good with charcuterie.

7. 1997 Napa Screaming Eagle Cab. Get your hands on this coveted item any way you can!

8. 1947 Bordeaux Chateau Cheval Blanc. A nice summer wine, good with almost any seafood. I prefer mussels and garlic.

9. 1995 Greenock Creek Shiraz. Not my favorite grape, but this one is most drinkable. At least it is NOT Merlot (as in the movie *Sideways*)!

10. 2006 Pomerol Vieux Chateau Certan. Earthy terrain. The gravel in the soil must do it.

11. 1986 Chateau Lafite-Rothschild. An effete wine if ever there was one. The name says $$$.

12. 2005 Russian River Hook & Ladder Pinot Noir. Limited production and so good to drink you won't be able to keep it in stock. My everyday wine.

13. 1973 Napa Stag's Leap Cab. The best of California. I used to serve this at my holiday party in the UN just to piss off the French. I told them it was French—then I told them the truth and they were caught.

10

CNN: RAW MEDIA POWER AND
A NEW GLOBAL SHERPA

And He said to them, "Go into all the world and preach the gospel to every creature."

—MARK 16:15 NKJV

Atlanta was a Southern town, but it was metamorphosing into something *very* different and more impressive by 1992. They were getting cosmopolitan and downright worldly. They had won the Olympic bid scheduled for 1996 (secured by Andrew Young at—you guessed it—Davos). Segregation was over and grits were hard to find.

One company had come to personify the newfound swagger and embodied the spirit of the New South. That company started as a small-fry radio station with a big signal and had grown into the powerhouse and the most-watched network on cable television. Its format was unheard-of: All News, All the Time.

After the Gulf War, Ted Turner, their CEO and founder, bragged that he had won. CNN represented raw media power as it had never been witnessed before.

When you met Turner, the smile, the pencil moustache, and the ability to speak his mind, he instantly mesmerized you. I went to dinner a few times with him and Jane Fonda, who looked younger than her age and had lots of plastic all over her body, to boot. In their Bugatti restaurant we had bison steaks and talked about his growing empire—worldwide.

Turner could get mad and was even known to throw phones, but when he wanted something, he went after it like an untamed bulldog. He invited me to a Braves game and we sat in the dugout, and when Chipper Jones hit a home run to win the game, they brought him the ball and he gave it to me.

Tom Johnson ran CNN, and he was a senior TV journalist who had been Lyndon Johnson's press secretary. He was also mentally ill, as he later divulged in a most honest account of manic depression. He knew his way around Washington but was often hidden away as if he were battling something. It turns out he was—his own deep depression. Our main point of contact at CNN was the colorful and ego-driven, Lou Dobbs. His star was ascending, and he wanted Ted to make him president of CNNfn. He was, in other words, as Lou often does, posturing. He thought a lot of himself, and his people in New York at the offices across from Penn Station were both afraid of him and yet oddly devoted to him. I was never sure which came first. I liked Lou and he was a good head.

The idea for a World Economic Development Congress was not mine. An entrepreneurial madman from Boston, who had bought and sold conferences before in health care and other industries, Vidar Jorgensen, originated the scheme and sought me out with my Davos experience to become president and run it. He took all my suggestions and did let me run it, even giving me a piece of the action.

Getting CNN to be the named marquee cosponsor and brand was not easy, and I was sent to sell them on it. The bumpkins from Atlanta were salivating, and the higher-ups thought it a no-brainer. Ted was quick to say yes because he wanted to flex his muscle after the Gulf

War coverage, and this fit his larger goals. We were assigned a working relationship with the maniacal Dobbs, the economics news chief, whom I met with regularly and talked to on an almost daily basis.

The scheme was, frankly, to compete with Davos. Plain and simple, I thought that by bringing the world's elite to a meeting just before the annual World Bank–IMF meetings in Washington, DC (Clinton would later do the same in New York before the UN meetings), we had an opportunity and timing to exploit. Many big shots were coming anyway, so all we had to do was build a compelling reason to attend our gig. The theme was chosen: *Building the Integrated Global Economy*. We wrote a clever script and CNN used its footage, and they played the invitation a million times or more all over their giant global network. You couldn't get away from it. It was on in every hotel room in the world, every hour.

We invited everyone on every list. Klaus Schwab got wind of it, and he was mad as could be. The one thing a monopolist hates is competition. He claimed we were using his material, stealing his ideas. There is no patent on such ideas, and indeed I had learned much in the mountains of Switzerland. We invited many of the same players, but because our price points were lower and we had a full-blown trade show, we extended far beyond any other like event.

I got DRI/McGraw Hill, the economics firm where I had friends, such as their chief economist, Roger Brinner, to do a *Directory of World Markets* for the event. It included definitive material on more than one hundred countries, and it came in a fancy bound book. They did it for a barter sponsorship. That was my plan to get as much in barter as possible and have to pay very little except for a few big-name speakers so as to have a windfall.

The sponsor side involved hiring a sales staff and my working with them to get meetings and close deals. It wasn't easy, but by the end of the day we had about thirty sponsors at different levels and raised more than $3.5 million. The big ones, like Sprint, Cadillac, and Digital, gave a bundle, and I got Europeans, even Swiss, and quite surprisingly, Japanese sponsors, to kick in. On a trip to Japan, we closed the giant

Fujisankei for a big check and got the Japan Club, Nippon Air, and many government officials to agree to participate.

CNN, while they had a say in the program, did not control it and got paid nothing. At the actual meeting, I was on the elevator with Ted Turner, who was quite disturbed that he got squat for lending his brand to our confab. He didn't even get a percent. What can I say? He wasn't exactly a great negotiator.

During the buildup I got to know and sail with Ted's son, Teddy Turner, who had blown his entire wad of inheritance on a used ocean-going sailboat that he was trying to get into the Whitbread Round the World Race. He had won some minor races, but he wasn't his father—in any form or manner. He didn't have the charisma or the drive. He was also a poor salesman. As a result of a budding friendship, I told him I would try and help him get a big-name sponsor. We took some potentials sailing with the tall ships in New York Harbor. But no one was biting.

I talked to a few CEOs who could take down such a price tag, but they were unsure about sailing, or about Teddy himself. We came up with a clever idea whereby we would attach a CNN camera to the back of the boat and provide coverage from around all of the seas in real time. Some people liked that association but often concluded that if this was Turner's son, why didn't his rich daddy just pick up the tab? He had the dough. That was the problem; Ted was so rich and had such a big mouth that it hurt his son's prospects.

Teddy was desperate. I had a last gasp idea, but it was risky. I talked to Sprint, where I had gotten to know all the top leaders, and they liked the idea and the cost was tolerable but expensive. One problem they had was that CNN was an MCI customer. So what they proposed was that if CNN would switch (at a discount) its large telecommunications account over to Sprint, they would sponsor the boat. We even came up with a cool new name for the boat: *Sprint Around the World*. It was doable and it solved everybody's problem. Except for Ted Turner.

When the decision finally got to him, he blew his top, swore pro-fusely, and said, "Not over my dead body. I am not giving my son one more f'ing cent!" End of race. The boat never sprinted, anywhere.

Meanwhile the building of our program was mounting. We had ten months to put it all together, and I had four full-time staff working with me night and day to get a who's who program together that would knock the socks off of everyone. We used my Rolodex (it was before social media) and every contact I had ever made to knock down speakers. It was ambitious. We had plenary sessions and keynote headliners, panels and six separate tracks ranging from fast-growing companies to regions of the world to specific industries to one exclusively for CEOs, some three hundred speakers in all. Nothing like this had ever been attempted before. We also had a staff of kids selling space in the exhibit area that kept growing and growing as we added exhibitors.

We decided spending real money was critical for some big-name draws. I got Margaret Thatcher to accept to be chairperson and to give a prime-time keynote. We had to pay her sixty thousand dollars, but it was worth it. At the Congress she was delightful in her coffered blue hair and grandmotherly dress, purse clutched in hand. But under it all she was an Iron Lady. At a private breakfast before she spoke with Tom Johnson, Lou Dobbs, and me, she acted matronly, yet confident. Dobbs, who was a chain smoker, blew a puff right at her, and she stopped in her tracks and said to him in a reprimanding voice, "Will you either stop that or leave the room?" Lou did and was utterly embarrassed. She was that tough.

She said she had had second thoughts on her speech, which was to go live on CNN in just minutes, and she had stayed up until 2 a.m. rewriting it. I could see it was all marked up with her red pen marks. I was surprised and had assumed she would give a canned speech written by speechwriters full of platitudes. We went out onstage, where I introduced her in the kindest of words, a bit of hagiography, and using some fantastic film footage CNN had assembled to intro all the speakers. It was a dark room, some music, and then these powerful one- to two-minute newsworthy bios, and the lights rose slowly. It elevated the audience, and the speakers themselves were awed—blown away. Thatcher's first words were, "Whoever put this Congress together is a genius and truly a 'global Sherpa,'" and then she thanked me. I have used the praise and moniker ever since.

Lady Thatcher went on to give a historic speech that did not mince words. It was a hammer blow to the stomach. It was, in fact, her now-famous Maastricht speech, which concluded against Britain being a full part of Europe and against joining the Euro. People were amazed and dumbstruck by her strong words, fortitude, and her sheer brilliance.

She took no questions, and as we raced to the men's room, I saw George Soros, the tycoon investor, who was moderating one of our tracks on global finance, and we entered the lavatory together and approached the urinal. He said, "Quite a speech." I said, "Yes, what do you make of it?" He said we'd have to see. That weekend he shorted the pound sterling in one of the biggest naked plays against a currency of all times. He made a clean $1 billion. I only wish he had let me in on it.

The other big name we paid significant money to speak was the inimitable former Nixon secretary of state and national security advisor, Henry Kissinger. He was surprisingly generous with his time and genuinely interested in the theme of the Congress. His keynote covered all the bases in geopolitics, save one, Africa. You could see how his deep Germanic professorial voice could be, perhaps, an aphrodisiac? It sounded as though he had marbles in his mouth.

He took questions from the large audience sitting at a table with Lou Dobbs on one side and me on the other. He didn't acknowledge Dobbs or his journalistic questions, it was obvious. My questions synthesized those from white cards collected from the audience. I had devised that plan because that way they (the paying audience) felt they too were being included. The failure to mention Africa elicited one question for which Kissinger was apologetic but he said that Africa would continue to suffer and had few prospects, which is why he had neglected it. He was bluntly persuasive.

The final question at the end of the hour was mine. I said, "I have a card here [I did not; it was made up] from a gentleman who is an Indian living in London with family dispersed throughout the US and the Middle East. His daughter has just given birth to her first child, a baby girl, this morning at 6:05 a.m. Greenwich Mean Time. She wants to know, will the world see peace in her baby's lifetime?" Kissinger, the stern, accomplished diplomat who had worked with the Vietnamese and taken Nixon to China, choked up. He was, you could see live on CNN, emotional. Touched by this final question. It showed a side of him that few before or after have ever seen: a human side. He said contritely, "I don't know, but I pray so."

At the reception that evening at the Smithsonian's Air and Space Museum, I rode with Henry in a rented limo and a security escort. In the back of the car we chitchatted and exchanged pleasantries. He wanted to know about the audience and how large it was. "Over twenty-five hundred," I said. He had a few more specific queries. Then, he paused and asked, in great seriousness, "Tell me, Ted: how much did you make on this thing?" It proved to me he was not just a brilliant strategist and a human being, but a shrewd businessman.

When tallied up, we had some 2,500 attendees, from 117 countries, 7 heads of state, some 100 ministers of government from finance and economy to industry and foreign affairs; we had more than 200 CEOs, the likes of Michael Dell, Akita Morita, and Dwayne Andreas, and many from overseas. We had so many bankers that it was standing room only on the track. The Japanese were there in droves.

We had succeeded beyond our wildest dreams. When it was over, there was a letdown and physical exhaustion. I had other offers to do 101 things, and I needed a break. The Norwegian funder, who always carried around a spiral notebook in which he made copious notes because he was so slow, wanted to keep most of the proceeds and claim all the credit. He was a selfish soul and had a definite sense of insecurity. We had built something of global significance, and all he could think of was the profits and shafting people, myself included, and all those who had labored nonstop for a year to build it. He refused to pay commissions, and his lawyers got involved. I later discovered he had a reputation for starting companies and shutting them down and sticking others with his debts.

Not only did I have many companies that wanted my talents, but also my home situation was difficult now that my wife had left and I had to raise three boys aged twelve, ten, and five, alone. My parents were helpful and loving, and I hired a Jamaican woman, Annette (who, ironically replaced our Lynette), who lived in the basement and did cooking, cleaning, laundry, and household chores. I felt like a modern-day Thomas Jefferson. I am sure the neighbors wondered what was going on at my little Monticello.

I decided to start my own company to take in all the consulting I could garner and to try and get a life again. A leading DC lobbying firm asked me to join and suggested they would house me for 50 percent of the take. I said no thanks and hung out my own shingle. At some point I started dating again after a lapse of about twenty years.

At age forty, which I had just turned, I questioned what lay ahead. Getting introduced to females was relatively straightforward but also very time-consuming. Every friend had someone in mind for me, it seemed, and I just *had* to meet them. A ballet teacher, a sister-in-law, the divorcee who lived next door. You name it; they all wanted "it."

Over the next year and more I started keeping what we—Skip Weitzen, my golfing buddy and sick Jewish humorist friend, and I—referred to as "the Database." It consisted of women I had dated and ranked by a number of categories. You can imagine what they were. The number of entries on the database lengthened. It grew and grew. No one was perfect. One human resources director had great season tickets to ice hockey games, but not much else. Another computer geek was, well, a geek. A don at St. Johns College wanted someone to write poetry to. A mortgage banker was sweet but had a young child and more than one boyfriend. A real estate appraiser looked like Heather Locklear and wanted to get married, but my kids couldn't stand her or hers. A half-black beauty dated baseball players—many of them simultaneously. Another, a chemical salesperson, was fit and a bit anxious but couldn't stop talking about her past!

I was ready to throw in the towel when in late 1993 I started consulting for the Aspen Institute and met a woman who worked there for Marriott Corporation, directing conference services. Her name was Beth, and she was eleven years younger than me, with flowing auburn hair and a gleaming smile. She had never been married before and was a pastor's daughter. The first time I met her, she spilled coffee on me. One of the other women on staff told me about her and said she'd like to meet me, i.e., date. We did. I invited her to go on a ride on my boat as the leaves were turning and the colder winds gusted late in October. It was a pleasant afternoon. In my living room, as dark set in, the large French doors mysteriously blew open and we had our first kiss.

I have never kissed another woman ever since. I asked her to marry me at Bridal Veil Falls in Yosemite National Park, and she said yes. We were married the next July on Pintail Point Farm in an outdoor wedding, with all our friends and families present, and led by a Scottish bagpiper. It was a warm day and the clouds got ominously dark at 2 p.m. as the service began; a few large drops of rain hit the ground. And then, as if miraculously, the clouds parted and the birds sang and the brightest sun ever shown through. Ironically, we moved into a house on Coachway, next door to where I used to live some ten years earlier. It was déjà vu all over again—only better the second time around.

This lesson is about perseverance. Sometimes you have to slog through darkness and high water to find heaven, which doesn't even exist—on earth.

MY THIRTEEN FAVORITE CLUBS IN THE WORLD

As a member of the University Club of DC and Oxford-Cambridge Club in London, I have reciprocity with many such fine establishments around the world. They are preferred over hotels and have large leather chairs to fart in, serve scotch neat (no rocks) and allow cigars, still. Some—well, most—now accept woman members and call it "progress." A gentlemen's club is a members-only, private club of a type originally set up by and for English upper-class men in the eighteenth century. Today, however, they are generally more open about the gender and social status of members. Many countries outside the United Kingdom have prominent (gentlemen's) clubs.

1. University Club of Washington, DC

2. University Club of New York City

3. Yale Club of New York

4. Lotos Club of New York

5. Union League Club of Philadelphia

6. Olympic Club of San Francisco

7. The Chicago Club, Chicago, Illinois

8. Oxford and Cambridge Club, London

9. The Vancouver Club, Vancouver, British Columbia, Canada

10. The Albany Club, Toronto, Ontario, Canada

11. Hong Kong Club, Hong Kong

12. The New Club, Edinburgh, Scotland

13. Athenaeum, London

11

THE BERLIN WALL: EASTERN EUROPE AND THE POST-SOVIET KLEPTOCRACY

And we know that all things work together for good to those who love God, to those who are called according to His purpose.

—ROMANS 8:28 NKJV

Going through Checkpoint Charlie into gloomy and dark, dank East Berlin was always frightening. The wall itself was ominous, the guards were the fiercest on the planet, and the barbed wire and landmines were right there for all to see. All of us have seen jaw-dropping spy movies about the infamous *Friedrichstraße* and what happens on the other side. They were Commies, after all.

I first went through the experience as a teenager in 1972 and have done so more than a half dozen times as an adult. It never felt any better. The DDR, as they called East Germany, was a former Nazi-land that was now Communist. And they did communism better than anyone else because they were authoritarian by nature. And the crossing guards were a special breed of person/animal, who could and did make life difficult, very difficult. Just watch *The Lives of Others.*

When I was a college student, I had to cut my hair at the border just to get into the lovely DDR. One of my mates had a bigger problem; after waiting the obligatory seven to eight hours and having everything you owned strewn out to inspect, they took issue with his passport picture. In the photo he had a beard, but in the moment he was beardless. They debated for an hour among themselves before they let him pass. The guards liked to confiscate cigarettes but were most fond of *Playboys.* But their absolute favorite thing to turn up was Bibles.

On another trip we were in a group, which I was leading, and we had VW vans. At the DDR border, which was always the strictest, with German shepherds and goons in long, black leather coats, our turn finally came and they deflated our tires, rolled mirrors under the vehicle, and strip-searched with *grosse frauleins* the woman first, and then intimidated the men.

They kept asking me, as the leader, "Do you have Bibles?" They were insistent. I knew the rule: that a person was allowed one in his or her personal effects. They asked two more times, never quite believing my answer. After the third time, I felt like Saint Peter denying Christ three times before the cock crowed after the scene at the Garden of Gethsemane. I loudly protested that I had *no* bibles except the one I kept in the glove compartment, which they had clearly noticed. It was a Good News Bible for popular culture and easy to read. The guard blurted out, "How could people of your level have a Bible?" Then they let us through, but the government guide assigned to us spent the better part of a day reading that thing cover to cover in the front seat of the van. They had a thirst for truth because they were not permitted any.

When that wall finally came tumbling down, and it did, there was an opportunity of historic proportion that followed after it. It wasn't just a German unification issue, although it was that; it wasn't just a European issue about defining the new borders of what was Europe, although it was that too. It was a Free World problem because we had fought so long, spent so much money, and prayed so hard for this day.

Could we seize the opportunity, or would it slip through our fingers?

I was at the Berlin Wall just days after the opening. I was in Europe as a senior diplomat just after when adjustments were made and discussions about probabilities quickly changed into term sheets for deals and marching orders for new economic relationships. Since all the old leaders fell or killed themselves one after the other and the new leaders were in almost every case our former drinking buddies, who suffered communism in less-than distinguished jobs, it meant I was well placed to move in this new orbit to assist and to recommend new options, as a consultant and advisor.

Claus Barbier was chairman of Arthur Andersen Worldwide, headquartered in Geneva but with boundary-less responsibilities. We had met at Davos and at various Geneva functions and dinners. He had hosted Eastern VIPs in Switzerland. He asked me to work with him on some new companies he was starting under the title CEO (he said it stood for *capitalist economic options*). It was based on the premise that these now freed countries in the East would be keen to search out new economic options. Barbier was a Frenchman with a much younger, cute American bride and two small children. He lived well and had homes in France and in Bermuda. I was invited to Bermuda for a week's vacation and to plot out targets. I traveled with him to Hungary and then to the Soviet Union, where he thought the biggest opportunities were to be plucked. We also knew Arkady Volsky and some of the Soviet economists whose careers had been transformed instantly and overnight as the tides shifted and the new economic realities came into play.

I made about twenty missions to the East and the Soviet Union, soon to be retitled simply "Russia," in a few years' time. In Hungary we helped the central bank become more bank-like. The assignment ran out of IASA, a scientific think tank in an old castle outside of Vienna where a number of Eastern country scientists were placed to learn the lessons of the West. They held a number of sessions there first for Hungary, then Poland, then Czechoslovakia, and finally Russia to get them up to speed on the banking sector and especially in the to do's and don'ts of running a central bank.

Our team consisted of senior and some older retired people who had run the Fed, been at Treasury, done research on banking, and spent time in money center banks. We would present. They would listen with simultaneous translation and ask questions. Most of the time was spent just going back and forth on what they did and then telling them what needed to be done differently. Their senior-most people were for the most part untrainable or too old to relearn new tricks. The younger ones were attentive and spoke some English and seriously wanted to get on with new forms of business. One of the Soviets was particularly bright, and it turned out he had spent time at Wharton in Philadelphia some years before, learning econometrics. Leonid Grigoriev was a definite keeper and did well. He could also drink like a fish—an Old Russian ailment.

The best trip I made to the East was with the Institute for East West Security and its colorful founder, John Mroz, who was a streetwise administrator who knew how to get things done. He had great energy and a super Rolodex to match. He asked a bunch of us to join him and Iain Somerville from Accenture in Poland for a week to help them and their new leadership do "change management and privatization." Sounded worthwhile, and the stipend was good. We flew over on LOT, the Polish airlines, and went directly to the offices of Leszek Balcerowicz, the new minister of finance, whom I had met years before in Germany at the UN meeting on economic reforms. Now he was in charge of making them. We were brought in to help him and his new juniors on privatization and transition to a market economy. Everything from A to Z had to be worked out and rationally ordered. Late that night they took our group to our hotel. It was not a real hotel. It was the headquarters of the former Warsaw Pact countries, the place where their generals met to plan war against us. They were very nice digs, but the air was creepy. I kept thinking about the mischief that had been orchestrated from those very rooms. It felt like a scene from *Dr. Strangelove.*

After working intimately with them and debating all kinds of options, we were taken to a dinner where we met the president of Poland, Lech Wałęsa, and he asked each of us one by one for our best recommendations.

It was a time when time moved fast and change was rushing in like an incoming tide. My recommendation was "Get on with it—don't delay the pain or the coming rewards." He nodded, approvingly.

In Czechoslovakia we made a similar visit, but this one had more formality to it with the seated dinners and few roll-up-your-sleeves working sessions. Vaclav Klaus wanted help, but he was cocky and thought he knew most of the answers. We had a state dinner in the castle with their president, Václav Havel, and he gave a philosophical lecture. They seemed much more poised and ready to go back into Europe than their other Eastern counterparts. They sent Vladimír Dlouhý over to the United States to meet with us. He was a bright new minister and later head of Eastern Europe for Goldman Sachs. It was coincidental how many of the people we worked with in short order jumped to the private sector and made a killing. Dlouhý had worked in the UN as a professional and was a politician. They lost his suitcase when he arrived at Dulles Airport, and I had to take him out to buy a whole new wardrobe so he could be seen in public. My own mother sewed his pants, making alterations in haste late one afternoon so he could make a big speech that evening. What we don't do for the cause.

The situation in the USSR around this time was most chaotic, as everything they knew was crumbling either from the dead weight of seventy-five years of communist rule or from plain Old Russian inefficiency and the jockeying that was going on for political and economic power.

Working with them was always frustrating, as nothing ever seemed to move. When the ball went uphill, like Sisyphus, it rolled right back down again! But there was wealth in them thar hills, and they knew it. Volsky and his cronies had money stashed away in numbered accounts; apartments in Paris and London, and in Russia they still wielded ultimate power. They could fly you to Siberia and get on a helicopter to see some oil wells or get you in and out of some dangerous places in Central Asia. They controlled the large Kombines and dictated who would run them and who would own them when they eventually went private.

On one trip with a small delegation, we saw all the new leaders and were the first and likely last people to see the autocrats who ran Gosplan, where all the centralization of the economy and of prices took place. Soon they would have nothing to do. Our delegation leader was an Uncle Sam–looking and–talking figure named Donald Kendall, who had been CEO of PepsiCo and was still very much an all-American salesman.

His real interest was seeing that the Kremlin picked Pepsi over Coke and built more Kentucky Fried Chicken stores where the lines went around the block; and later he made a deal to buy the leading vodka maker, they say to get his rubles out and converted. His sidekick was a short, tough-looking dark guy, named Roger Enrico, who himself later became CEO of the company. We met with all the economists from Bogomolev to Griginsky and Chubias. There were so many theories and personalities it wasn't clear who would come out on top now that Yeltsin was taking over. A pack of Marlboro cigarettes was still a good bartering tool to get a taxi or to buy those ever-present Babushka nesting dolls. My favorite one had a tiny Lenin, inside a small Stalin, inside a bigger Khrushchev, inside a larger Brezhnev, inside a larger yet Gorbachev, and all contained inside a largest Yeltsin. Very Russian—you like? It cost me a carton of those smokes. And it still sits on my bookshelf.

On that trip we were allowed for the first time outside Moscow to a forbidden area that contained secure military installations. Our destination was the old and very beautiful Russian Orthodox monastery at Zagorsk. We were the first Western visitors and were shepherded around by an old and a young priest, both with long beards, one gray and the other jet black. I think the translator was going out of her mind, as she too had never seen this other side of Russia. It was touching and emotive to see the art collection, the icons, and all the religious memorabilia still intact after so many years of total neglect and atheism.

In the end some countries with our help made an easy and direct transition to the market. HCP were the three that made it and the break was clean. The others further east were messier and were Slavic in culture and had closer ties to the Russians. Many used the same alphabet and had the same mores. For them, change was slower and more painful.

And in most of these cases the dictatorships of the proletariat gave way to the kleptocracies of the instant capitalists. Entire industries and large firms were looted, gutted, or merged with others in acts of instant privatization that saw wealth transferred from the state to the kleptocrats and their cronies or relatives in one fell swoop.

In 1992 I got involved, given my background, with the Soviet-soon-to-be-Russian entry in the America's Cup sailing races. Tom Griffin, a heavy vodka-drinking friend in Annapolis, was the key organizer, and I helped raise funds for the Red Star entry, captained by an Olympic medal–holding Georgian. We were set to bring the boat to San Diego when the Soviet Union collapsed and the KGB thwarted the effort. Yeltsin wanted to come himself, but there was just too much chaos to leave his shifting situation. We have some great sailing memorabilia from those days and were made members of the Leningrad Yacht Club before it too was revamped and renamed. You have to admit that St. Petersburg does sound a lot better than Leningrad.

We did sponsor Yeltsin when he finally had his tanks surround the parliament to take office. He came to New York, and we met him and ushered him around. He was sober only a few minutes during the entire visit, but I do recall that he made two very good, new American friends—Jack Daniels and Jim Beam.

The lesson in this yarn is that when you least expect it, as the saying goes, stuff happens. Never say never!

MY THIRTEEN FAVORITE GUNS I HAVE OWNED

1. My Remington 12-gauge shotgun, the all-time favorite shotgun for every use, but stay out of a goose blind with Dick Cheney.

2. My Remington 16-gauge shotgun: the gold-trigger version is a classic and works every time.

3. My Remington 10-gauge shotgun, great for shooting geese over a long range, but a heck of a kickback. My shoulder still hurts.

4. My 20-bore Purdey over-and-under shotgun, very expensive and actually my brother's, but a real beaut.

5. My Benelli pump shotgun, sort of the Dirty Harry of hunting.

6. My Ruger 77/22 gauge rifle, long range and accurate. Pick the right caliber bullet depending on the target.

7. My Benelli Super Black Eagle shotgun—the American Armed Forces version works in war and peace.

8. My Mossberg 935 turkey gun: you need a special setup for this strange sport, and the camo to match.

9. My 16-bore Purdey side-by-side shotgun, Churchill's favorite and one that the English gentleman still prefers for grouse and bird.

10. My 30-08 Springfield rifle, this is the one (older version) Charlton Heston held high over his head in the NRA meeting with the quotable line "from my cold, dead hands."

11. My German Luger P08 pistol, a wartime collector's item. My uncle had one he got during the big war while in Patton's tank corps.

12. My Browning .22 rifle, my first as a youth, for shooting cans, right?

13. My Glock 19mm semi-automatic pistol, the most accurate and lethal handgun ever invented.

THE ASPEN INSTITUTE: THE ANTITHESIS OF LEADERSHIP

"Whoever wants to become great among you must be your servant."

—MATTHEW 20:26

Founded in 1949 after the big war to ensure that the democratic capitalist system survived and prospered, the Aspen Institute was invented when America was trying to set the new regime for both postwar democracy and global capitalism. The country, it was argued, needed values to guide it in its newfound responsibilities as world leader.

The Institute began as a celebration of the anniversary of Goethe's birth in a small silver-mining town in the Rockies of Colorado, more or less owned by Walter Paepcke, a wealthy Chicago industrialist of German ancestry and the then CEO of Container Corporation of America. He teamed up with Robert Hutchins, the classics scholar who had become president of the University of Chicago, and Mortimer Adler, the philosopher and founder of the Great Books and Paideia approaches to education. This troika made for a most formidable team.

The initial conference was attended by a who's who collection of hundreds of notables, including Albert Schweitzer on his only visit to the United States. He gave the keynote address in German, translated simultaneously by Thornton Wilder. At the conclusion of that first meeting, the decision was made to continue the conversation and to formally launch what had to be called the Aspen Institute.

It became, in its own words, "an international nonprofit organization dedicated to fostering enlightened leadership and open-minded dialogue."[1] Through seminars, policy programs, conferences, and leadership development initiatives, the Institute and its international partners sought to promote nonpartisan inquiry and an appreciation for what they euphemistically called "timeless values."

The Institute was later headquartered in Washington, DC, and acquired campuses not only in Aspen (forty prime acres downtown), Colorado, but also on the Wye River, near the shores of the Chesapeake Bay in rural Maryland. Its international network came to include partner Aspen Institutes in Berlin on the Wannsee (at the infamous Hitler haus, where the "Final Solution" was launched), Rome, Lyon, Tokyo, and sometime later, New Delhi, and Bucharest, and leadership initiatives in Africa, Central America, and India.

Aspen always prided itself on being nonideological, or at any rate including both known liberals and conservatives; Democrats and Republicans. Nonpartisan, as long as you were part of the eastern liberal establishment, was its badge and mantra. In time, the latter (conservatives) were in somewhat short supply. In many ways Aspen was, simply, the ruling elite, with all its distinguished fellows, a large board of names of the good and the great, and its various policy programs, Congressional Program (for junkets overseas), and especially those of the Aspen Strategy Group which consisted, by invitation, of only former this-and-that's, and mostly secretaries of defense. Aspen embodied what sociologist C. Wright Mills would have labeled the "American ruling class." It was mainline establishment—no kooks, crazies, radicals, extremists, or nuts of any stripe were allowed.

The landed gentleman-intellectual Arthur Houghton (of Corning Glass fame) on his death bequeathed his entire estate to the Institute. Consisting of twelve hundred pristine waterfront acres, including a scientific herd of Black Angus cattle, on what was his historic Wye River great house, it was ironically a former plantation that used slaves and where the first Governor Paca of Maryland is buried. It also had a newer, river house, both of which were ideal locations, removed from the hubbub of normal life for profound conversations. The CIA met there every summer with its top leadership, the North Atlantic ministers rededicated NATO there, and most notably, Clinton used it as a staging ground for the failed talks between the Israelis and the Palestinians. It was also free to rent to the highest bidders.

The so-called Executive Seminar was at the heart of the very being of the Aspen Institute. It began jokingly as the "Fat Man's" seminar at the University of Chicago and was led by Adler himself to school chief business leaders in the ideas that formed the emerging, hopefully more democratic world. At first, it was a two-week total submersion effort that resulted in an educated and cultured person who discovered his own values in conversation with those of the greats of the past. It was literally a classical education—in no time, creating "instant Aristotles," so to speak. It culminated in a reenactment of the play by Sophocles, *Antigone*.

In time, as society got more rushed, the seminar was collapsed to a week, then five days, and when I was involved, a shorter, hyper-version that took just three days was uncorked. We in jest said it went from the Great Books, to the great paragraphs, to the great sentences, to the end— the great words. Flash cards for the unread. But there was a constant market for the exercise, and the cost was high, at five thousand dollars or more per reeducated person. Aspen had big donors who wanted their names on things, from the Crown family, who owned skiing in Aspen, to the Lauders, to the bra lady (and worst CEO) Linda Wachner of Playtex. Money always speaks.

Moderators of the Executive Seminar, a literal who's who of public intellectuals who were well read and who could carry a debate, always prodding with the right or profound question, were told never to lecture. They had to bring out the ideas in the dialogue itself. "Dialogue" was the magic word—an ancient formula of Socratic origin. People like Mark Van Doren and Jacques Barzun and of course, Mortimer Adler himself, well into his nineties, made a second living just moderating these seminars. The USC professor of leadership, James O'Toole, was leading the ranks when I entered the scene. Moderators, past and present, formed a sort of closed club of illuminati, as priests of the very elite of the elite.

My parents had a lovely retirement house on the Wye River, a bucolic spot of total tranquility if ever there was one in the vicinity. The only problem was beating the traffic over the notorious Bay Bridge on a Friday night and back to the city on Sunday evening. I attended a few Aspen sessions and got to know the Wye director, Sandra Feagen, who was nice and very leggy but flighty and a disciple of W. Edwards Deming, the production guru. She was a weak administrator.

The president of the institute during that period was David McLaughlin, who had a troubled past as CEO of a few companies, including Toro, the lawn mower maker, which he ran into the ground, and of Dartmouth, from which he had himself graduated. The college trustees fired him once they lost trust in his leadership.

But fortunately for David, who was a miserable, cranky fellow, he had a friend who always seemed to bail him out. That was Fred Whittemore, the legendary investor and moneyman from Morgan Stanley. They were, it turns out, college Ivy League mates together, Big Green (where the motto is *Vox clamantis in deserto*—"a voice crying out in the wilderness"). Fred got David dropped into the Aspen Institute when its previous president, a Yale Divinity School dean type, utterly failed from an endowment perspective and had to sell off parcels of land just to balance the institute's books. David could at least glad-hand people and raise money.

It was agreed that I could as a consultant help poor Sandra Feagen and try to resurrect some of her forlorn programs. It started as a set fee for a number of hours and quickly turned into a few days a month after only a few months, as there was so much to do.

Finally, Sandra decided it was time to leave and to move with her jumper horses back to courtly life in Charlottesville, Virginia, from whence she came. The best seminar she ever put on was using Deming's true production principles to guide American corporations. She had a few people from Ford and the drug companies, the Society of Human Resource Management, and various hangers-on. My favorite by far was Patti Kluge, the divorced wife of media magnate John Kluge. The former well-endowed belly dancer put on quite a show in the pool in the late hours of the evening. Sandra's prime program flopped and earned, after expenses, nada, not a cent. Aspen was a not-for-profit, but it had to make something to cover its considerable expenses, as it had twelve hundred acres gifted to them by the Houghton family—who also donated the library at Harvard to maintain.

The Institute and David were in a bind and asked me to step in as vice president of Wye Programs, but because O'Toole was cutting back his commitment, at least for a year, to serve as head of all national seminars, as well, I said yes on the proviso that it be only 80 percent of my time. I had other clients and didn't want to be stuck, lock, stock, and barrel on Maryland's empty and agrarian Eastern Shore. There were lots of ducks and geese but too few people to interact with of any intelligence. David was rarely there himself, as he served on five or six corporate boards from Chase Manhattan to you name it.

David was a big name-dropper and not an intellectual in any knowable form. He had no degrees and was not well-read. His forte was bossing. Boy, could he boss. He went through many secretaries, and everyone was afraid of him because he was known to have a huge and impetuous temper. You never knew what or when it would be set off, then explode, which meant people stayed clear of him as much as possible. He was also very dismissive and never accepted criticism of even the constructive kind. David had a penchant for throwing telephones or telephone directories and notoriously hit one of his sycophants one day.

In reality he thought himself much more important than he actually was. Humility was his long shot. He didn't like to sit in meetings and paced around the room wherever they wore on. He told me he wanted to be secretary of the Air Force (in which he had served) but Bush 41 passed him over for some flunky. He was disgruntled, at the end of his tormented career, and now sought to torment everyone else who crossed his threshold.

One day he and I were driving in my new Lexus sports car, complete with a built-in telephone, around the Beltway to northern Virginia for a meeting with Nortel, with whom Aspen had a big program. He got lit off about something and cursed a blue streak and ended with a sour comment about why and how I could afford such a car when he was driving an older Pontiac. I wondered, not out loud, how such a person came to inhabit such a position in the world's leading leadership institute, for he surely didn't exhibit much of the quality himself. God forbid we should produce more copies like him.

Nortel was a huge multinational put together with majority interest from Bell Canada to compete in the United States and globally in telecommunications. They were a clever but not always successful company. One thing they did was beat out AT&T by partnering with the Aspen Institute to offer what was called the Institute for Information Studies.

It was the beginning of the digital era, and the world was one of near-constant change and disruptive innovation for large companies. The idea was to fuse some of the timeless values-based leadership of the Aspen history and legacy with some of the newfangled technological and big-picture industry overviews of the immediate term of Nortel and to create a safe space where chief information officers (their clients and targets for future business) could meet to engage in a thoughtful two-and-a-half-day program and come away saying, "Thank you," and "Where do I sign?" It couldn't be salesy. It had to be driven by content—rich content.

I was very involved with Nortel, which assigned three to four senior executives a year to this project; it was that important to them. They also made a significant contribution to Aspen and the use of its conference facilities and their maintenance and upkeep. The idea worked so well they did it nonstop, from ten to fourteen times a year for about four years. They owned the attendees and held them captive in this remote location. They treated them like kings (a few queens). All expenses were paid; first-class everything was included, gratis. One idea they incorporated was very impressive. They bought multiple copies of all the "hot" books on information strategy, and IT and made them available, without charge, for any CIO attendee who would take them home. Actually they Fedexed them for free, if you asked. There was only one caveat: you had to promise to read them!

Senior execs like to be treated to this kind of feast, listened to, and to learn as real peers. I cohosted the entire program and ran a segment of the program on the second afternoon right after we took the guests to a skeet-shooting outdoor recreation time. Many had never held a gun before, let alone a 10- or 12-gauge shotgun. It plain energized them.

My session was based on Aspen's *Executive's Compass*, which led people to consider their leadership traits along two axes or four quadrants. These are the tips of the kite, so to speak. They include: *liberty, equality, efficiency and community*. The readings are very enlightened, and there was a role-playing game that drove it all home, which we wrote based on a hypothetical telecommunications company. The case study was tight and believable and the options real. We got the participants to buy in completely, and in the process they spoke out of their own real experience and chosen values. At the end they were able to create and show everyone their own "values kite for leadership." It was as useful as any Myers–Briggs inventory.

The participants loved the exercise so much they couldn't stop. It opened them up in a way few had felt before, like a can of worms. It showed weaknesses and strengths. I was more or less convening them in a self-identification process of deeply held values. The game was extremely interactive. It was always a huge hit. We did the program at Wye and in Aspen, Colorado, and then I was asked to do about a dozen in England—at Lea House south of London off the A9 road—for their European counterparts; and it worked there as well.

I often wondered if David McLaughlin had honestly taken the test how large, or more likely small, his leadership kite would have measured. He was never prone to such self-study and practiced the destructive tendencies of the Jack Welch school of command-and-control leadership, instead. He was more neutronic than Jack himself in terms of bad behaviors.

O'Toole, head of all the Aspen moderators, and I were good friends, and we enjoyed each other's company. He went out on my boat on the Chesapeake for crabs. He once rented a Cadillac (no other car was available at Hertz, he said), and we drove it at over one hundred miles per hour on a dirt road just to remember our youths, and we talked shop a lot. We also came to agree that McLaughlin was what we called "the antithesis of leadership."

Ironically, the leadership hall of fame was being led by the equivalent of the black team, the bad guys. One fall weekend we had to go to New York to the annual, large Aspen fund-raiser, a black-tie event at the upscale Pierre hotel abutting Central Park. McLaughlin would give out some impressive awards to his friends, typically, and the high and mighty would pay big bucks to look "leader-like." The Lauders and the Rockefellers would be there, and so on. David would get to be the center of attention, for a *gala* evening, which was most important to him.

O'Toole and I were asked to come to rub shoulders with the high and the mighty. Brains on order, so to speak. We rented tuxedos to look like all the other penguins and performed our task. A week or so later, McLaughlin hit the fan when he found out that O'Toole and I had expensed the tuxedos. He couldn't believe we could do such a thing. But since neither of us owned one and it was a business function we were told to attend, what was to be expected? McLaughlin owned an old tux, so what did he care? Whose pennies was he pinching anyway? Or was he just looking to flex his small muscles?

McLaughlin was notorious for always booking two seats in first-class wherever he traveled. He was so antisocial he refused to be near another person. I think the DSM psychological manual has a category for this kind of behavior: deluded antisocial. While his wife was popping pills to keep peppy while married to him, our leader was spending lots of time on the road, poking the development director. They always traveled together and "had a thing going on," which was well covered over by his office. Such doings are not only horrible for morale, and set a bad example, but over time they erode all legitimacy.

One of the leadership decisions I made that McLaughlin actually liked was giving Marriott Corporation the contract for food and beverage, housekeeping, and sales and marketing. He inherited a system from the former plantation owners going back a number of years that kept on a whole string of incompetent and lazy local employees just because they had grown up on the property—sort of like freed slaves who choose to stay on as sharecroppers. Bonnie Messix was the ringleader who with barely any education was put in charge of things way over her head and pay grade. She hired relatives and friends, and it all looked like a family tree from West Virginia. The property was in disrepair, the food mediocre, and the marketing was a total joke. Marriott did all of this as a core competency and excelled at it. In no time they brought order and upgrades that paid off in more room nights. Remember this was a 501(c)(3) not-for-profit, which for all intents was operated like a for-profit hotel and hospitality business, without the encumbrance of this small charge, i.e., paying taxes. If only the IRS knew.

The old colonial Manor House at Wye and its stables was historic and full of ghosts, which always made for some good breakfast stories. Not only did we grace guests' night stands with books of the scariest titles, which we told them had been specifically chosen for them (made them start to wonder what we knew and what was their true self-portrait), but in certain rooms, especially over the library, a kind, blue-haired apparition often appeared late in the evening. She was the dead mother of two sons who had lived in the house, each of which had chosen to fight on opposite sides in the tragic Civil War.

The Confederate son, who called it the War of Northern Aggression, had died, and rumor had it he was killed by none less than his very brother, an officer in Lincoln's cavalry. It made for ghoulish tales. The ghostly mother lamented her son's passing, carrying his severed head, and beckoned the sleeper into her travails. It was a very good historical tale, fitting for Maryland's Eastern Shore and a modern-day leadership academy that prepares today's top executives for fighting the next battle in their own mighty corporations.

Aspen had some great and highly intellectual programs. One in which I participated one summer in Aspen for two weeks was the seminar on "Asian values." It was lead by Tu Weiming, the top Neo-Confucian scholar from Harvard, and involved many business leaders of rank and mostly Japanese CEOs and their ambassador to the UN, Wasadea-son. He was an amazing bicultural thinker, and his daughter, one of twins, later became the emperor's wife. Her son will be the next Emperor of Japan. Insight often arises out of the profound dialogues of this sort, and friendships endure. We all went white-water rafting one afternoon on the fast Colorado River and had to work together just to stay dry and to avoid the rocks. It was perhaps a metaphor for global society as we were coming to know and experience it.

One of the notable programs, among many, was the Young Leader's Program—you guessed it—for young leaders, but in this case only men and women of color, mostly African-American, who had been selected by their companies for management development at the cost of ten thousand dollars each.

The ten-day exercise brought together speakers of quality who related their own life experiences. Some were from government, others from the academy, but most were those who had succeeded already in business. It was the brainchild of Edith Wharton, a petite bolt of energy who was both opinionated and distinguished. She was the wife of Clifton Wharton, a university president many times over that as a black had served on many boards, from Ford to Kodak. He was at the time the deputy secretary of state for President Clinton, but soon to be fired.

I remember being marched into his office by the enlightened McLaughlin to meet the dynamic duo, with whom he was scared to death to lock horns. I was to salvage their program and get better speakers and serve as the Aspen moderator, a thankless job if ever there was one. It was too much: black aristocrats were paid big bucks to gather wannabes and to form a network indebted to them, all on the site of a former slave plantation, now a leadership institute. I couldn't imagine a novel with such a plot.

My parting shots at Aspen took place in the fabulously lavish ski town now famous for Hollywood actors and Disneyfication. McLaughlin was getting older, and the board was pressuring him to find a successor. He had hesitated for years. O'Toole thought he should have it, and he did deserve the job, based on acumen, if that be the standard. That wasn't the criterion. David wanted "his" man, someone he could own. He had selected S. Fred Starr, a likable and bright former Oberlin College president, who was a master of many trades, an author, architect, bon vivant, jazz clarinetist, and student of Russia and Central Asia. I had met Fred before at Davos and generally liked him.

David hired him and introduced him to everyone, and he gave nice speeches on how he was going to continue the tradition and yet make needed and substantial changes. David's eyebrows went up. What changes? David was going to manipulate the situation as a good (bad) leader always does, and fully planned to stay as chairman of the board, put his man in as crony, and then control him like a puppet. Independence or autonomy was not part of this well-worn formula.

The action was right out of the books of old. Machiavelli or Napoleon could have written the script. But Fred would have none of it and let it be known. So David fired him and then me on some trumped-up charges of insubordination. And O'Toole quit, leaving David as president for yet more years until a castle coup finally did him in.

The tales of the Aspen Institute School of Leadership were so worthy and laudable but not lived or practiced by example. The last word: Fred sued and I gave testimony on his behalf, and all that money David had raised at his puffed-up black-tie events ended up in the pocket of the injured. Justice wasn't part of the executive kite. But it is in the real world.

The lesson in it all is what my mother told me long ago on her knee: be nice; it is no more difficult—and pays huge dividends.

MY THIRTEEN FAVORITE CIGARS

1. Ashton Distributors, Inc.

2. Fuente Newman Cigars

3. La Flor Dominicana

4. Monte Classic Churchill

5. RyJ Real No. 2

6. Cuvée Rouge Toro Gordo

7. Vegas Imperiales

8. Habana Cellars / Tatuaje

9. Oliva Cigar Company

10. GURKHA Presidente

11. DAVIDOFF No. 2

12. Arturo Fuente Churchill Maduro

13. Cohiba Black Churchills

13

PEKING DUCK: CHINA IN TRANSITION

And the Lord will continually guide you, and satisfy your desire in scorched places, and give strength to your bones.

—ISAIAH 58:11 NASB

My Chinese is very inadequate (although one of my books appeared in Mandarin), but I said, "Let me begin by saying, '*Da jia hao*—greetings to you all and—*Xie xie*.'" I said it like I meant it—very staccato. "Thank you for this privilege to address this prestigious business conference. I am truly honored to be your keynote speaker. I have only two messages for you; so let me state them up front, before I begin.

"First, China is today a full member of the world economy.

"And second, China is in *transition*."

This was my tenth visit to mainland (Communist) China (Hong Kong is still my favorite Chinese destination, but it is free), land of the CPC, and I was addressing some three thousand Chinese managers (whatever that means) at a large convention center outside Beijing. I had been asked to come by the office of then premier Wen Jiabao to talk about a dirty, not so little secret: *corruption*.

BLOO, M P

0157

Thursday, February 13, 2020

China needed a dose of morality he thought, so I was the cure. He said to me, "I have read Adam Smith twice, but most of your countrymen have not read him once. We need his *Moral Sentiments* in China as soon as possible. Can you do it?" I said, sure—but in fact I knew it was impossible.

Since my first visit in 1982, every time I returned—China was a different country. Same old ideology but development was rampant, thanks to ramped-up state capitalism. Every time I revisited they had built a new ring road around Beijing. I think they have ten or twelve now, but the system remains structurally flawed, even if the Peking duck is great.

China's transformation into a dynamic private sector–led economy and its integration into the global economy have been perhaps the most dramatic economic development of recent decades. I'm an economist, remember.

Indeed, China's growth performance over the last two decades has been, well spectacular, with GDP growth averaging over 9 percent annually. China now ranks as the largest economy in the world. The expansion of China's role in the world trading system has been no less remarkable—its overall share in world trade rising—from less than 1 percent in 1979 to more than 8 percent in 2008 to well over 10 percent now. But it comes at a political and social cost: that cost is freedom.

There are strong prospects that China's rapid economic growth and trade expansion will be sustained well into the future. However, a number of macroeconomic and structural vulnerabilities need to be addressed for this potential to be fully realized. Given the size and complexity of the Chinese economy, many of these reform challenges are, I argued, interrelated. If they are not executed, China will implode. I said as much on a US talk show, and the host's jaw dropped.

With its rapid opening up to the world economy, a more concerted, multifaceted approach to the reform process is crucial to maintain rapid growth and manage the challenges associated with the process of global integration. Is it possible? I doubt it.

The expansion of China's international trade has been the most noteworthy aspect of China's rising prominence in the world economy. China's exports and imports have grown at an average rate of 15 percent each year since 1979. Trade reforms and the general opening of the economy that have led to a surge in foreign direct investment and increased integration with the global trading system, especially since China joined the World Trade Organization in 2001, have facilitated this process.

There appears to be every prospect that China could maintain relatively strong export growth for a number of years into the future. Given China's very large population and still substantial development potential, as reflected by its current per capita income, China could have a bigger impact on the global economy than all the other Asian economies. But will it, or will the bubble burst?

China's trade expansion also reflects greater specialization in production within the Asian region, with China now serving as the final processing and assembly platform for a large quantity of imports going from other Asian countries to Western countries through China. These changes have resulted in a shift in China's bilateral trade balances, with its increasing trade surpluses with Western industrial countries, especially the United States, being offset by rising trade deficits with many Asian countries. Reflecting its growing prominence and rising appetite for imports, China has been one of the most important sources of growth for the world economy even during the recent global slowdown.

China now accounts for about 25 percent of world growth (using purchasing-power-parity-based GDP). China's imports are growing rapidly from all trading partners, and it is now the third largest importer of developing countries' exports, after the United States and the European Union. China has even contributed to the recent strength in world commodity prices; it is now the world's largest importer of copper and steel, and among the largest importers of other raw materials, including iron ore and aluminum.

While China's integration into the global trading system benefits both the global and regional economies, there are no doubt some short-run distributional effects across countries. The countries most likely to benefit from the expansion of China's trade include exporters of capital and resource-intensive products, while countries that specialize in labor-intensive exports similar to those of China will have to undergo significant adjustments to increased competition from China.

Trade expansion also poses some domestic challenges, within China itself. Expanding trade increases regional income disparities, while foreign competition aggravates social pressures arising from job dislocation and rising unemployment.

As a result of its increased integration with the global economy and continued domestic price liberalization, prices in China are increasingly market determined and traded goods' prices have achieved substantial convergence with international prices.

For three decades after the 1949 revolution, China followed a policy of socialist economic development based primarily on the centrally directed allocation of resources through administrative means. By the late 1970s, this approach was increasingly recognized as being untenable and unsustainable, and an overhaul of the economic system was initiated.

China's approach to economic reform has been gradual and incremental, without any detailed "blueprint" guiding the process. This incremental approach is best depicted in a metaphor attributed to Deng Xiaoping as "crossing the river by feeling the stones under the feet" and is still applicable to many of the reforms being carried out by China today.

This incremental approach has been characterized by a number of features commenced thirty years ago. First, reforms have tended to be undertaken first on a pilot or experimental basis in some localities before they are applied to the whole country. In the view of the authorities, this minimizes disruptions to the economy, allows deficient policies to be modified based on experience, and provides time to build the necessary institutions for full implementation. Second, another strategy frequently employed has been the use of intermediate mechanisms to smooth the transition to a market-oriented economy. One example of this is the setting up of special economic zones in the early 1980s as a way of gradually introducing foreign capital and technology. Finally, the Chinese leadership has consistently tried to preserve the social character of the economy while introducing market-oriented reforms. For example, even though policies have been conducive to the rapid growth of the non-state sector, state enterprise reform has been gradual with few signs of a mass privatization strategy for large and medium-sized enterprises as pursued by other transition economies.

A great deal of recent debate has focused attention on China's exchange rate regime. China maintains a de facto fixed exchange rate regime, with the renminbi linked to the US dollar within a narrow trading band. China's strong export growth, expanding market shares in major trading partner countries, and rapid accumulation of reserves have raised questions about whether the renminbi's link to the US dollar may have resulted in an undervaluation of the currency. However, estimating a currency's "equilibrium exchange rate" is a very complicated matter, with the difficulties greatly compounded in the case of a developing country like China that is undergoing substantial structural change.

The currency's value will be inexorably linked to the ongoing structural reforms of the economy, and will reflect further opening of domestic markets to foreign goods and services in line with World Trade Organization commitments. Moreover, the medium-term movement of the exchange rate will depend on the nature and pace of liberalization of capital controls. Discussions about attaining a particular level of the exchange rate may be less productive than focusing on the broader benefits of exchange rate flexibility for China.

As China's economy has opened up, domestic macroeconomic policies have a more prominent role in reducing vulnerability to external shocks. For an economy with a tightly managed exchange rate, fiscal policy is therefore of considerable importance. With relatively low explicit government debt and a modest budget deficit, China may not face immediate concerns of fiscal sustainability. However, the government faces a number of possible obligations associated with potential losses in the state-dominated banking system, the future funding requirements of the pension system, and rising expenditure pressures, especially for education, health, and other social programs. Resolving the substantial quasi-fiscal liabilities poses a significant challenge.

This challenge increases substantially as macroeconomic conditions, especially growth, become less favorable or if structural reforms are not forceful enough to prevent the accumulation of new contingent liabilities. This highlights the urgency of undertaking structural reforms since many of these liabilities could otherwise pose an even greater burden in the future.

China's stock market is relatively thin, and there is a small corporate bond market. Banks have a crucial role in intermediating the substantial amount of private saving in China, which is estimated to be around one-third of total household income. Bank lending has supported the high level of investment growth, which has made an important contribution to China's growth performance in recent years. Stability of the banking system is therefore crucial for promoting sustained growth. Financial sector reforms undertaken recently highlight the remaining challenges. The urgency of financial sector reforms has increased as domestic banks face intense competition under WTO accession commitments; the financial sector opened up to foreign banks in 2006.

Many of the inefficiencies in the Chinese economy are ultimately manifested in labor market outcomes. Unemployment and "under-employment" of a significant portion of the rural population remain pressing concerns as the economy adjusts to the effects of state-owned enterprise reforms and WTO accession. Even with strong output growth, the unemployment problem has in fact worsened over the last few years due to restructuring in the rural and state enterprise sectors and the global downturn. How soon the unemployment problem will be brought under control will depend in large part on the degree to which the reforms are undertaken and world growth resumes.

To mitigate social pressures as labor is shifted from agriculture to other parts of the economy and from the state sector to the private sector, further progress is probable in strengthening the social safety net, including the pension system, unemployment insurance, health care, and the minimum living allowance. Needless to say, these measures have fiscal implications as well, again reflecting the interconnectedness of required reforms on various fronts.

Overall, China's economy has good potential for sustained robust growth over the medium term, based on its attractiveness as a destination for foreign investment, a high domestic saving rate, underlying improvements in productivity stemming from reduced barriers to both internal and external trade, and significant surplus labor. Fulfilling its potential for high growth and continued integration with the global economy depend largely on successful management of the diverse set of financial and social risks that China faces. The growth is by no means guaranteed. This, in turn, depends crucially on the pace and effectiveness of core macroeconomic and structural reforms. Implementing a broad and concerted reform agenda, and doing so in an expeditious manner, under the difficult conditions of a contracting global economy due to severe recession and market revaluations remains the crucial challenge facing Chinese leaders today.

To my eyes, everything is progressing in China, changing nearly overnight, except political change and democratization. Building continues apace following the historic 2008 Beijing Olympics, which were viewed by the globe with absolute wonder as they showed off China's accomplishments to the entire world. Massive and dramatic changes are today under way everywhere, in every corner of China—from the gilded skyline coast to the remote far west.

I have been to China ten times personally, since my first visit in 1982 as a young American diplomat to my visit with the Bush presidential delegation a few years ago to my trip in October 2012 to celebrate China's scientific advancements. Every time I return, I find a new country, yet another new ring road around Beijing, more skyscrapers in Shanghai, and more progress on almost every front.

What is China becoming? How exactly is it advancing? How are freedom of conscience and economic growth now viewed in a country with a communist government and increasingly capitalist economy? Past president Hu held a number of summits over the past few years with Western leaders. They have been meetings of equals and significant proportion, always ripe with historic opportunity. China is now rightly viewed as a full partner in world peace and economic development. But will it carry its weight and match expectations?

In a recent interview with the *Financial Times* of London, then Premier Wen said he was reading Adam Smith. He recanted that China very much needed today such a demonstration of moral business to undergird what is being achieved economically.[1] This is a great insight from a very wise leader. China needs to have honesty and virtue in its business dealings in order to become a more wealthy and prosperous nation. But that is no easy or automatic process.

There is potentially a win-win plan that appears to be emerging, all sides willing, in China's relations with the rest of the world, and particularly with the United States. Arguably, nothing is more critical to the project of the twenty-first century than Western-Sino relations. The United States has pivoted east. And China is now woven into the global, interdependent economy. How can formerly tense relations be so improved? Is it possible to build a new dynamic that would give both sides a further boost, improve economic conditions, allow more freedoms, stabilize political relations, and affect the future of the world for good? Will China step up to the task, away from some of the Orientalist trappings of the past and its ensnarled bureaucracies and outdated ideology? The signs, I think, are mostly mixed.

China boasts one of the longest single unified civilizations in the world. All of us need to have enormous respect for China's rich, five-thousand-year history which has been characterized by dramatic shifts in power between rival factions, periods of peace and prosperity when foreign ideas were assimilated and absorbed, the disintegration of empire through corruption and political subterfuge, and the cyclical rise of ambitious leaders to found each new empire. Yet for the last three hundred years China has seemingly more or less been asleep. The error and mistake of Mao's disaster are all too evident today. (I offered to help find funding for a Museum of Mao's Killings, but China refused the offer.) It appears the sleeping dragon empire is now reemerging in a vibrant dynasty. China is attempting changes on a scale never before achieved and at breakneck speed. A new, so-called harmonious society is the stated objective, and today nearly everything in China is in a constant state called: *transition.*

Twenty-five years after Deng Xiaoping's reform and opening policy allowed the West back into China, the country remains as mysterious, beautiful, and undiscovered as it was in the nineteenth century, when gunboat diplomacy forced the last tottering dynasty to open up the country to trade and exploration. China's vast population has also grown from 400 million to more than 1.3 billion in less than a century. (Even if the demographics oddly include a shortage of girls—for some reason.) This has driven a boom in consumerism most evident in the cities where advertising abounds and an entrepreneurial and materialistic China is literally, bubbling up. The Chinese can shop!

Many analysts and students of China's culture see four gigantic transformations happening in China, simultaneously. No country has ever, in all of human history, been involved in such dramatic change. But in this case, given China's size, power, and integration into the global economy, the risks and rewards involve the entire planet.

I think the four transformations or transitions are:

the change from a rural to an urban population

the change from state-owned enterprises to private enterprising

the change from a Communist to a consumerist society

the change from an antireligious culture to a spiritual culture

The West should be well prepared to comprehend and ponder each of these concurrent transformations in attempting to understand modern China. And China would be well advised to realize the nature and scale of the changes it has itself embraced.

The emerging, dynamic China surely involves combating rampant corruption, enforcement of intellectual property laws, assistance by way of expertise on reforms, an open admission that ideology is both wrong and dead, and realization that consumers increasingly come "first" in China's emerging "harmonious society."

This is not to suggest that there are no problems in or with China or that it magically can assume an instant overnight superpower status, become America's keen rival or eventual enemy. It is simply time to recognize the facts and seize the day. There are many hard questions to ask, and I did, some of which include the following:

The economic growth question. Is China's boom of the past quarter century extendable into the distant future? Or does China's large and growing dependence on global markets mean that external markets could damage its economy by disrupting resource flows, obstructing market access, or slowing the growth of global demand for Chinese products? Will international conflict within East Asia or over offshore oil deposits or even conflict in the Middle East undercut China's economic prospects?

The reform question. Long-neglected institutional deficiencies constrict seemingly promising growth prospects, as history has repeatedly proven. Is China's reform, while broad and deep, uneven? Vital institutions affecting important clusters of activity in banking, land allocation, dispute resolution, business regulation, exchange of property, corporate governance, capital markets, public finance, investment decisions, and administrative structures surrounding these segments of China's economy have witnessed only limited reform. How can China, with help, make progress on reform over the coming decade?

The intellectual property question. Large multinational companies and especially their CEOs are anxious to see results on the contentious issues of IP protection in China. I have personally been sold copies of bootleg movies for seventy-five cents (repeatedly); purchased pharmaceuticals in a large drugstore with the Pfizer label and logo that are not Pfizer products; bought clothing such as Vuitton and Ralph Lauren Polo that are imitations; and discussed with a major beverage company how its designs were ripped off in China in just days. What should we tell global corporations about trademark and IP infringement in China? Is it worth doing business here without such assurances?

The corruption/morality question. Widespread corruption, now often linked to transactions involving land in China and a vibrant black market, have tilted market outcomes toward select groups within the Chinese population. In recent Transparency and Opacity indexes for all countries, China has been ranked poorly.[2] What can be done to more actively combat corruption and promote the rule of law?

The finance question. The dominance of China's state-owned banks have increased since the 1990s, raising renewed questions and global concerns that non-performing loans are worsening. The continuing unwillingness of the big state-owned banks to make loans to entrepreneurs limits the growth of private business and exacerbates China's already serious problem of unemployment. How is China planning to avoid the kind of economic lethargy that affected Japan's formerly dynamic economy for about a decade?

The information question. Most in the world agree that as the maxim suggests, information is power. While we were in China, articulate, young, professionals repeatedly approached us asking if they could view BBC.com or CNN or surf the Internet in our hotel. They relayed that Chinese authorities block many websites, including news sources. Why? What does China fear from the free flow of information, if its intention is to build a knowledge-based economy and populace?

The America question. How has China's perception and understanding of America's role in the world and global economy shifted over the past few years? Is it China's view that the American century has ended and the Chinese century has begun? What is the role and responsibility of a superpower? Is China America's friend or rival? Why is China building up militarily? Can America and China live in peace and cooperate together and for the global good?

The ideology question. Marxism-Leninism has been defunct as a philosophy for many decades in intellectual circles, and since the collapse of the Soviet Union, its empire no longer holds sway as an ideological system. What has China learned from the Soviet example and the void it has left as a result? Must China be authoritarian and repressive to human, and especially religious rights? China is also increasingly a consumerist society. Therein lies the contradiction. Is China likely to be a communist country in ten, twenty, or fifty years? How and employing which means? Could it also implode, or fall apart, like the former Soviet Union?

Confucius, who lived from 551 to 479 BC, is still one of the foremost Chinese thinkers and teachers. There is a huge Neo-Confucian revival under way in China. He is once again coming back into favor. A real interest in religion—Buddhist, Taoist, Neo-Confucian, Muslim (not allowed), and even Christian—is sweeping through China like a tornado. Confucius taught a philosophy of *ren* (benevolence) and *yi* (righteousness). Perhaps, enjoined in meaningful dialogue, China can rediscover these. The world depends on it. Spiritual pluralism may be the critical key that unlocks China's future and assures its smooth transition to the future. There is little evidence that it is maturing at any depth or with any speed.

Let us look at how China is making its many and simultaneous transitions. These are not easy or automatic, but China appears to be making progress on all sides. If I were to make a documentary movie of all this for the whole wide world to see, there would be four episodes. Let's pretend and visualize each of them here and now. Here is the movie: *China in Transition.*

RURAL TO URBAN
People on the Move
This story is about China's urban coastal cities and the loss of innocence. It demonstrates how the experience of living in modern China has reinforced new ways of thinking, living, and working. We could follow a young man from a primitive state of subsistence farming in the distant countryside into the urban jungle, without his wife, children, or traditions. We would notice the effects and record the scale of massive demographic change over the last decades for some 300 million such Chinese people.

STATE OWNED TO ENTERPRISING
Central Planning Is Giving Rise to Corporations
This story could best be filmed first in a Wal-Mart in the middle of America and then at various Chinese factories across this gigantic country. It demonstrates how China has become connected to the global economy. It could trace a number of commonplace products back to their origin in China and document the new industrial life that has come to define the emerging and robust Chinese economy. We would meet workers, as well as CEOs, and trace the route from factory to ship to store. The end of central state planning has brought a flood of new companies competing for the future and trading with the world, but too many are still state-owned enterprises.

COMMUNIST TO CONSUMERIST
The Power Is Shifting to the All-Powerful Consumer
This story could be filmed on Shanghai's equivalent of LA's Rodeo Drive. It would discuss how the pursuit of the self and material gratification has given rise to the modern Chinese consumer culture. Old ideas about the soul and character have been gradually replaced by the appearance of considerable wealth. It would conclude with observations about the new celebration of self and end in the collapse of self; but not before it becomes a surrogate divinity and the new object of

idol worship. We would talk to Chinese celebrities, the newly minted billionaires, and all the constant shoppers.

ANTIRELIGIOUS TO SPIRITUAL
From Official Atheism to Limited Spiritual Choice
This story could be filmed in the five different faith communities in present-day China. It would discuss how the object of spirituality has been changed from something closed and persecuted to something slightly more open and respected, even valued for its contribution to a "harmonious" society. Such views and forms of worship could be observed from the temples, shrines, and house churches, where real believers live and pray. We would see firsthand how spirituality is transforming China in every faith community as lived experience. Spirituality leads to moral health of both individuals and society. China's rapidly expanding economy both domestically and externally needs to be based on honesty and fair dealing as well as the rule of law. These are born in spiritual well-being. The Chinese know this but find it most difficult to permit.

You have to agree, this would be quite a dramatic movie. It would prove hard to document because it is actually transpiring on such a grand scale, here and now. China is in transition, and everyone in the world is taking notice. They are also excited by what is happening—celebrating with every success.

Our then secretary of state, Hillary Clinton, recently used the aphorism *tongzhou gongji*, which, as you may know, means roughly "when on a common boat, cross the river peacefully together." You probably didn't know that, right? The proverb was of course made famous in *The Art of War*, the book by the brilliant ancient Chinese philosopher and military strategist Sun Tzu. The United States and China have common problems and we should and could work together. Like most Chinese proverbs, this one contains four characters (and four syllables) but it is loaded with historical and literal meaning about our course together—which we could, I believe, make as a joint effort and in a concerted way. We could . . .

I ended my speech with "*Zai jian.*" Truthfully, I have seen unbelievable development in China in this relatively short span of time and also severe repression in a still one-party autocratic State. I have three personal stories to relate at the close of this chapter that best tell this wider story.

In the mid-eighties on one trip to coastal China, near Qingdao, I was taken secretly through back alleys to a Chinese Christian house church. Some people estimate there are 100 million "Jesus believers" in China, and this concerns the authorities greatly. They prayed in earnest and were afraid of the police but stalwart in their faith. They held my hand and sang out loudly, not caring about the consequences, even though they said they were harassed and their pastors arrested regularly.

The second story came decades later. I was at a Templeton Foundation confab in Beijing to celebrate the invention of the telescope (I thought the Dutch invented it, but, heck, now the Chinese take credit). Fenggang Yang was our host; although he is a professor at Purdue, he goes both ways (culturally, that is). I was asked by the CPC (the same folks who had confiscated my suitcases on other trips for closer inspection) to come to the Party headquarters to meet with their new top political director. I thought this an incredible invitation, so I accepted and they sent a black limo, complete with those little red flags, to pick me up at my luxury hotel. When I arrived, after going through many security posts, they had an older woman greet me and usher me into a large modern conference room, with fancy knockoff Aeron chairs. The director appeared within moments, but she was a tall, slender, very attractive woman in her early forties wearing a close-cut designer outfit, with a Prada bag, and beautiful white pearls, as well as Dior Jadore perfume. I know that smell! I was astounded, expecting some party hack in green army cloth with a worn Mao army hat. She spoke perfect English and just wanted to spend some "quality" time getting to know me and ask about the contours of the new US administration and who would likely be in which cabinet posts and what that implied. Wow . . . On my exit the older woman took me back out through all the security to the street for my return limo ride. But before I left she whispered in my ear surreptitiously, "I have a son graduating high school this year; can you possibly help to get him into the best American college?"

My last saga is equally telling. After our ten-day presidential-level visit we saw everyone, including the nutty defense minister who wants to nuke LA. I said, "Go ahead; do us a favor" after our cordial lunch at the Peking Duck restaurant, where you eat the beak and web feet as well. The secretary of homeland security led the mission, Tom Ridge (the former Pennsylvania governor is a great all-around guy), and we made a super business deal while striking up a lasting friendship. No politics involved—it was all commerce. I would negotiate the price on two identical Oriental silk rugs (huge red ones) at the famous Silk Market. One for him, and one for me.

I got them down quite a ways, and then I landed the deal of a lifetime. I told the merchant I would buy one, but *only* if they gave me two for the cost of one. They were more than mildly shocked, even angry, so I walked away. They chased me down the crowded aisles and said, "Well, yes, OK, for you." They put each rug in a large, black "body bag," as they were really heavy to carry. Tom was pleased and very impressed with my negotiating skills, since I had just saved him three grand. We checked them in, and when we got to JFK International Airport in New York, all the Homeland Security and TSA folks rushed to greet Tom and have their pictures taken with him. I went through customs with the group of dignitaries and declared the rugs. The border guard said, "Oh, no, for you we estimate the value to be $125, so no customs are due." I protested and said that is not what we paid. But they had their way and said that in the end, "we determine value."

So a hard lesson learned: who is more crooked—them or us? Better read Adam Smith again!

MY THIRTEEN FAVORITE FOREIGN DISHES

1. Nasi goreng (Indonesian): the peanut sauce and flavors are to die for. Go to a *rijsttafel* next time you are in either Jakarta or Amsterdam.

2. Peking duck (Chinese): eat the whole thing, including webbed feet and beak, like they do in China. The crispy skin is the best part!

3. Sauerbraten (German): meaty and sour, it is best with red cabbage or sauerkraut.

4. Choucroute garnie (Alsatian): with all those meats, it makes a vegetarian mad.

5. Raclette (Swiss), freshly prepared at your table: what could be more pure than new potatoes and heated Gruyere cheese?

6. Bouillabaisse (French): let it cook all day and savor the shellfish and stock. Soak it up with a baguette.

7. Summer red pudding (British), only in summer and only in England: the fruits, berries, and currants make for a mouthwatering treat.

8. Haggis (Scottish): sheep's stomach is not for everyone. Have the guts to try it, and if necessary, do it with some scotch. Good with neeps (turnips).

9. Huevos rancheros (Mexican): love to have breakfast in Mexico or the US Southwest, and I always start the day with this feast—then run to the loo.

10. Jerk goat with ackee (Jamaican), very Caribbean: jerk anything is good. The side dish grows on the local trees.

11. Falafel (Israeli): fast food Middle Eastern–style, and healthy, too.

12. Goan vindaloo (Indian): wow—watch out! You've heard of superhot and spicy? This dish will take your head off!

13. Macadamia-encrusted tripletail reef fish, served with conch soup (the Bahamas): for pescatarians this is heaven. Reef fish in nut batter. Couch is the local favorite and tasty in soup or stew.

14

BOARDS OF DIRECTORS:
KEPT IN THE DARK?

"So you also, when you have done everything you were told to do, should say, 'We are unworthy servants; we have only done our duty.' "

—LUKE 17:10

There is what you know, and what you don't know, and what you don't know you don't know. Right? But what about what you don't care to know or don't want not to know? Corporate governance is all the fad these days after the many corporate and accounting scandals and the notorious theft at United Way, not to mention Madoff, MF Global, the Libor scheme, and Volkswagen.

It wasn't always so. For hundreds of years business, for-profit and not, was done differently. It was more or less done behind closed doors, sealed off from public scrutiny, and conducted in smoke-filled back rooms without accountability or much transparency at all. The world survived and most institutions thrived or labored through; some even prospered and lasted. But that practice wasn't good for society or for corporations themselves; and therefore it started to change, slowly at first, and now more rapidly.

I have had the pleasure, fiduciary duty, and responsibility, I would say, to have served on some thirty-six boards to date. I counted them up and eight were for-profit companies, three were mutual funds or asset management related, five were related in some fashion to universities and higher education, most were not-for-profit corporations, and three were philanthropic foundations. I have chaired three boards and served as president for another for five years. I started three companies and served as chairman and CEO, and founded another not-for-profit where I served as chairman and founder. So, I do have some limited experience with boards of directors, what they do or don't do, and how they are and often are not run and organized or governed.

Corporations are critical to modern life, and they emerged in the Middle Ages as groups of people sought to organize around the labor of guilds and the education of universities and in contradistinction from the omnipotent church. What we call "civil society," or the mediating structures between the state on the one hand, and the individual on the other, is made possible largely due to the definition and formative powers of these corporations. They have unique legal status and serve to organize much of what we do and how we spend our time, treasure, and talent.

Think of it: schools and universities and voluntary associations and charities and clubs and religious parachurch organizations, and most important, companies, where most of us work, are all corporations. We simply couldn't live without them. They would have to be invented to get anything done. It has only been in the last decades or so that many of us have become more concerned with their proper and good governance and have started to articulate best practices, rules, and even laws on how these corporations are to be ruled. The headlong march in this direction is mostly for the good. But there is still much more to do and the tide is always ebbing, in and out, on what and how to accomplish the best ends by employing the best means. I doubt this will change appreciably into the distant future.

My honest experience with boards has been, in all truth, *very* mixed. Some boards are far better than others, some are led well, some are rubber stamps, and some are meaningless or worse; and the worst are corrupt and often do harm. I still believe they are necessary.

Here are half a dozen stories of my life on boards, which are illustrative of both how important they can be, and how, when poorly managed, they too can become destructive. I will offer a typology of boards using my own real-life placements as examples to guide you.

I would rank boards from 1 (lowest) to 6 (highest) with these identifiable characteristics and names.

THE DESTRUCTIVE BOARD (1 STAR)

I was on the Chesapeake Wetlands Trust Board for three years, before a group of us resigned in protest. The outfit inherited a large parcel of land, mostly endangered wetland, on Maryland's Eastern Shore, at Kent Narrows. Development had run amok and trampled all the ecosystems and the wildlife. The Trust was supposed to protect it, educate the public, and be a sort of touring ground for school and scout groups to experience their pristine environment in all its natural glory.

Some rich person gave an aviary, another wanted to bring in canoes for tourists, and still other board members wanted to sell the land for a big profit and walk away. The Trust had very weak and too democratic leadership and almost no science. The bird watchers wanted one thing and a developer just wanted to look good for his own selfish PR purposes. Eventually, the budget went to near zero. We cooked up a decent plan to merge the Trust with the larger and well-run Audubon Society. When the board couldn't decide and the interests were at loggerheads and the crabs and terrapins suffered, it was time to say good-bye, and three of us, "real conservationists," left in protest. This board was self-destructive and was probably doing more to hurt the Chesapeake environment than to help it. The only worse board I served was Liberty Fund—but since I started a whistle-blower case with the IRS against them, I can't say how bad it is; but it is nearly criminal!

THE MEANINGLESS BOARD (2 STARS)

I was asked by then crocked Governor Schaefer of Maryland to chair the Maryland Information Technology Board. Don't ask why. I am neither a Democrat, as was he; a ward Baltimore political hack, as was he; or a contributor to his campaigns. Here is how it went down. Frank Knott, a friend and a telecommunications *guru* whose family was 100 percent inner-city Baltimorean, was to be appointed to this job and ran into some political flak because of his ties to the governor when he was mayor. It didn't look good—sort of an IOU political favor. So Frank told the governor to appoint me, which would look very bipartisan and neutral, and I was clean. Frank would work, then, behind the scenes. I was appointed and my picture was taken. It was never certain what this board was supposed to do in the first place. In the end it met in Annapolis just one or two times, and the bureaucrats from the state in the end did what they wanted to, anyway. It was a totally meaningless effort. At least it did no harm, and unlike most government initiatives, spent little money.

THE LEND YOUR NAME / HONORIFIC BOARD (3 STARS)

I have been on a long list of honorific boards (I am told I am clubbable, too), one of which was the Pew Trust FASTNET Board. Honorary boards are nice because in essence all the entity wants to do is use your name. There is no quid pro quo. Names show gravitas and merit and are used to demonstrate power and reach or diversity and span. Nothing wrong in all that—if some good comes of it. Pew Charitable Trust is one of America's largest philanthropic foundations, and they have many program areas.

This board grew out of their religion division under Louis Lugo, the short, rotund Cuban who was an evangelical until he reverted back to Catholicism. He wanted to form a board around a program on financial and technical support to the faith-based community. The idea was sound and they had oodles of money to spend. And they did, including many nice consultative meetings in places like Miami and Washington, DC. The problem was they picked bad partners (The National Crime

Institute for a project on faith?) and hired weak people who didn't know the first thing about technology, business, or communities of practice. The grant went through about five iterations and as many partners, all of whom sucked out cash but delivered few tangible deliverables. It ended badly when the Hudson Institute, the final partner, left Indianapolis and Jay Hein tried to pull things together with a remnant group, the newfangled Sagamore Institute. They were not up to the task either. More than $5 million was spent and hardly anything existed to show for it, except a long list of advisors and a very honorable but completely frustrated—and in truth, embarrassed—board.

THE GIVE-AND-GET BOARD (4 STARS)

I served on both the Yale Divinity and Berkeley Episcopal School of Divinity Boards, which are a part of the larger Ivy League, Yale University. Yale is an incredibly rich institution, steeped in history, and is normally ranked either number one or number two among all research universities, worldwide. Their then president, Richard Levin, is a scholar and a gentleman who went from economics to administration without batting an eye. He led the school very well in the eyes of the larger community. It is today an international university with about $28 billion in endowment and some excellent graduate schools, including their schools of medicine, law, and management. The Divinity School is historically at least the core of the university, as Yale was founded to train Congregationalist ministers in the earliest days. Revolutionary minister Jonathan Edwards got his start there. The lovely quad where the school is housed on Prospect Street, in New Haven, Connecticut, is a tranquil and aesthetic site. The dean of Berkeley was a friend and a superb intellect. The Reverend Dr. Philip Turner was sharp as a pencil and asked me because of my business experience and religious sensitivities to serve on his board. I was willing to do it for him, but there was a condition everyone on the board respected. I had to get others to serve, and more specifically, to give to the cause.

The board was well run and had committees that achieved a great deal.

I think it was a model board. It even enforced term limits. I was made chairman of the nominating committee, which did two things: chose new board members and suggested the choices for the awarding of honorary degrees. I argued for some choices that otherwise would not have been made and helped find some interested donors, while giving myself.

On a later watch, after Turner left due to retirement, the incoming dean got caught with his hand in the cookie jar and was fired over writing checks to himself and for his child's Harvard education. I don't know where the auditors were on that one, as I too had moved on after two terms (more than enough, I would add, for service on any board) to the larger Yale Divinity School Board.

Dean Wood was a renowned scholar and former college president at Earlham. I went on doing the same thing for two more three-year terms and many trips to New Haven, where at least in the latter days I had a son matriculating and rowing. In fact, Ian became rather better known than his father at Yale, as he was All Ivy and captain of Yale Crew, who were national champions for three years running. They even won the Temple Cup at Henley, as you know from chapter 1. He was given the Yale "oar" as the winningest rower in the history of the university upon graduating. It turns out it was easier to raise more money for rowing and boathouses at Yale than for God. But then, Bill Buckley had already more or less predicted that in his controversial 1952 classic, *God and Man at Yale*, better known as GAMAY (maybe after the grape?).

THE ACTIVE, ACCOMPLISH THINGS BOARD (5 STARS)

I was for nine years on the advisory board of the John M. Templeton Foundation for three three-year terms, but nonconsecutively. The Templeton Foundation grew out of Sir John's vision to work at the nexus of science and religion. He put billions and billions of his funds that were made in investments over the years into research and gave out various prizes. Last year it awarded more than $100 million dollars in grants to a slew of recipients, mostly world-class universities and top-notch scientists, to search into what he called the really "Big Questions."

The mission of the John M. Templeton Foundation is to serve as a philanthropic catalyst for discovery in areas engaging life's biggest questions. These questions range from explorations into the laws of nature and the universe to questions on the nature of love, gratitude, forgiveness, free enterprise, poverty, and creativity.

Its vision is derived from John Templeton's own commitment to rigorous scientific research and related scholarship. The Foundation's motto, "How little we know, how eager to learn," exemplifies its support for open-minded inquiry and a hope for advancing human progress through breakthrough discoveries. All of this is most laudable, and I have been extremely proud to be asked to be even a small part of it. The board is not only run like clockwork, but it is seriously and often consulted. They pay for expertise, peer reviews, and strategy. This is an organization that gets a great deal accomplished for the good of mankind, and it does so in part due to its large and expert advisory board. I am personally most proud of the work we (Barnaby Marsh, who is a Rhodes scholar and like a brother to me, and Chuck Harper, a polymath whose mind travels at the speed of light) did in the Lyford Cay Summits at that club in the Bahamas. There, over a series of seven years, we brought some of the world's leading philanthropists together to share ideas on innovation, to venture and partner together, and to leverage what the foundation was itself doing.

THE SERVANT LEADER BOARD (6 STARS)

I served for five years and for two years was chairman of the Board of Great Dads. Great Dads is a not-for-profit on a specific and important mission. Its vision is: to encourage fathers to turn their hearts to their children. Its mission is: to equip fathers through practical training, supportive resources, and inspiration to make and live out lifelong commitments to be Great Dads. In turn their challenge is: to combat pervasive Father-Absence in America—both physical absence and emotional-psychological absence—by continually fanning the flames of a Great Dads movement.

The founder of the entity is Bob Hamrin, a friend from my Senate days (and along with his wife, Carole, from the State Department) who gave up his day job as a practicing economist and instead followed his heart. Bob is a devout but nondenominational Christian and believes in the notion of "calling." He is also a disciple of the servant-leader form of leadership. His very life is a testimony to it. Bob came to care deeply about the state of fatherhood in America, especially in the African-American and prison populations and in the ranks of US troops, particularly those serving abroad on long and dangerous combat missions in harm's way. He partners with other organizations to help fathers in prison who rarely even see their own children. Bob is a terrific and caring person who leads by example and is fully dedicated to purpose. He is wise and humble and uses a board in a prayerful way to help and to counsel and to grow the organization. There are other boards of this type, more in private charity, unfortunately, than are found in business, but they exist to accomplish something, and more importantly, to serve others; they are purpose-driven. If I did anything at all to help this cause, I know that my crown is in heaven.

The lesson is *serving*—be of service wherever and whenever you are asked; add value. It pays personal and societal dividends.

MY THIRTEEN FAVORITE BOARDS ON WHICH I HAVE SERVED

1. Great Dads

2. Polaris FT

3. Spiritual Enterprise Institute

4. The Hudson Institute Center for Religious Freedom

5. The Four Ancient Development trust

6. Zeron Group and Shogun Funds

7. The Roosevelt Group

8. World Economic Forum

9. University of Toronto Global Governing Council

10. Meridian, Inc.

11. Association for Public Justice

12. Global Fiduciary Governance LLC

13. Foxhall Capital

15

CEO STRATEGY: INVENTING THE FUTURE?

"Behold, I stand at the door and knock; if anyone hears My voice and opens the door, I will come in to him and dine with him, and He with me."

—REVELATION 3:20 NASB

The Roosevelt Group, Inc., the company I founded, has two and a half decades of experience in strategic advisory work and corporate education preparing and leading Summits, Forums, and CEO level Roundtables and doing business strategy; what Will Ferrell called, "srtategery" in his SNL bit on Bush '43.

I am sitting in the swank conference resort outside of New York City that is closed to the public. Here is what the president of International Paper just told me.

"The Roosevelt Group demonstrated its unique value to our firm in staging the most important thought leadership event we ever hosted involving our top executives and those of our most significant client companies—resulting in fantastic new business activity and e-business opportunities along the entire supply chain."

Paul was the number two guy at PwC, and we just got off the golf course at Silverado in Northern California with a raft of tech CEOs who are clients. He said this: "Because intellectual capital is the most appreciable asset in the new knowledge economy, companies are striving to be competitive—based on what they learn. Today the best professional service providers are not only business advisors but learning partners. The CEO roundtables created in the Learning Partnership series co-branded with the Roosevelt Group over the last eight years have proven to be provocative experiences, a rare opportunity to probe fundamental issues and to spend time with colleagues from some of the world's most influential companies. We have retained many of our most important clients and obtained tens of millions in new business from this activity."

The Caliber CEO got me to get them mindshare, and he said, "We gained our largest single business relationship from the contact and access of the Roosevelt Group, which literally helped create our business in its formative stages, providing us with a $6 million client relationship with one of the world's largest professional service firms."

We just left the Savoy Hotel in London, and the president of CNA Insurance, Carol, was pleased. "We have received many accolades and dozens of new client relationships that resulted directly from our sponsorship of the International Corporate Governance Forum, organized and produced by the Roosevelt Group."

John Bailey, who ran SwissRe Capital, has just given the concluding remarks in the Cash Room of the now new W Hotel in Manhattan. "An eye-opener! Excellent, current, relevant discussion. This was the best format I've seen, and I've seen a lot. Good chance to talk about deals and find new ones. Great to be with people who are really in the business."

At the Aspen Institute in Colorado, the CEO of Pier 1 Imports said, "The Roosevelt Group CEO roundtables make for an unusual opportunity to test ideas with other CEOs and leading industry experts. A global view underpins each roundtable, and one leaves with scores of implementable action items."

After dinner at the Reynolds Plantation in Georgia, the CEO of DuPont-Merck bragged, "Pharmaceutical companies are forced to find a more global infrastructure, and our industry is seeing many mergers, joint ventures, and a great deal of acquisitions. The Roosevelt Group CEO roundtables have helped me focus on coming trends."

At the Darden School, the then dean of the University of Virginia business school admitted, "Like profound knowledge, the quality of learning is unsurpassed at the Roosevelt Group events. Chief executives today want to be part of such a continuous learning exercise."

Walking on a starlit night in the Sonoran desert at the Boulders resort, in Carefree, Arizona, the CEO of Colonial Penn stated, "This industry-based CEO roundtable reminded me of a high school prom, once you got up the nerve to start dancing, it was great—and most valuable!"

I have delivered a wide range of economic and business, legal, governance, financial, business-to-business, and industry-sector custom programs and solutions in places as remote as Bangkok and as intimate as the New York Yacht Club—which, as you know, is not only in New York, but also in Newport, Rhode Island. We even did one on a Navy aircraft carrier!

I have done events at most of the top resorts in the world. Tough work if you can get it! The critical benefit that it has provided is extraordinary networking opportunities for senior business leaders, mostly CEOs, facing competition for market share, mindshare, reputation, and capital through related print, electronic, and other products. I started the company in 1992, and I own it 100 percent. It is my baby, and has provided the bulk of my income, and is part of my lasting legacy, even though I now teach more and practice less.

As modern global Sherpa (thank you, Lady Thatcher, for my moniker), the Roosevelt Group has had the good fortune to have guided a who's who list of corporate organizations in strategic thinking, client and business development programs, and related learning, knowledge management, and business development exercises. It has specialized in fostering "thought leadership" (a term I used first, and nowadays everyone does) in a process of "perpetual learning" (another phrase we trademarked) at the highest level and has maintained relationships with some seventy-five hundred CEOs and other "C-level" senior executives (CFOs, CTOs, CIOs, CKOs, COOs, whatever "C" you can think of) in companies worldwide.

It doesn't quite seem possible, but since I had both the access and created the content, it just came together, mostly between my two ears. It always surprised me that people, smart people and at the highest levels, would pay me so much to do something I rather enjoyed doing. Indeed, the market had real elasticity, as an economist would put it. And the market is nearly infinite, at least in good times.

In strategy, the Roosevelt Group has conducted or owned four different but related types of thought leadership and strategy products covering a host of topics and industries, which map directly onto a consulting services strategy that approaches the enterprise with a unified voice. Essentially, it can conduct an unlimited number of conferences, colloquia, and forums and fosters thought leadership and extends brand awareness to the highest-level corporate community, regionally, nationally, and globally. It works in various industry groups and lines of business (twenty-three in all for PricewaterhouseCoopers), and often by partnering, as sponsors, and through consultative arrangements, that finance these events and assignments. More recently we have also initiated a series of audits covering everything from corporate governance to ethics to Dodd-Frank to enterprise-wide risk and corporate culture (through a subsidiary called Global Fiduciary Governance, LLC).

As chairman and chief executive officer of the Roosevelt Group, I built and have sustained this leading strategic management and thought leadership company. In 1994, I cofounded and directed the CEO Learning Partnership for PricewaterhouseCoopers LLP. This was a program that has developed some eighty topics across twenty-three different industries. It has run more than 115 times in every region and in many parts of the world. The theme was always "Inventing the Future." Fortunately, there is always some future scenario to talk about in a world of near-constant shifts and change.

With a client list of more than 150 leading multinational companies and some not-for-profits as well as states, agencies, and other governments, the Roosevelt Group obtained an advantage to see what was happening in the global economy, and particularly in the CEO corner suite. It benefited from an advisory board of leading thinkers and doers from academe, government, and particularly from the ranks of business. The products and services it has provided run a wide gamut.

Many leading companies and organizations have either retained our services or partnered with us to do valuable things and to build both relationship and what is termed "reputational capital." There are many noteworthy and diverse illustrations.

The Conference Board called on us to inaugurate its Leadership Series for senior executives. We served as program director and developed sponsors for many programs held at resorts around the United States and abroad. We also have directed some of their major conferences on intellectual property rights.

The Economist has engaged us to advise, program, and seek sponsors for major government roundtables.

The Peter F. Drucker Foundation involved us in the significant conferences we co-developed and executed on the social sector.

CNN was the sponsor of the World Economic Development Conference, which we conceived and presided over. That meeting was the largest CEO-level business meeting ever, with 2,500 attendees, 250 CEOs from 117 countries, and more than 100 ministers of government and heads of state. The corporate underwriting and fees totaled nearly $3.5 million.

Visualization Research Institute engaged us to conceive the Visualization Forum, held in the United States and the UK. We found two major sponsors, a global corporation and a financial fund, and ran all logistics and co-moderated the meetings.

Watson Wyatt Worldwide has involved us in numerous projects from organizing a major meeting with top government leaders on public-private experiences on restructuring to articles in the *Communicator* to a major research study, and associated products on leadership.

Zeron Group, the Japanese merchant and investment bank, has retained us for highly proprietary work with many of their large Japanese client companies, their offshore mutual fund, and on work with the leading US technology companies in whom they invest and or structure strategic alliances.

American Reinsurance: for this large global insurance company and its subsidiaries we developed and helped execute a series of CEO-level seminars on insurance and financial services in the emerging markets.

A. T. Kearney: for this executive search and management firm, which is owned by EDS, we developed and directed a study of COOs and executed a number of forums on topics of interest on operations, which culminate in the COO of the Year Awards.

Business Week: for this preeminent business publication owned by McGraw Hill Companies, we have assisted in programming for executive meetings and locating corporate sponsorship.

Computer Sciences Corporation: for this system integrator and defense contractor, we were the organizer, on a turnkey basis, of a five-session seminar. With the Council for Excellence in Government, this program, for the senior-most federal government managers of agencies, permitted a dialogue on "reinventing and rightsizing government."

PricewaterhouseCoopers LLP: for this world leading Big Six accountancy firm, we co-founded, developed, and direct the CEO Learning Partnership, their key learning program for leading partners and CEOs on the future of industry. This multiyear program consists of dozens of programs from health care to insurance, and from retail to diversity and intellectual property on subjects and industries of interest to CEOs.

Federal Express: for the world's leading logistics and delivery firm, we have been involved in corporate sponsorship and the delivery of content programs for their customers on topics of world trade.

Chief Executive magazine called on us to co-develop a CEO retreat, to do the timely program, moderate, and find corporate underwriting.

Healthy Companies: for this well-known and Macarthur Foundation–supported not-for-profit involved in engaging companies in conversations on the high-performance workplace, we have been involved in membership development, network and program delivery, and in the sponsorship of a PBS special on leading people.

Change Labs International: for this highly innovative consultancy and software developer, we have been active in their learning labs and working with their clients on knowledge management and content authoring.

Fortune: we assisted this highly acclaimed business magazine in founding its Conference Division, and programs for the first Fortune 500 CEO Forum.

Moody's Investor Services involved us and an affiliate in conceiving, programming, and executing a major investor-related conference with extensive media coverage, on the future of California.

National Education Association secured our services as senior advisor, program director, and in seeking corporate funding on its major project, "The Next Generation of Teaching and Learning." The multiyear project consisted of five dinner parties with renowned authorities on diverse learning topics and a major forum with educators, businesses, and think tanks.

National Association of Manufacturers has involved us in numerous undertakings, including the sponsorship of a PBS television series, *Making It in America*, and a major summit on economic growth.

Nortel, formerly Northern Telecom, the transnational telecommunications company, has sought us out for the execution of numerous programs, including involvement in its Institute for Information Studies for CIOs , in both the United States and Europe, and for other programs on executive development, leadership, and the information highway.

PEPCO Energy: we have worked with senior executives of this large utility to develop leadership programs and in-house training.

Society of Human Resources Management is a membership organization of seventy thousand human resource executives and professionals with whom we have been engaged in numerous capacities from developing their CEO Partnership Forum to sponsorship and developing new sessions for their large annual and international meetings.

Coca-Cola asked us to develop and execute a number of proprietary programs for their senior-most executives and international strategy teams.

Cambridge Technology Partners had us develop a proprietary series on issues of interest to chief technology officers.

e-Gov was a multi-client large conference on Capitol Hill on the future of the Internet in government and public services.

Golf & Travel had us as partners to do meetings on golf and resorts, spas, and real estate development.

Korn Ferry had us do a CEO forum involving their largest global clients.

Heidrick & Struggles has done CEO and CTO forums related to the needs of their clients in talent and search.

KPMG asked us to work on three conferences jointly on deal making, anti–money laundering, and Sarbox.

Marsh Crisis had us work on a number of engagements with them on security and combating terrorism in some of their largest clients.

The US Navy gave us a contract to do three forums in Annapolis at the naval Academy, at the Naval War College in Monterey, and aboard the USS *Intrepid* in New York Harbor on reengineering the Navy to today's circumstances.

Standard & Poor's had us do a program on the metrics of the new economy for senior executives.

MIT Tech Review had us develop the program for their famous ECT conference series on emerging technologies.

XL Insurance had us do an exclusive CFO forum in Bermuda, where they entertained new and retained old clients.

ACE asked us to develop a CEO roundtable for their clients on insurance-related issues.

Pfizer allowed us to use their facilities and underwrote a major conference on corporate governance.

The Templeton Foundation engaged us in multiple events, advisory meetings, and the Lyford Cay Philanthropy Summits in the Bahamas for the world's leading philanthropists, seven times.

The Indiana Humanities Council hired us to plan and run their Leadership Summit over five years. Its head, the dubious Scott Massey, who had a beard, became a friend. We even got Ford Foundation to give us a cool $1 million to write a book and do a big conference in Aspen. We spent six weeks in a villa in Tuscany writing that book. Hard life!

The Aspen Institute has had us moderate many Aspen programs and served in various capacities to develop new programs and seek funding from both corporate and foundation sources.

For the **Liberty Fund, Inc.** an operating foundation, we built colloquia, directed conferences, and served as discussion leader at more than a hundred events.

And the list goes on and on . . .

As you see, as modern day Sherpas, we have literally guided an impressive list of chief executives and other chief corporate officers for over two and a half decades as they set out to invent the future and think strategically.

Specializing in fostering peer exchange and thought leadership at the highest levels in a new category of executive education we have created, we dubbed it "perpetual learning." Our success can be attributed to unparalleled ability to what some have called "hit the C-notes," referring to today's chief officers . . . executive, financial, information, operations, technology, legal, human resources, and other functional titles, such as the newest C-notes, knowledge and privacy officers. We have, as impresario, played host to thousands of C-notes each year.

There is no secret formula, just a few guidelines I am willing to share here.

DO WHAT WORKS

Lady Thatcher in 1992, for my designing the World Economic Development Congress, bequeathed me the title "Global Sherpa." That event, sponsored by CNN, which drew twenty-five hundred executives from around the world, helped me establish my business mission: to fulfill the needs of sponsoring and host organizations through CEO roundtables, summits, conferences, forums, learning partnerships, institutes, and other custom events and products.

I have facilitated perpetual learning at the highest strategic business levels by bringing together CEOs and senior executives, thought leaders from the nation's top universities, business schools, and think tanks to meet in an atmosphere of open dialogue to explore new developments, policies, strategies, and issues facing all key global industries. I tried to marshal the leading thinkers, gurus, business executives, and policy makers to produce substantive programs that result in a rare commodity today: "real insight, learning, and business development," explained a recent attendee at an event.

We have been able to develop intellectual properties for clients, for a myriad of reasons. Some simply want to attract CEOs; others want to explore a new intellectual or industry topic in detail; others want a high-level laboratory or focus group to test an idea or explore the potential of a market or supply chain; still others want to interact with their best clients or potential sponsors; and others want to serve association members in a more profound way. Whatever the need or reason, the overriding thrust is perpetual learning and thought leadership, the twin pillars of this rarefied industry. Think of the picture where dialogue leads to profound insight and you will have described this temple of reason.

INVENT THE FUTURE

Senior executives who are charged with leading have looked for a decade now to our group and to me personally to help them invent the future. They trust me with unprecedented access to their thinking and concerns. So, the clients know what drives, motivates and captivates them.

In a world now completely transformed, the issues addressed by businesses really do determine the course of this new millennium. Corporations are the agents of global economic change. CEOs choose perpetual learning and thought leadership to design business and trade relationships, explore market forces, and develop competitive strategies and investment opportunities, within and across industries. This is particularly true in the dawning of digital business, where old economy firms have been blown to bits as new entrants re-create the landscape and innovation wins every time.

We have articulated and facilitated peer exchange. This shared know-how from real practitioners establishing best practices is essential to competing in today's global economy and for inventing the future. Few people walk the footsteps of CEOs and other chief executive level officers. Surprisingly these people are often lonely, and they listen to, open up, and share with others in the same predicament.

ANTICIPATE CHANGE

The universal theme facing businesses across all industries is the need to anticipate rapid and constant change in today's global marketplace. The ability to manage the increasing volume and complexity of information needed to make wise strategic decisions in a climate of continual change is critical to survival in today's economy.

For the past twenty-odd or so years, dozens, dozens, and dozens of global companies have entrusted their brand reputations to us. These include large, world-class entities, PricewaterhouseCoopers' CEO Learning Partnership, CNA Insurance, Unilever, and International Paper, to name but a few. Our clients and products have themselves evolved over the years. Learning-on-demand, e-learning, globalization, and intellectual property were major themes; today spirit at work, globalization, and various forms of sourcing and digitization have risen to the top. Media giants such as *Fortune*, the *Economist*, CFO, Business 2.0, Conference Board, CNN, and various technology and services companies have knocked on our door to develop the next generation of proprietary products, such as the Supply Chain of the Future, digital CFO, Visual Future of the Internet, the Global Privacy Summit, the Tax Policy Summit, Rebuilding the Humanities, and Venture Philanthropy.

DEVELOP CONCENTRIC CIRCLES

We have developed perpetual learning as concentric circles based on my own diverse background in corporations, academia, and government. I served on the executive board of the World Economic Forum, which hosts the renowned Davos meeting in Switzerland. I held an ambassadorial level position in the United Nations in Geneva between 1989 and 1991, watching the Berlin Wall fall from a ringside seat. I headed consulting at Wharton-Chase Econometrics; has worked in international capital markets at the investment bank, Salomon Brothers; has served in senior policy positions at the US Senate Committee on Foreign Relations and in the US State Department. My PhD is in international political economy, and I have taught at universities around the globe. These served as viable credentials.

We have executed for and with clients, which include corporations, professional services firms, associations, media organizations, academic, and not-for-profits, special events at the pinnacle of decision making. Because intellectual capital is the most appreciable asset in the new knowledge economy, companies are striving to be competitive—based on what they learn. In words that have often been quoted, "Today the best professional service providers are not only business providers, but 'learning partners.'"

HAVE THE COMPETITIVE ADVANTAGE

There is an appropriate venue for every meeting. We know them all. Since I have traveled for business, diplomacy, and pleasure to more than 145 countries, I know the world. We place programs at retreats, resorts, historic properties, nationally recognized conference centers, and leading institutes. We also have access to places that are private and closed to the public.

The Roosevelt Group has worked on a turnkey basis—from program content to audience development to sponsorship to logistics and execution—allowing for a four- to six-month lead time in preparing new forums. The programs we have directed are annual, take place quarterly, or are repeated for multiple groups throughout a given year. Many produce distinct learning products that continue throughout the year or webcasts and white papers or op-eds.

Many CEOs say, "If you're invited, drop everything and attend, because you'll be with people who move the world." Your most important clients and prospects will perceive you as being head and shoulders above your competition. Most important, you'll be engaged in learning with leading thinkers, you will share strategic insights with your peers, and you will actively invent the future of your given industry. You may also get to play golf at Pebble Beach, visit a hacienda that is a private villa, or have a picture taken with a prime minister or cabinet member. We have worked at every resort, golf club, and corporate strategy and retreat center known to man. It has been a wonderfully rich and rewarding episode, a ride that just keeps going on.

Like Atlas in the Greek myth, or if you prefer, Ayn Rand's 1957 classic of objectivism with the same title, this kind of heavy lifting is work. Thinking and getting others to collaborate in it alongside you is actually quite unique work. The world is heavy and may be getting heavier. The theme of *Atlas Shrugged* is the role of the mind in man's existence and, consequently, a forceful but, I would argue, inaccurate presentation of the morality of rational self-interest.

Inventing the future is moral; it is at times slightly scientific, also slightly artistic; it is international in scope nowadays; and fortunately, for me at least, it has also proved to be highly profitable. I have gotten to know a ton of very senior executives, particularly CEOs, in the process, and to peer into their minds and know their souls. Some are dark, many are burned-out, and a few are greedy, but most just want a friend and a "Sherpa" to help them scale the pinnacle of success. More recently we have also done business as Global Fiduciary Governance, LLC, as so many clients and boards wanted our advice and audits in regards to better corporate governance, enterprise-wide risk management, and on ethics.

The lesson in all this strategizing is to find your *niche*. In fact, be a "son of a niche," instead of the alternative with a similar handle.

MY THIRTEEN ALL-TIME FAVORITE COMPANIES

1. *Cargill,* the world's largest private company and a powerhouse that is vertically integrated and based on an old Presbyterian motto, "Our word is our bond."

2. *Chick-fil-A,* the best sandwich out there and a company based on gratitude. It does not deserve the criticism it has taken.

3. *ServiceMaster,* the servant leadership model, is most applaudable.

4. *PepsiCo:* I liked its leadership, especially when we traveled to the then USSR. Uncle Sam—in action.

5. *Miele,* the German *Mittelstand,* is arguably the backbone of the German capitalist economy, and its motto is: *Immer Besser* (Always Better and always innovating).

6. *Herman Miller,* the most admired company because it treats all it workers from top to bottom with respect!

7. *Tata,* this company is synonymous with India and is structured to give rewards to the greater society. They recently acquired Jaguar and Land Rover.

8. *Tyson Foods:* John Tyson is a humble leader who practices forgiveness—a novel business idea.

9. *Walmart:* what's wrong with everyday low prices? Without them America would have less thrift and higher costs.

10. *Infosys:* I studied and wrote a case study on their consensual form of management and appreciated their business model.

11. *Grameen Bank* won the Nobel Prize for microfinance and is the originator of "social business."

12. *Whole Foods*, perseverance from small to huge while always abiding by the principles of Buddhism and "conscious capitalism."

13. *Toyota*, lean manufacturing and total quality control—not to mention profitability and Shinto worship.

16

PALM BEACH SHAKEDOWN OF THE
RICH AND THE DUMB

"For my thoughts are not your thoughts, neither are your ways my ways,"
declares the LORD.

—ISAIAH 55:8

D riving down Royal Palm Way, lined with palms, of course—what
else?—you are likely to encounter more Bentleys and Rolls Royces
than you would anywhere else in America, maybe the world.
BMWs and Mercedes are way too commonplace to be noticed, and
anything less is downright suspicious. Poor people drive Audis.

On both sides of the road you have, one after the other—all the
private banks, wealth advisory firms, and the likes of Bessemer Trust,
Northern Trust, Citi, and JP Morgan; all the players are present and
doing a brisk business. The zip codes in Palm Beach County, Florida,
especially on the Island and in Jupiter, are among the wealthiest in the
land. By wealth I do not mean the millionaire-next-door, garden-variety
type. I mean real *high net worth*. Tens, and likely hundreds, of millions

and even billions in the vault or invested, are all that really count here. Anything less and you are just a "climber."

It's funny: Palm Beach, with all its old money also lays claim to more nouveau riche, social climbers, and wannabes than anywhere else on the planet. And then there are all the people and professionals that cater to this ilk, from accountants to estate and trust lawyers to insurance hucksters, zillions of high-end real estate agents, and the ever-present "financial advisors."

There are really three Palm Beaches: the truly rich; the want-to-be-perceived-as-rich; and the throngs who service and live off them like lemmings and leeches, who themselves believe that someday, they too will become rich.

Henry Flagler, the industrialist who invented and built Florida out of the hot swamp it was, had an idea that he brought to fruition. As a railroad magnate, he bought land cheap, built rail lines, and then built a string of hotels to let the Northern rich escape to "paradise" for the winter months.

In those days, in the 1920s, there was no such thing as air-conditioning. Yet more and more bluebloods took up this offer, the condition of "wintering." The "snowbirds," as they were later called, got away from the ice and cold and frequented resorts built especially for them, like his famous The Breakers, overlooking the sea. Those from New York and New Jersey tended to go to the east coast of Florida, along with some prominent Canadians, while the Midwestern crowd preferred the quieter, slower, sedate Gulf west coast.

Segregation has always been part of Floridian culture. The blacks were not permitted in Old Dixie to do much beyond menial and servile tasks. Latinos own Miami now, but in the rest of the state they cut lawns. The Jews, who did come, could not join the WASP clubs, so they started their own. Boca Raton came to have in time a higher Jewish population per capita than anywhere, save Israel itself. The ethnics were not part of the original Florida, but once they had made it in cash-based American society and had sufficient money, room was made for them at many new places with Tuscan-sounding names or Mizneresque villages. Mizner was the original architect of Florida.

And the celebrities were always welcome because the only thing better than being rich is being "rich and famous." Heck, they even made a TV show about the phenomenon! It shouldn't surprise anyone that West Palm Beach airport has more private jets, G5s, and Gulfstreams than any airport in the world. Nor should it surprise anyone that the *Forbes* 400 Most Wealthy List is overrepresented with the likes of PB locals: Kluge, Arison, Glazer, Huizenga, Frost, Abraham, Lindemann, Fanjul, Williams, Ansin, Koch, Desai, Ross, Clark, Johnson, and Heisley—and this is just the top tier. House prices range from more than a hundred million to the low twenties, with a few real bargains in the high teens (that's millions, of course).

Jupiter Island just to the north on a seventeen-mile barrier island is a tropical sanctuary and also winter home to some of the wealthiest "old families," from presidents and CEOs to new sports heroes. The Reeds started the island and handpicked the members. Mrs. Reed is said to have had knitted black sweaters and put them in the rooms of those who interviewed for admittance but were rejected. The island has families such as the Johnsons, Fords, Davises, Scaifes, Bells, and a raft of others from the pages of the *Social Directory*. The directory is useful because it names, names and tells the monikers of boats, plane numbers, and names of one's children and pets. But you can't get a copy unless you are duly "registered." We were.

The nearby Hobe Sound Yacht Club is replete with former CEOs with nothing to do but sail or catch sailfish on their sixty-foot sport cruisers. One day I caught sixteen of them, so what do I know? I was so exhausted I came home at five o'clock, ate a hamburger, and went right to bed. Such are the days in South Florida.

More recently, celebs like Tiger Woods and Greg Norman have bought in, destroying older one-story houses and paying $40, even $60 million, for a single residence that they immediately gut and refashion into even larger personal palaces. "Celebrification," to make a noun into a verb, is occurring at breakneck speed in the Palm Beaches. Whether it is tennis stars the Williams sisters and Chrissie Evert (now married to Greg Norman); football hall of famers such as Joe Namath and Ahmad Rashad (newly married to and quickly divorced from the very old-money Johnsons); golf giants Jack Nicklaus, Raymond Floyd, Ernie Els, and Gary Player; rock stars such as Rod Stewart; or, most recently, basketball great Michael Jordan (who moved in down the street from us, building a forty-thousand-square-foot monstrosity, replete with an indoor basketball court—what else?), all claim fame to life in the *fast lane* of the Palm Beaches.

There is *no* intellectual life to speak of in Palm Beach. It is a gilded, swank place built around the beach and the sun, not the mind. The Four Arts Society makes a pass at an occasional lecture from some has-been, and the fancy, new, and very expensive Kravits (thank you, Henry) Performing Arts Center brings in a few classical performers for less than well-attended performances, but Palm Beach is *not* about high culture. Rachel's strip club is better attended.

The Palm Beach Pundits, a sad group of older (honestly, very old) men that meets on Tuesdays during season for lunch, offers up speeches by still other has-beens on weighty topics such as the fall—or was it rise?—of the dollar and the coming or past recession, neither of which seems to have great impact on Palm Beach, except that house prices have stagnated in the $20 million range and foreigners from Europe and—God forbid—Arabs are able to buy in on the cheap.

Palm Beach is, like its counterpart, the Hamptons, on Long Island, about just one thing—*vanity.* The very name of the expensive shopping street is Worth Avenue, lined with every pricey store imaginable, from designer this to art galleries to Saks and Ralph Lauren. It is all about names, logos, and being seen. Eavesdropping is an art in Palm Beach, and the local rag has a special so-called "Shinny Sheet," complete with color photos of the who's who and what dress they wore at what benefit ball. You wouldn't believe the jockeying that goes on to get included and thereby become the talk of the town.

"The Season," when everyone who is anyone arrives, begins after Thanksgiving, heats up in January, and ends in mid-April. For about four months the elite of the elite are to be found in only a few square miles on Florida's east coast, regaling in a delightful temperature, swayed by cool ocean breezes and rocked by decadent living.

At the center of the scene are the many charitable balls, luncheons, black ties, and polo. Polo, of international quality, technically takes place in horsey Wellington, and other equestrian events, like jumping and dressage, likewise occur in that nearby vicinity. The horse people are a separate but overlapping set, which is these days increasingly glitzy. My own brother, Rich, a president at a huge media company, was a dressage *aficionado*, with horses at a cool one mil each. But polo is Argentine and global in makeup.

Each year there are well over five hundred fund-raising events held at places such as Donald Trump's Mar-a-Lago, the Brazilian Court, the Breakers, or the Ritz, in Manalapan, to raise money for mostly "worthy causes." You name it, they have an event. Heart, Cancer, Red Cross, March of Dimes, every disease, Fashion Week, schools, causes from A to Z and everything in between. It is estimated that annually over $5 billion is raised on the Palm Beach circuit for these needy causes. The balls generally have an honorary (old and very rich bitch patron), chair-persons (slightly lesser), and a bunch of committee members (lesser still) who do much of the work. The balls are particularly elaborate affairs, with fine cuisine, silent auctions, live auctions, (selling hundreds of thousands of dollars of items, exotic vacations, and puppies, always cute little puppies) to the assembled cast of the rich and richer.

I have done the math, and most every ball or event costs 70 percent or more of what is brought in. So in effect these end up being elegant doings of a social nature, encouraged by the tax code, as they are deductible (or up to a point), so that in the end they give little to the named charity but make for a *heckuva* good party that allow a lot of rich people to feel and look "special" and generous. The A-list types who can get their friends to come and give or buy (a table, perhaps) are coveted in Palm Beach.

I once was invited to a charity event at the Healys' mansion on the beach, a newish, $30 million-plus estate of nearly ten acres. The beneficiary was some foundation the host had created, no IRS status— I checked—and it put on a really big show that went on until early breakfast, supposedly to help children, always the children. They had vodka bars, whiskey bars, and even an oxygen bar to get a quick hit. The fact that they made money, paid themselves a bundle, and put on an air of helping others is, well, hypocritical. Most of the attendees were even bigger hypocrites trying to show off and be seen. Wearing skimpy little gowns and dancing on a glass-topped extra-large swimming pool to a live rock band to tunes like "I Wanna Be Somebody" more or less sums it up. But the be-all and end-all was reached (climaxed) when the hostess, a former Victoria's Secret underwear model with an East Ender English accent (and all that that implies), showed me their impressive paneled library. I thought I was gonna "get done." When I went to take a closer look at the books on the shelves, I discovered that they were all painted on. There were no real books at all. Like so much in Palm Beach, it was faux. Everything is faux! That is the operative word, FAKE.

Faux breasts, faux teeth, faux marbleized painting, and the collection of Botox-specializing dermatologists and plastic surgeons in Palm Beach runs pages and pages in the Yellow Pages. One woman we met through school, a doctor of dermatology (or so she said) was, it turned out, neither a Harvard graduate, as she claimed, nor of Japanese descent. When we met her parents later, they embarrassingly confessed they were Korean. Of course Koreans are of lesser stock than Japanese, which perhaps explains the exaggeration. But she had a long list of facial clients who needed their weekly shots and who knows what kind of injections.

One of the many dubious financial advisors we encountered in the Palm Beaches, who worked for a series of firms, one after another, as he couldn't keep a job and lost people's money, claimed he was a CFA— which he wasn't. He also said he was a close friend of the former vice president Quayle, who it turned out hardly knew him. Worst of all, he confessed to hating Jews in an anti-Semite diatribe. We later found out from his first wife, who now lived in the Mid-Atlantic region, that he was himself, Jewish. His second wife was a pretend model from eastern Europe (really, the Midwest) with whom he had an illegitimate child before he finally, after seven years, got the courage or suffered the guilt and asked her to move in and get hitched.

Another bogus character was a guy who'd built a castle-like structure in a development called Steeplechase. Yes, all the streets are named after horses. He claimed to be a friend and tennis opponent of Andre Agassi, but it all came crashing down when his lovely wife committed suicide. It turned out he not only had a violent temper but also was quite abusive. His demeanor as a pious Opus Dei Catholic did not match up to the reality.

Palm Beach is all about the people—who for the most part want to be reimaged. Lon and Sally were social climbers but it turns out from hillbilly origins. He had lost millions of others people's money (always OPM) in stock schemes in the health industry, and he just kept coming back for more and sucking any naïve taker from the Palm Beach elite in with him.

The Bradfords were perhaps the classic case, and not atypical for Palm Beach. Buddy was a college dropout many times over who lived off his family trust and golfed moderately well. He looked like Elmer Fudd, balding and hairy, and could barely put a sentence of two cogent thoughts together. I got him invited to private golf clubs in Scotland and he thoroughly embarrassed me asking for "that whiskey with the deer's head on it" and failing to wear a sport coat as is required at such places as Muirfield, a proper and hono(u)rable gentleman's club. His vivacious younger wife (who later left him for a Chicago mobster–type), Sonja, was a nymphomaniac and acted like a college slut behind his back. She was in real estate although she was illiterate—seriously, she could not read. Her partner, Ralph, and she had a ten-year affair going on behind dumb Buddy's back, but it was Palm Beach, where everyone was on the make/fake. I do owe her, because in the housing bubble she sold a couple of condos I owned, one in a grand total of five minutes (a simultaneous closing) where I made $750,000. Good work if you can get it—until that bubble burst and the housing market stalled and then collapsed, and poor Sonja left dumb Buddy for that much younger stud she always wanted and moved away to Portland. She called us one Christmas unapologetic and said her new name was now Angelina. Total remake.

There is far too much of everything in Palm Beach, but drugs, sex, and money would top the list. Drugs, recreational ones, are rampant, and the police pretty much look the other way. Supposedly, even a radio talk show host who lives in town reportedly had an infamous oxytocin problem/addiction and engaged in doctor shopping. Another acquaintance, a woman of some notoriety, who made designer handbags, all bejeweled, always wanted to remain anonymous. She went through detox and alcoholic rehab so many times it became ritualistic. She was finally arrested in a bad neighborhood, buying crack. Her rehab was an annual affair. But we felt particularly bad for her young daughter, who, like so many spoiled brats, grew up in this decadent environment. It was no surprise that so many children came to imitate it themselves before their sixteenth birthdays. One mother gave her daughter condoms at age thirteen because she said she knew "she was going to hook up anyway." Another family with a big name in automobile dealerships spent $300K on their daughter's sweet-sixteen birthday party and gave her a new baby blue Porsche convertible to top it off.

By far the best story on this front happened right next door to our very own house. Seth Tobias, a minor hedge fund star, was not only doing coke and mixing it with Ambien (countervailing forces?), but he was a flaming gay before his wife allegedly killed him (she got off scot-free). She had supposedly served him a potent cocktail in the form of purple pasta and enticed him into the pool and left him floating in their swimming pool, head down and drowned. (He was heavily involved at Cupids, a gay joint, with a male stripper-prostitute named Tiger. Appropriately named, Tiger had stripes tattooed all over his body.) It was his wife's fourth (in this case fake) marriage, and the day after he drowned, she had the pool resurfaced and her personal trainer moved in with her and her kids, each from a different, previous marriage. Filomena, or Phyllis, as she was known formally, was a truck stop type with a mouth to match. But she was a force to contend with on the Palm Beach social scene, especially after she inherited all of her gay husband's loot. The story was well documented in a CNBC special titled "For Love of Money: The Death of Seth Tobias."[1] Watch it and weep.

A few months after the death, we were on our loggia one Saturday night, and at about 9 p.m. my daughter and wife came running in saying they had heard a bang and then another two loud bangs at the former Tobias house. They believed they were gunshots. We called the Bears Club security force, largely made up of old men without weapons, whom my young daughter referred to as "grandpa cops." They were so scared they would not go to the house but instead called the real Jupiter police. Four cars came racing through the private gated community and burst into the neighbor's house but found no guns. There was just a loud party (no swimming though) going down. They left. The next morning Phyllis called while I was still in the shower, before 8 am. I took her call, and she went on a rant about why the f*** this, and how the f*** that, and "did you call the f***ing police? I told her my wife did call the club's security, alarmed by the loud bangs, and knowing what had happened there only months before—we were compelled to do so. I said in a calm and diplomatic, measured voice, "Never, ever dial our phone number again" and I hung up the phone.

That neighborhood was the Bear's Club, which consisted of just fifty or so $7 to 30 million-plus homes, in a secure gated community (although it got robbed a lot), all on two acres or more and surrounding the highly rated, slope 143, Jack Nicklaus championship golf course. Membership was $400,000, and money, not handicap, was the exchange of entry. Europeans who visited would often ask, "Which one of these houses is the clubhouse?"—they were all so large. One was thirty-five thousand square feet and looked like Buckingham Palace; another was nicknamed "the Hotel"; still another had a retirement wing complete with a medical facility (for just two older people). The caddies referred to one ugly yellow house as Taco Bell, which it vaguely resembled. Michael Jordan was building a "Taj Mahal" there (forty thousand square feet), and another house housed a $300 million modern art collection—in a separate wing. The owner was a dubious individual. Jack himself got very upset and had to ask a few rambunctious members to leave when they organized a single, onetime $200,000 Calcutta golf game with the winner taking all. Jordan and his athletic crowd played the game of choice. It was called "whip it." You had to whip out a cool thousand dollars and pay off on the spot if you lost the hole. There was just too much money circulating. These were for the most part second (or third or ninth) homes, not primary residences, although some too-clever-by-half people did live there six months and a day, to beat the IRS and gain Florida residency. Some skirted the law and obtained Florida Homestead status, which meant nothing and no one could pry them free from their home.

When the big crash of 2008 came, it hit Palm Beach hard, very hard, and not just shopping on Worth Avenue—in all the fancy Rolex brand outlets, and not just in the deflated and large over inventory of mega real estate. It hit the net worth—the wallets, trust funds, and stock portfolios—of the rich and dumb. It hit them hard. It devastated many. Many lost more than half of all they had accumulated. When you have a lot and take large risks and get all leveraged up, you fall hard.

One hedge fund mogul lost $2 billion in a weekend and lost it all when the banks squeezed him to fold. Another big real estate player got stuck in the game of musical financial chairs and was "long" in the Miami condo market and went bankrupt when it turned south. A developer we knew was so leveraged in land deals that he went bust after being a highflier; and his sidekick, an ex-football player, got so beat up in the market he almost disappeared altogether.

All the real estate agents lost their incomes, and the financial services market players imploded with massive firings; and "puff" Lehman Brothers was gone in just days, an old institution left without a bailout.

Dick Fuld, their CEO, exited with more than $300 million personally (he was a member at the Bears Club, too), but the government wants his head and he doesn't play golf much more in this part of Florida. Many of his folks lost their considerable net worth in a week, as they had so much of their own wealth tied up in Lehman paper. One fat, bossy Lehman broker we knew not only lost her seat but also her McMansion. It couldn't have happened to a nicer person. So many deals gone badly and so much wealth washed down the drain. When Madoff made off with $65 billion in Jewish wealth, it made international headlines. Many people wondered how such a Ponzi scheme could be continued over more than a decade. Several of the people on the short end were Jews from Palm Beach, where he preyed.

My favorite capper was a billionaire Minnesotan, Tom Petters who claimed he owned about sixty companies, including regional airlines, Ubid, Fingerhut, and Polaroid. It turns out he had created one of the largest Ponzi schemes in history, totaling some $10 billion over fifteen years, based on selling fraudulent receivables. He took down a number of hedge funds that had stupidly but (un)knowingly invested in his fraud, and the FBI discovered, then outed him. It seems one of his employees who executed the scheme wore a wire exposing his doings, and now he has gone away to the big house for the rest of his life. His oceanfront mansion in Manalapan, just south of Palm Beach, previously owned by Amway magnet Richard DeVos, went on the chopping block along with everything else he owned ill-begotten, from Bentleys to multiple houses, and from expensive jewelry (fifteen high-priced watches) to his boat and private jet. What a shame—or sham? We knew him because my youngest son dated his only daughter for a while—until the government clawed back all the gifts she gave him. Poor Tom was sent away for seventy-five years and will never see the light of day again.

Rich and dumb makes for a curious and at times, deadly combination. Brain-dead can be life shortening, and great wealth can only compound it. When all you have to worry about is who has what, lives where, is doing whom, and is seen with whom at the Everglades Club, the B&T, or the Beach Club, life becomes, well, consumptive. Even I was sucked in by a so-called premium insurance slickster who took my loot and left me holding the bag. All I have to show for it is a bunch of costly lawsuits and a $20 million charitable gift to my wife's alma mater in Ohio.

My final story relates to the expensive, private Benjamin School, where our daughter attended, swam, and did well academically, despite having a drunken teacher one year and kids experimentally doing drugs at age ten, another. The girls were particularly cruel—*mean* is the word! I think they made a movie about them! They formed what they called "crews" (really, gangs) based on exclusivity—race, religion, class, and ethnic origin—that were as hateful as any inner-city gang. They were abusive and spiteful and hurt individuals with and without discrimination. It was what the social psychologists refer to as "odd girl out" syndrome.

One day my young daughter, whom we tried to keep above it all and her head screwed on, came home in tears. It wasn't that she had played with an African-American or Indian Muslim girl; or that she had befriended an overweight girl; or that she didn't take advantage and taunt a weaker child; or her lack of the right "designer" clothes. The crime this time was over what cars the parents used to pick up their kids from school. God forbid. We had a Mercedes SUV G-Wagon (as well as a few other cars), and they are somewhat rare (but actually quite expensive), and the other girls made fun of her for driving a truck. Well, "truck you," I said. It was past time to be rid of the petulance and the social maneuvering and to reenter a saner, less faux world. The real estate crowd says: location, location, location. This was no longer a tolerable location.

The lesson of this sordid life is, don't be superficial. Reality is complex but very deep and variegated. Try to find your *noble* purpose. Get real.

MY THIRTEEN FAVORITE GOLF COURSES

1. The Bears Club, Jupiter, Florida

2. Royal and Ancient "Old Course," St. Andrews, Scotland

3. Royal Dornoch, Dornoch, Scotland

4. Carnegie Club Course, Dornoh Firth, Scotland

5. Muirfield, in Muirfield, Scotland

6. Turnbury, Ailsa Course, Ayrshire, Scotland

7. Pebble Beach, Carmel, California

8. Ballybunion, Ireland

9. Lyford Cay, the Bahamas

10. Winged Foot, Mamaroneck, NY

11. Stanwich Country Club, Greenwich, CT

   (tied) Pacific Dunes, Bandon Dunes, Bandon, Oregon

12. Penha Longa, Portugal

13. Trump International Golf Links, outside Aberdeen Scotland—This classic links-style course raises golf in Scotland, if not the world to new levels. It took someone as bold as Donald Trump to do it. The championship golf here makes for the best golfing experience in Scotland, if not the world. Maybe this is why America needs Trump in the Oval Office. He gets things done that other people cannot even imagine, let alone execute! You're hired.

17

STILL, NO GOD OR MAN AT YALE

But seek first his kingdom and his righteousness, and all these things will be given to you as well.

—JESUS, IN MATTHEW 6:33

In 1951, a twenty-five-year-old Yale graduate published his first book, which exposed the extraordinarily irresponsible educational attitude that prevailed at his alma mater. That book rocked the academic world and catapulted its young author, the aristocratic William F. Buckley Jr., into the public spotlight.

This seminal work, of one of the most courageous conservative thinkers of the twentieth and twenty-first centuries, also laid the groundwork on which numerous other media voices over time were built.

Buckley described how it all started when he was an undergraduate at Yale University from 1946 to 1950. He wrote from his conscience. Buckley was very precise in describing how he felt traditional American values were being ignored, undermined, and distorted by academics. He made his case by citing specific classes, instructors, and textbooks.

Bill Buckley earned the right to be the quintessential role model for conservatives and tradition because of his courage and gift of clearly communicating his argument in a logical manner. His special accent and style didn't hurt either. There were no ad hominem fallacies. He confronted issues head-on. He even discussed his motive for writing the book (which caused quite a flap) by saying it was tied to his love for his alma mater and the country in general. By that he meant his desire was for constructive change. It was in pointing out the errors that he hoped to achieve the positive resolutions he sought. Buckley remained a voice worthy of an audience in the marketplace of ideas for six decades to come.

In many ways, *God and Man at Yale* was the book that launched him and the conservative movement in America. No one has had the stature, voice, or credibility of Bill Buckley since. His award-winning television show, *Firing Line*, was something I grew up on in my household, as well as his opinion rag, the *National Review.*

I met Bill a number of times, first as a debater of some acclaim early in my undergraduate days in Boston, and then at various NR events. We had one long exchange of letters over a speech I gave at St. Andrew's School in Delaware on the themes in the movie *Chariots of Fire.* I quoted the lines of the film, and Bill, it turns out, particularly respected the nobility of the character who played a British lord. I still have those letters and covet the true intellectual exchange. He also liked that I used the phrase "Don't immanentize the eschaton," a kind of hallmark of his own best thinking!

Buckley, frankly, set the stage for what has become the most vibrant political and cultural force of our time: conservatism. Many forces made this phenomenon happen, and those forces have influenced American culture, politics, economics, foreign policy, and all the other sectors of American life. Without Buckley and that first missive, now referred to as GAMAY, none of this would have transpired.

The rise of conservatism in the United States over the past half century has been one of the most important political developments of the age—not only for America, but also for the world. My story does not go back in time to see how or where it all began—at Yale—but instead moves into the present time frame to see how much *worse* things have gotten at that same institution of Ivy League fame—the venerable Yale University.

Yale's deep roots are traced way back to the 1640s, when colonial clergymen led an effort to establish a college in Connecticut to preserve the tradition of European liberal education in the New World. That vision was fulfilled in 1701, when the charter was granted for a school "wherein Youth may be instructed in the Arts and Sciences [and] through the blessing of Almighty God may be fitted for Publick employment both in Church and Civil State."[1]

In 1718 the school was renamed Yale College in gratitude to the Welsh merchant Elihu Yale, who donated the proceeds from the sale of nine bales of goods together with 417 books and a portrait of King George I to the fledgling school.

Today, Yale has matured into one of the world's great and global universities. Its eleven thousand students come from all fifty American states and from 108 countries. The thirty-two-hundred-member faculty is supposedly "a diverse group of men and women who are leaders in their respective fields."[2] The only thing lacking is intellectual diversity, as Leftism has become the agreed creed, not the Hebrew Bible, as etched into the original college seal.

This is my tale about Yale. I had served on the boards of both the Episcopal Berkeley Divinity School at Yale and Yale Divinity School for six years each and was well known to the administration, fund-raisers, and faculty alike. My Waspy sensibilities and pedigree fit well into their paradigm for Yale. For years they had a strategy to loot the high net worth of the East Coast families and Yale alums in the establishment and run with their money—in precisely the opposite direction. I call it stealing from the rich to support the Left. It is an arrogant and obvious theft and, unlike Robin Hood, it is quite well camouflaged.

Nearly everyone knows about the Bass family gift to Yale on promoting "western civilization"[3] that was returned by the president because such a cause was, well, not academic enough for Yale's notorious leftist faculty. My story is equally wicked.

I left the board at Yale just before the dean was charged with embezzling funds from their accounts to pay for such things as his daughter's education—at, of all places, Harvard—and padding his own pocketbook. The story broke in the *New York Times* and all hell broke loose. This deed occurred in a divine school, albeit, one that no longer believed in such a transcendent destination, let alone an omnipotent God who created heaven and earth.

My son (recall chapter 1) Ian, the world-famous, All Ivy rower, was a Yalie and into the secret society lure as well as the prestige of wearing the big Y on the blue shirt. He had so many victories in rowing we used the multiple tee shirts from his opponents to wash and dry our cars. Clearly at our house, Yale was number one—*Lux et Veritas*.

When I received a large, multimillion-dollar grant and then two smaller ones, I urgently needed to find a university at which to place the funds and conduct the research. So even though I am a sorrowful, admittedly "recovering academic," I naturally chose Yale. I knew them, they knew me, and it felt right, even though I had some deep-seated suspicions.

I met with Professor Miroslav Volf, a thin, bald, bespeckled Croatian, who was *Time* magazine's theologian of the year and had started something he dubbed the Center for Faith and Culture. He was co-teaching a team course with the former British New Labour prime minister, Tony (lapdog) Blair on "Faith and Globalization." While he was an eastern European of the neo-Marxist type, he was also a Pentecostal Christian. This was an odd combination, to say the least, I thought. Anyhow, while his ideas bothered me a bit, I decided to fit into that perch and park the project there so long as Yale gave me a contract for multiple years as a full research professor, with all the salary and benefits one would presume. They caved and gave me everything but the free parking place (that cost a hundred bucks a month). I too was now at Yale—in the very belly of the beast!

It turns out Volf was a toxic person of the worst sort (ask his former executive director, the nicest guy on earth). Volf, while pretending to be a humane guy, was ugly, disrespectful to his underlings and assistants, and as bad as Tito (a fellow Yugoslavian) himself—where likely he learned his nasty tricks. As it turned out, I discovered he was an Islamophile and penned a controversial book on Allah, saying we all worship the same God. On the side it was later disclosed he took lots and lots of clandestine funding from the Muslim world, and one emir in particular—which I suppose made him "unbiased."

Yale, it turns out has sailed way left of where Buckley departed it in the 1950s—way, way left. Its right wing truly starts with Barack Obama and moves quickly left to the anti-American diatribe, victimization crowd, GLBTists, and enviro-madness that is American university life today. This is the strangeness of post-postmodernism, I suppose. And parents pay for this. At Yale they pay a lot!

While I was at Yale, out of the entire gigantic faculty I could name only six who had even a moderate conservative perspective. That's less than two hands. One was a Straussian political philosopher who actually voted for Obama but believed in the American Founding—a radically brave notion, I must say, for Yale. Another was a Law School Professor who wrote on corporate reputation and belonged to the Federalist Society.

One close personal friend, who is a conservative, was almost fired for his worldview. He was targeted by his boss, a kooky leftie dean who said he could find him a position in Abu Dhabi instead. Imagine that: exiled to the Persian Gulf because you are a conservative at Yale. That's how the system works nowadays. There is no intellectual diversity. It is Left or else. When Yale got $4 billion, that much, to open a non-degree granting campus in Singapore, the faculty voted 99 percent to turn it down because they had an "authoritarian regime." But Yale's then president Levin, took the money and ran anyway.

When Buckley was at Yale, he noted where things were right and where they were headed south. Today, there is only the Deep South and Antarctica. It is a virtual monopoly of one opinion. There is no God (at all), and human beings are viewed as nihilistic, materialist beings, soulless, and progressing to some kind of socialized future—once enlightened and tamed by the force of an all-knowing elite called The Government (mostly run by former Yalies, I suppose).

My research at Yale was on virtuous (good) companies. The idea that companies might be "good" upset a lot of people who believed especially that all big businesses were radically evil. I only taught one course at the graduate level with the management crowd and PhD students, called "Virtue and Business." One student who took the class actually asked, in all seriousness, "What is virtue?" He had never before encountered the term.

I did my own thing, published books such as *Doing Virtuous Business*; *The End of Ethics*; and *Practical Wisdom in Management*, based on all the case studies we were collecting at the Yale School of Management. Fortunately, my grant paid for four post-docs. I also coauthored a polemical treatise entitled *America's Spiritual Capital* with the (in)famous Catholic philosopher Nicholas Capaldi, from Loyola, who is—God forbid—libertarian. That angered a lot of people even more. How could a Yale professor defend America and write with an alleged right-winger? We even thought there was some Providence at work in our founding. Such utter nonsense!

My theoretical contribution (appearing in scholarly journals) on what we termed "spiritual capital" did not go over all that well either with the social scientists or those who believed religion had waned (or should—and the sooner, the better).

The dean of the Divinity School, a Catholic of the most liberal sort, was embarrassed to see me publish so much and speak all over the world. When my PBS documentary *Doing Virtuous Business* (which had a million dollars in sponsorship from leading foundations) was nominated for an *Emmy Award* and aired on 150 stations to 15 million "*viewers like you*," it was just too much publicity. In an airing of the documentary at Yale, the faculty, not the students, questioned it, as *too* positive on capitalism.

That dean, old Harry nefarious as he was, tried to cook my goose by queering another grant I was offered by a big Catholic foundation and had his Yale bureaucrats reject it. Conservatism or anything pro-business should not be funded, was the foregone conclusion at Yale. I had to literally sneak a smaller grant (from Jewish patrons) onto the books to fund my work on crony capitalism and the financial debacle because Yale would not like that either. When I attended Liberty Fund colloquia or the Mont Pelerin Society or the paleo Philadelphia Society, Yale would not pay my freight. No, these were deemed "political" in nature, as if what they professed was not. But their sentiments were approved as defensible, whereas mine were Waspy or traditional, and not.

Neither could I approach donors—some Jewish, others Evangelicals—who wanted to support my work. Yale would not find it respectable to take such contributions. One day, I brought a potential $50 million gift to the head of Yale Development, a lanky sophisticate of Germanic descent, Inge Reichenbach. Her office, high in the office tower with the best view in town, looked across the Elm City and its famous green. She said that to take such a grant, the faculty would have to choose the topic, and even then that could change every five years to fit the needs of the university as it evolved (i.e., leftwards). The donor and I got up, shook her hand politely, and said both good-bye and good riddance.

The one thing, however, Yale did better than any other state-run institution, even the old USSR, was bureaucracy. They had three full-time drones, who were literally unemployable in the real world but unionized, run my grant. They worked twenty hours a week but got salaries of over fifty grand each as full-time employees, and lots of benefits and long vacations. Their boss, an ironclad battle-ax autocrat, supposedly trained in finance but who hadn't a clue, let alone a degree, became my nemesis. Only threats of lawsuits forced her to back off. She was like those old East German (DDR) border guards where power went to her head. "Stasi" is what they called her—behind her back.

When I left Yale after four years in a purgatory of sorts, I felt as though a chain had been lifted off my back. I screamed, "Free at Last" like MLK—or was it Mel Gibson, in the movie *Braveheart*?

Yale had degenerated into Sex Week (yes, just ask and you shall receive), endless gender studies, and streams of anti-Americanism, far worse than anything poor Mr. Buckley would have remotely recognized. The Buckley Society, a student-led group, could quietly invite speakers to campus, but only if they kept it a secret, lest there be protests around the likes of Steve Forbes (a capitalist tool) or the notorious Charles Murray (of the dubious *Bell Curve*).

Only behind closed doors, and certainly not in the classroom, could we openly discuss ideas—which used to be the very basis of any university. Today the basis of that purported education is simply and blatantly *indoctrination*. Debunk everything, deconstruct reality, rid the students of the diseases of religion and class, and for God's sake (oh, there is no God; I forgot), by all means redistribute the wealth (which of course was, as we all know, stolen).

My parting shot at Yale came my final term when the famous Yale Political Union invited me to be the keynote speaker in their esteemed debate program stretching back centuries. In front of about eight hundred students, the resolved was: "Embrace American Exceptionalism."

Here is the case I made that night.

American exceptionalism is the view that the United States occupies a special role among the nations of the world in terms of its national ethos; political, economic, and religious institutions; and its being built by immigrants. The roots of the position date back to 1630 with John Winthrop's "city upon a hill,"[4] although some scholars also attribute it to a passage of Alexis de Tocqueville, who argued that the United States held a special place among nations, because it was the first working representative democracy.

Belief in American exceptionalism has long been characteristic of both conservatives and liberals. The radical Marxist Howard Zinn, however, said that it is based on a myth, and that "there is a growing refusal to accept" the idea of exceptionalism both nationally and internationally.[5] But he of course is dead wrong!

Many intellectuals, across disciplines have argued that to deny American exceptionalism is in essence to deny the heart and soul of this nation.

In essence the exceptionality of America, politically, economically, militarily, and culturally is based on these facts:

1. The Protestant American Christian belief that American progress would lead to the Millennium

2. The American writers who linked our history to the development of liberty in Anglo-Saxon England, even back to the traditions of the Teutonic tribes that conquered the Western Roman Empire

3. Other American writers who looked to the "newness" of America, seeing the mass of "virgin land" that promised an escape from the decay that befell earlier republics

Because America lacks a feudal tradition of landed estates with inherited nobility, it is arguably unique among nations. The Puritan Calvinists who first came to Massachusetts had a strong belief in predestination and a theology of Divine Providence that still has affects down to this day. Since God made a covenant with his "chosen people," Americans are seen as of a different type. This "city on a hill" mentality is still evidenced in American folklore, song, and customs, such as Woody Guthrie's 1944 anthem "This Land Is Your Land"). With its particular attention to immigration, America has generation after generation been a beacon to the world.

The Statue of Liberty itself is an embodiment of that ethos. America was also created on a vast frontier where rugged and untamed conditions gave birth to the American national identity and the narrative of a continent of exceptional people—explorers and adventurers. Think of my relative Teddy Roosevelt on winning the West!

The economics of the American Founding was very much a Lockean affair: the protection of property rights in what was "the largest contiguous area of free trade in the world." But you recall there were two competing views of America's economy: a Southern Agrarian view, championed by Jefferson, and a Northern industrial or commercial view, championed by Hamilton. It is this same difference in visions that was at the economic root of the American Civil War, a war that saw the ultimate industrial and commercial view victorious.

Hamilton, as secretary of the Treasury, prevailed. He established the credit of the United States by consolidating state and national debt and paying the interest on it and transformed it into capital by issuing certificates on it. He established a national banking system and thereby encouraged what he called "the spirit of enterprise." Hamilton used the freedoms of the Constitution and its protections to create a capitalistic, free-market economy and ensured that the United States would "become the richest, most powerful, and freest country the world has ever known."

The role of the government in such an economy was well described by James Madison in Federalist no.10:

> A republic . . . promises the cure for which we are seeking . . . the same advantage, which a republic has over a democracy in controlling the effects of faction, is enjoyed by a large over a small republic.

To be a fit participant in a modern republic and market society, like America, it is necessary to be a certain kind of person in a particular kind of culture. This kind of person is one who internalizes his or her values and makes them work: a person of virtuous character. It is no accident that Max Weber identifies none other than Benjamin Franklin as the epitome of the "Protestant work ethic." Nor is it an accident that America remains the most philanthropic country in the world. Franklin was the quintessential American, an entrepreneur in every sense of the word and a proponent of both thrift as a virtue and generosity as a practice.

Finally, as Nobel Prize–winning author, V. S. Naipaul has put it, the "idea of the pursuit of happiness . . . is an elastic idea; it fits all men. It implies a certain kind of society, a certain kind of awakened spirit. I don't imagine my father's Hindu parents would have been able to understand the idea. So much is contained in it: the idea of the individual, responsibility, and choice, the life of the intellect, the idea of vocation and perfectibility and achievement. It is an immense human idea. It cannot be reduced to a fixed system. It cannot generate fanaticism. But it is known to exist; and because of that, other more rigid systems in the end blow away."[6] One does not impose personal autonomy, and that is the secret of America's real and lasting power.

Human flourishing is an American moral theory that links virtue and happiness, specifying the relation between these two concepts as one of the central preoccupations of ethics. Virtue ethics today has been revived, and largely on account of the American spiritual capital built up as a legacy over many centuries of eudemonic thinking and practice. American exceptionalism is the very embodiment or the exemplar of the logic of modernity.

In Reagan's famous words, "the United States remains the last best hope for a mankind plagued by tyranny." And, to the extent that the logic of modernity is rooted in Judeo-Christian spiritual capital, America is unique in preserving that connection. Americans continue to identify themselves overwhelmingly with the Judeo-Christian spiritual heritage, long after it has disappeared as the cultural foundation of western Europe. That is why most Americans subscribe to the Lockean liberty narrative, not the social democratic equality narrative that now dominates Europe; it is why America can combine a secular civil association with a religious culture instead of the belief in a theocracy; it is why America celebrates autonomy instead of the Asian belief in social conformity.

Early American settlers gave voice to a specifically Anglo-Protestant identity (yes, I am a WASP). As Harvard scholar Samuel Huntington has argued, American identity has had two primary components: culture and creed. The creed is a set of universal principles articulated in our founding documents: liberty, equality, democracy, constitutionalism, limited government, and private property.

Our culture is Anglo-Protestant, specifically, dissenting Protestantism. Moreover, the creed is itself the product of "English traditions, dissenting Protestantism, and Enlightenment ideas of the eighteenth-century settlers."

One way of characterizing the early United States is to say that it inherited the logic of modernity and all of its institutions (the technological project [from Francis Bacon], economic freedom [from Adam Smith], political freedom [from John Locke], and legal freedom [common law] [from Great Britain]). What distinguished the United States from England were three crucial things: (a) the lack of a feudal class structure, which dominated Great Britain down into the twentieth century (yes, we all love *Downton Abbey*, but . . .); (b) an extensive virgin territory for applying it (the Louisiana Purchase); and, most especially, (c) the opportunity for a multitude of dissenting Protestant sects, Catholics, and Jews to engage the new world with a religious fervor largely absent from the feudalistic state churches of Europe. It is important to remember how many of the original settlers were from dissenting Protestant sects, such as the Puritans, Methodists, Baptists, and Quakers.

This early influence can be seen in the sermons preached during the American War of Independence, the Declaration of Independence, and throughout the rest of US history. Here is a brief sampling.

- In the *Mayflower* Compact (1620), "In the name of God, amen . . . having undertaken, for the glory of God, and the advancement of the Christian faith . . . a voyage to plant the first colony . . ."

- The Declaration of Independence asserts that "all men . . . are endowed by their Creator with certain unalienable Rights, that among these are Life, Liberty and the pursuit of happiness." The last sentence asserts "a firm reliance on divine Providence."

- The Liberty Bell contains a verse from the Torah: "Proclaim liberty throughout the land."

- George Washington's 1790 letter to the Hebrew Congregation at Newport: "May the children of the stock of Abraham who dwell in this land continue to merit and enjoy the good will of the other inhabitants—while everyone shall sit in safety under his own vine and fig tree and there shall be none to make him afraid. May the father of all mercies scatter light, and not darkness, upon our paths, and make us all in our several vocations useful here, and in His own due time and way everlastingly happy."[7]

- John Adams said, "Statesmen . . . may plan and speculate for liberty, but it is Religion and Morality alone which can establish the Principles upon which Freedom can securely stand."[8]

- In his classic *Democracy in America* (1840), Tocqueville identified America's unique religious heritage derived primarily from the Puritans, the importance of the Hebrew Bible, the transposed belief that America was a chosen nation whose founding gave Americans a sense of moral mission. Most especially, Tocqueville observed that the biblical outlook gave America a moral dimension, which the Old World lacked. "I have said enough to put the character of Anglo-American civilization in its true light. It is the result (and this should be constantly kept in mind) of two distinct elements, which in other places have been in frequent disagreement, but which the Americans have succeeded in incorporating to some extent one with the other and combining admirably. I allude to the spirit of religion and the spirit of liberty" (chap. 2).

- Lincoln's Gettysburg Address concludes with: "We here highly resolve . . . that this nation, under God, shall have a new birth of freedom—and that government of the people, by the people, for the people, shall not perish from the earth."

- In 1952 President-Elect Dwight Eisenhower acknowledged that the "Judeo-Christian concept" is the "deeply religious faith" on which "our sense of government . . . is founded."[9]

- "Under God" was added to the pledge of allegiance in 1954.

- The national motto (since 1956), which appears on US currency, is "In God We Trust."

- Presidents take the oath of office on both an Old and New Testament Bible.

America exemplifies the logic of modernity par excellence. That is why there is such a thing as the American Dream—which continues to draw people to our exceptional shores from the world over.

For those among you who are wont to pose the question empirically, "Do Americans see themselves as exceptional?" you can look at the results of a very recent December 2012 Gallup Poll.

It turns out that Americans widely agree that the United States has a unique character because of its history and Constitution that sets it apart from other nations as the greatest in the world. This view, commonly referred to as "US exceptionalism," is shared by at least 80 percent of Americans in all party groups, including 91 percent of Republicans.

One of the extensions of the belief in American exceptionalism is the notion that, because of its status, the United States has an obligation to be the leading nation in world affairs. Americans generally endorse this position, as 66 percent say the United States has "a special responsibility to be the leading nation in world affairs." Republicans, Democrats, and independents generally agree, with fairly modest differences among party supporters.

My friends, Yale students and pundits everywhere along the Yale Political Union party spectrum, embrace American exceptionalism.

To my utter surprise and in part due to a clever debate technique employed in rebuttal (I quoted Barack Obama), we won.

Yes, we won, but just by one single vote. America is exceptional—by one vote at Yale. *All praise to thee, Bill Buckley!!!*

The lesson here is ideological: might makes right. Surely, a sound idea always triumphs, eventually.

MY THIRTEEN FAVORITE HYMNS

1. "The Old Rugged Cross," sung by George Beverly Shea at all the Billy Graham crusades; it is an old revivalist hymn.

2. "How Great Thou Art," based on an old Swedish melody and poem written in 1885.

3. "Crown Him with Many Crowns," sung at my summer camp every Sunday, penned by Matthew Bridges in England in 1851.

4. "Rock of Ages," the great reminder of saving grace, written in 1776.

5. "Abide with Me," written by Henry Frances Lyte and first sung in 1849 to the tune of "Eventide."

6. "Faith of Our Fathers," English hymn written in 1849 by Frederick William Farber in memory of the martyrs of the faith.

7. "Lift High the Cross," nineteenth-century text to proclaim the love of Christ.

8. "A Mighty Fortress," from an old German song entitled, "Ein Feste Berg," by Martin Luther.

9. "Be Thou My Vision," an old Irish hymn set to the tune "Slade."

10. "What a Friend We Have in Jesus," written by Joseph Scriven in 1865 to comfort his own dying mother.

11. "Jerusalem." England does not have a national anthem, but this is the unofficial version. The words are taken from Milton.

12. "Holy, Holy, Holy," written by Reginald Heber and sung on Trinity Sunday, based on the scripture text from Revelation 4:1–11.

13. "Amazing Grace," authored in 1779 by John Newton about his own conversion from slave trade captain to parish priest.

18

THE PHILANTHROPIC ENDEAVOR: WHAT'S GIVIN' GOT TO DO WITH IT?

For God so loved the world that he gave his one and only Son, that whoever believes in him shall not perish but have eternal life.

—JOHN 3:16

Supply meets demand; demand matches supply. Economics is all about the intersections along this crucial curve. "Supply-demand" describes relations between buyers and sellers of any good or service. We all learned that much in Econ 101!

The model determines prices and quantity sold in a given market. In a competitive market, as is capitalism, prices function to equalize the quantity demanded by consumers and the quantity supplied by producers, resulting in an economic equilibrium. Where and how does "generosity" fit into the equation? Or does it? Is generosity/charity valued or a good virtue? I think so.

Herbert Gintis, a self-described former Marxist economist at the University of Massachusetts, has been one of the leading economists taking up the matter of economics and generosity. Gintis is codirector of the Preferences Network team. His team's research is dispelling the myth of happy generous savages that are corrupted by contact with markets and modern societies. It turns out that the more the savages actually participate in markets, the more generous and filled with apparent "fellow feeling" they tend to be.

Based on his research, Gintis believes that history traces humanity's rise from tribal selfishness to more cosmopolitan liberality. I was at a conference with him at Harvard Business School and he said, "Market societies give rise to more egalitarianism and movements toward democracy, civil liberties, and civil rights," He pointed out, "Market societies and democratic societies are practically co-extensive." And it appears they are more generous too. Wow—what a breakthrough. What did he say?

Gintis speculates that markets bring strangers into contact on a regular basis, encouraging people to develop more concern for "others" beyond their family and immediate neighbors. Instead of parochialism, being integrated into markets encourages a sort of spirit of ecumenism.

In a classic treatment on the subject, *Generosity: Virtue in Civil Society*, the libertarian philosopher Tibor Machan both makes a case for generosity as a "civic virtue" and denies that law can enjoin it. Even the Bible does not make tithing a law but rather a matter of self-donation or what used to be called *agape* love. Grounding this argument in a rational-egoistic, natural law–based "virtue ethic," we can present what may be the best argument yet offered that the virtue of generosity is a constitutive part of a well-lived human life.

I wrote a book entitled *Being Generous* on this topic and spelled out how the virtue crosses all traditions and religious persuasions and is perhaps best captured in Saint Paul's litany about "gift." We could then proceed to demolish the view that generosity may properly, or can be effectively, enforced by a "welfare state."

I also try and practice the virtue. In fact, in my family, giving was so essential that it was, well, sacrificial. Giving was the meaning for living. We were made into philanthropists from birth. I even structured my entire personal financial and wealth model around a set of insurance policies so that when I die I will give $30 million to various charities. I guess that's why people can't wait for me to pass away!

One of the first principles of economics that I learned long ago suggests that material prosperity depends on moral convictions and moral dealings. You say you never heard *economics* and *moral* in the same sentence and it sounds like an oxymoron? No? Adam Smith, the principal founder of the dull economic science in the eighteenth century, was himself a professor of moral philosophy. He took it for granted that moral beliefs should and did affect economic doings. The success of economic measures, like the success of most other things in human existence, depends on certain moral habits. If those habits are lacking, the only other way to produce goods is by compulsion—by what is called slave labor.

In my work, I have examined some of the moral qualities that make possible a prosperous economy (see my book *Spiritual Enterprise*), as there is a strong connection to being generous. I argue that there is an actual *cycle of virtue* that starts with wealth generation (what a novel idea!), moves through thrift to investment with a long-term horizon, on to being generous (charity), and ends all over again with the renewal of culture.

The hard data finds that human beings as economic actors actually show considerable generosity toward strangers, people with whom they share economic and social relations but whom they don't know. This economic reality speaks volumes about generosity in real life—not in some research lab.

In 2012, over $300 billion was given to US charities, with $199 billion (77 percent) of this given by individuals. The absolute amount of charitable giving is not only high, but the proportion of income donated has grown. In 1954, the average individual in the United States gave 1.9 percent of after-tax income to charity ($222), while in 2007 giving averaged 2.2 percent of after-tax income ($656, inflation adjusted). In 2012, approximately one-third of this giving was directed to religious organizations, followed by 19 percent to health and human well-being as money. In 2012, according to Giving USA, more than 65 million Americans volunteered to help charities. Ninety-six percent of volunteers said that one of their motivations was "feeling compassion toward other people." In the midst of all this giving, the physiologic mechanisms that support altruism and generosity are little understood. Human beings routinely help strangers at costs to themselves. Sometimes the help offered is generous—offering more than the other expects.

According to a survey by Giving USA, there is a link between attendance at weekly worship services and giving, and since attendance at weekly worship services in the United States is declining, nonprofits are concerned. Here are some findings from the survey:

- Seventy-four percent of those who participate at least occasionally in worship services give to charity, while only 50 percent of those who never attend do so; and the more often one attends, the more likely one is to give.

- Religious households give 87.5 percent of all charitable contributions, averaging over $2,100 in annual contributions to all causes.

- Persons of faith are 25 percent more likely to donate money and 23 percent more likely to volunteer time than the general population.

- Persons of faith are 33 percent of the population but make up 52 percent of donations and 45 percent of times volunteered.

- Religious practice by itself is associated with $1,388 more in an individual's giving per year.

These numbers tell a bigger story, one I have witnessed firsthand, of faithful, even sacrificial giving that needs to be retold again and again. The cultural effects of giving extend to both the recipients and back to the givers, as well. We know this in America, but they have forgotten it in Europe today as the State usurps all power.

There is a catchy line in a television commercial for men's suits, which rather slyly state, "An educated customer is our best customer." It's true. Nothing works better than perpetual learning to cement a relationship or to build a habit or good practice. The monasteries were full of what they called "disciplines" that were less physical and more spiritual, including prayers at 3 o'clock every morning. When you talk to profound givers of any of the world's many traditions, religious, new social entrepreneurs or humanists who think a great deal about the ultimate grounds of human behavior, they all come down to one thing: *formation.*

People need and really seek to be formed—to take shape. Anyone who has a regular regimen of exercise or who has ever trained for a sport—any sport or event, not just the Olympics—or studied for a big examination or a test like the bar exam, knows this as well. We know it with our bodies; we school our minds; but what about our souls in an era of moral laxity and spiritual searching? Who and what cares for, forms, our souls? For it is the soul that ultimately guides our decisions on giving.

"Formation" is an interesting and often-employed word, used in a wide variety of fashions in every language. Aerobats, like the Blue Angels, of course, fly in formation. So do geese and ducks. Military units march and deploy in formation. Footballers get into formation on both offense and defense on each play before the ball is snapped. Geology has its rock formations and strata. Governments form coalitions to rule. Even business is conducted according to contract formation under the law. It is not surprising, then, that all of the world's lasting traditions—and I have visited all of them—contain elements of formation for adherents and those who lead worship. This formation is a kind of nurturance in the experience and practice of personal and social holiness. The goal is a deepening of spiritual awareness, growing in moral sensibility, and building character.

In a postmodern culture like ours, where identity is today primarily grounded in what a person "does," giving is often perceived as a kind of "performance" that requires the acquisition of a body of knowledge, an adequate level of intelligence, several skill sets, and sufficient training to be able to weave all of this together in effective ways. In such an atmosphere, givers, young or old, any color, can gain the whole world of knowledge, intelligence, skills, and abilities and still lose their souls.

Rarely is giving perceived as a matter of being—being in union with nature or with God—from which "doing" flows. It is like a doxology. Unless knowledge and intelligence, skill sets and training, are grounded in a life of loving union with something beyond ourselves, for the sake of others, they can become subverted by personal, cultural, social, political, or ecclesial agendas; they become manipulative, coercive, and even destructive although ostensibly employed in the service of the good.

John Wesley, the seventeenth century divine, in his own life and ministry, later called Methodism, underscored the value of integration on the way to spiritual maturity. His "conjunctive" theology called for a symbiosis of law and grace, of personal depth and social expression, of developing the life of the mind and that of the soul, and of serving one's neighbor as well as glorifying God as the highest end of life. There are many examples of this same dedication, from the ancient church fathers right through to Mother Teresa and Pope John Paul II. At the very core of this kind of formation is the giving of oneself—which is what "dedication" literally, means—and the gratitude that is the reciprocal aspect of that gift.

I am not a priest or a mystic, as you know, nor am I trying to make converts to any particular spiritual dogma. Nevertheless, I would not be doing my subject justice if I left it without offering some aids to the art of effective giving in this season of stewardship. And the two that I offer from experience, in all deference to the complexity of any individual life, are aids that I myself have found useful. The first involves some suggestions on setting the stage. It is a process and it can be taught and learned wherever and whenever the person is open and ready to be taught, to commence the learning. But recall that *learning*, like *forming*, is an active verb and implies the right state of mind and a perceived need from which the doing emerges. So here then is my personal guide to generosity:

GUIDE TO GENEROSITY

Is there a process to generosity? Would such a process, regardless of who we are or where we come from, suggest a more genuine, scientifically based, even universal form of being generous? Such questions are worth considering in the context of the arguments about the virtue of generosity and philanthropic endeavor.

What would a "process of being generous" look like? Decisions about giving are like other human decisions. Decision making is an outcome of a mental process involving cognition leading to selected courses of action(s) producing a final choice. Clearly, all integrated action decisions (like giving) impute a commitment to action. And we would all agree that diagnosis must be properly informed if treatment is to be appropriate. In general, intuitive elements, when combined with informed analysis, will lead to decisions that are both more effective in achieving the goal, and more honest in expressing their motive.

However, cognition styles and cultural attitudes differ across societies, even in a more globalized and integrated economy in this twenty-first century. Hence there may be no easy or single way to promote generous living and giving. But here are six techniques that have been used with good result in everyday life and by many thoughtful philanthropists, to help guide effective decision making.

1. List the advantages and disadvantages of any giving option(s).

2. Use random or coincidental methods to demonstrate the effect of acts of kindness.

3. Accept the first option for giving that achieves a desired result.

4. Acquiesce to a known authority or expert and act on that advice for giving.

5. Calculate the expected value or utility of each giving option.

6. Make a decision and follow it through.

In the case of giving, it is the last of those that is most often neglected.

It is easy to think that you have succeeded in giving something when you have gotten rid of the intended gift—say, by handing it to some official charity, church, temple, or agency, which may be entirely self-appointed to the role of distributor. But a "gift" is only a gift when the one in need of it has received it.

To be generous and to be an effective giver, therefore, it is not sufficient to give money: you must also give time and energy—the time needed to follow things through and the energy needed to convey your gift into the hands of the one whom you wish to help. Rather than give your money to an agency, why not join with your neighbors, associates, or social network in a project of your own? Travel to the place where your help is needed; work out how to establish a school or hospital; raise the funds; set up the network of support—and then enjoy the prospect of success, as the initiative grows before your eyes. It is my thesis that human nature itself unites all peoples in their need to be generous, but being effective in that virtue requires patience and faithful soul work.

This generous economy of ours is large, real, and measurable. This economy, and the society it spawns, is also rooted in religious and moral values, with liberty at its core. It should be remembered, for instance, that my mentor Sir John Templeton's favorite holiday, among all others, was Thanksgiving. He annually sent out cards and personalized letters reminding friends and colleagues how much they had to be "thankful for." And in so doing he also restated his deeply held spiritual view—that life begins in gratitude, runs through thrift, and ends in generosity.

Thanksgiving is a long-standing, ancient harvest festival. Traditionally, it is a time to give thanks for the harvest and express gratitude. While many countries the world over have their own versions of harvest festivals and worship, today it is a holiday celebrated primarily in Canada and the United States. While religious in origin, Thanksgiving is now identified chiefly as a secular holiday.

The date and location of the first Thanksgiving celebration is a topic of contention. Though the earliest attested Thanksgiving celebration was on September 8, 1565, in what is now St. Augustine, Florida, the traditional "first Thanksgiving" involving the Pilgrims is, as we all know, venerated as having occurred at the site of Plymouth Plantation in Massachusetts, in 1621.

Today, Thanksgiving is celebrated on the second Monday of October in Canada and on the fourth Thursday of November in the United States. Thanksgiving dinner is held on this day, usually as a gathering of families and friends, with a turkey and a sense of thanks. It always was in my house. We need Thanksgiving, but we need it *every day*, not just on that day in fall as a harvest festival. We need it as a reminder of the One from whom all blessings flow.

Now, I have been involved in philanthropies for a very long time. I have served on so many boards and given to so many others that they are hard to count. But there are three stories related to my philanthropic experiences I'd like to recount as instructive of three different things: lessons learned.

The first is about innovation. I was involved in a startup by my good friend Dennis Whittle, who used to be with the World Bank, called Global Giving. It is a web-based site that allows anyone to give online by PayPal or credit card to more than fifteen hundred needy projects on nearly every continent. This disintermediation cuts out the middlemen and all their bloated administrative costs. My daughter, then aged twelve, was a young ambassador for them, and we started the Global Giving birthday party for rich kids who don't really need more "stuff," so the kids give and get cards to donate to the things they find most worthy online. It teaches good principles and also involves people directly with things like disaster relief or girl's schools in Ethiopia.

The second lesson comes from my serving on a board of the Pew Charitable Trusts, based in Philadelphia and of considerable size and stature. It is about what I'd term "responsible stewardship or not."

Just because you have a lot of money to throw around at problems or a platform of global significance, that doesn't let you off the hook for your actions. Pew did a horrible job literally throwing money at problems in a fit-and-start fashion without much oversight and never accomplished the good goals it set out to achieve with its millions of charitable dollars. The intellectual who ran the projects for Pew was talented and committed, but they constantly choose the wrong partners and went through so many bad iterations that in the end they simply threw up their arms and said, "Enough!" They failed.

Pew did something even worse in my estimation soon thereafter. A venerable institution divorced itself from its long family heritage and deep-seated traditions and changed itself from a grant-making institution into one that took all its charitable dollars and did research itself. In other words, it paid itself—a lot. This is just unforgivable.

My final story is a sordid one. A philanthropist I knew gave millions to a great little Catholic college and wanted his name pasted all over everything from the auditorium to the dining hall to the dormitory. They were grateful and like so many such places lacked endowment and depended on such donors. When he was arrested for fraud, the government clawed back all the money, and the school was farther behind than when it started.

The lesson here is that giving, you see, is *very* hard work. It is most definitely a virtue, but it takes constant attention and a heart connected to a head (as Adam Smith reminded us in his *Theory of Moral Sentiments,* written seventeen years before his better known and appreciated *Wealth of Nations.*)

THIRTEEN BIG MALLOCH IDEAS NEVER IMPLEMENTED

1. The whole wide world goes on the Eastern Standard Time Zone
I proposed this in the UN, but the Asians found it wanting, as they'd have to work in the dark, but so what?!

2. Dictators retirement retreat in the Caribbean
I proposed this seriously at the State Department after seeing so many tin-horned kleptocrats from Marcos to Noriega who would not leave power. Suppose we had a Ritz Carlton resort for them to retire to—all expenses and vices paid—in some idyllic isle in the sun, complete with golf and a spa? Who could refuse the offer to leave office? And think how much blood and tears it would save! Sounds like a Steve Allen dinner party sketch.

3. Thrift Week
After penning a book on the frugal subject both public and private, I suggested to Templeton that we get Congress to declare an annual Thrift Week to re-practice the old-fashioned virtue. Congress could do fiscal conservatism a week a year!

4. Divide Iraq into three
I wrote to Ambassador Jerry Bremmer the day he became our vice consul for Bush 43 in Iran—I knew him from working together on "crisis management" at Marsh—to suggest forcefully that Iraq—which is a fake nation anyway—be divided into three parts: Sunni, Shite, and Kurdish. It could be a loose federalism, if he insisted, but the important thing was to declare American victory and leave immediately. He didn't do it, and the cost was over a trillion dollars and hundreds of thousands of lives lost. What a shame. I deserved the Nobel Peace Prize for this idea!

5. Create a dozen more Hong Kongs

I wrote a piece that appeared in the *Weekly Standard* saying the world needs at least a dozen more Hong Kongs, if not more. With free markets, the rule of law, and trading cultures, these dozen new free cities could create a world of commerce and freedom from which we would all benefit.

6. Divorce insurance

After suffering the plight and seeing so many others I know go down this road, it hit me that since over half of all marriages now end in "splitsville," there should be a strong and growing market for divorce insurance. Think of it as something you purchase when you sign your prenuptial agreement.

7. Reestablish Glass-Steagall

In our tome *The End of Ethics*, we actually rue the day the Chinese wall came down in the last decade when investment banking and commercial banking were allowed to combine. If you want to avoid conflicts of interest and "too big to fail"—reinstall the Act!

8. The North Korean sandwich

After my presidential delegation to China with secretary Tom Ridge, I wrote an op-ed suggesting we give in on Taiwan (two-China policy) if China gives in on North Korea and pulls the plug on the irrational regime. North Korea reunites with South Korea and all its wacky ways cease, as does its dangerous nuclear weapons proliferation!

9. China's impending implosion

On MaxTV I said in all seriousness during an interview that I thought it rather likely that by 2025 China would *implode* much as the Soviet regime did, either from bad economics, internal revolt, or ethnic rivalry in country! Let's hope so!

10. The Shadow G-20

In a proposal to the Legatum Institute in London (they have a very tony HQ in Mayfair), I suggested the formation of a Shadow G-20 Council made up of leading businesspeople from the same countries that would meet one month each year before the real G-20 meeting/summit and issue business-based recommendations. I thought the world would have to take this seriously!

11. The Oath of Virtuous Capitalism

I penned this oath for all MBA students, but no one ever signed it. It can be found at http://media.wfyi.org/DoingVirtuousBusiness/oath.asp. Students promising to be good—what a novel idea!

(tie). A Philanthropy Index Exchange

If philanthropies, which tend to be bloated and inefficient, were treated more like for-profit companies and their records compared or ranked with peers, we could have an exchange whereby people, especially donors, could invest in the best in class. Market-based philanthropy!

12. College 2.0 plus free upgrades

I have long suggested since coauthoring the book *Perpetual Learning*, that colleges and universities every year invite their graduates back to campus for a two-day extended session to learn everything new in their major field. This, like software updates, would keep them current, establish alumni relations, and acknowledge that there is no such thing as a terminal degree!

13. The Spiritual State of the Union

I started with the late George Gallup in 2003 a survey of the nation and with extensive analysis on the "spiritual state of our country." The idea was that the president would present these findings right after or included with his annual State of the Union speech to the combined House and Senate, every January.

19

FINDING THE SPIRIT

Since we live by the Spirit, let us keep in step with the Spirit.

—GALATIANS 5:25

It started out a number of years ago on a beautiful and balmy, tranquil spring day as we flew into the Bahamas and went through the gates of the lush private Lyford Cay Club.

My heart raced, as I was about to encounter the world's greatest investor for the first time. I was not there, as so many before me had trekked, to gain some useful perspective on the market or to discover which global companies to invest in. My conversation was even more profound. Over time, I was privileged to have many conversations and to embark on a friendship that turned into a challenge.

Sir John Templeton was a humble, yet penetrating soul. His gaze was truly like that of a sage, of a person both entirely otherworldly and so infused with spiritual information that he exuded, well, *joy*. I recall his first words to me after introductions. He said, "Always remember how little we know and be eager to learn."

He and his lieutenants, Chuck Harper (a brainy Oxford

astrophysicist) and Arthur Schwartz (a Harvard-trained moral psychologist), enjoined me in a direct yet simple challenge: to demonstrate how a spiritual force guides enterprises and the entrepreneurs who started them, itself rooted in faith. This work was to be about virtuous companies. I took up the challenge and with his generous support and my own endowment, founded the Spiritual Enterprise Institute. That Institute became a multidisciplinary, business-academic center, dedicated to exploring and analyzing the modern phenomenon of spiritual entrepreneurship and spiritual capital in the context of globalization. It sought to approach its activities within a values-based framework that—while explicitly held and applied—is very broadly defined, and which values the perspectives of all faith traditions. The Spiritual Enterprise Institute (SEI) became, in short order, a world-class, high-visibility center that would have a major impact on corporations and other organizations, as well as the broader worlds beyond academe and commerce.

Serving a catalytic role, SEI sought to help integrate the spiritual principles and practices of virtue and faith into the mission, values, planning, and operations of businesses and institutions in the United States and worldwide. The impact was far-reaching since it is changing for generations to come, how corporations operate and transact business in the global marketplace for the betterment of man and the glory of God. One of the earmarks of the successful integration of spiritual entrepreneurship is the renewed freedom of religious expression in the workplace.

The Spiritual Enterprise Institute's role as catalyst for spiritual transformation was made available to corporations, media, and governments worldwide through its web presence. This electronic nerve center provides resources, content, and communities to support institutions seeking to tap into the power of the Creator to transform their company, community and country. Spiritual Entrepreneurship Institute workshops, forums, and leadership summits are conducted around the world. Their content is digitized and made available to any company, college, or training institution anywhere in the world, through PDF and streaming media. The best-selling breakthrough book, *Spiritual*

Enterprise: Doing Virtuous Business, published in 2008, depicted how people of faith built their virtuous corporations. The book set the standard, told the stories, and provided the blueprint for a new expression of faith and good deeds in the marketplace.

The purpose of the Spiritual Enterprise Institute was straightforward: it had a clear vision that comes directly from conversations with the legendary financial entrepreneur and philanthropist, Sir John Templeton.

The Spiritual Enterprise Institute focused on the research, lessons, and potential value of understanding spirituality as an essential component of economic development and progress. It carefully targeted opinion leaders to learn more about the significance of spiritual capital and the enterprises it generated, across a range of issues relevant to leaders and the media in the private, public, and social sectors.

The Spiritual Enterprise Institute's activities included the following:

Research. The Institute undertakes and encourages research on the phenomenon of spiritual entrepreneurship and globalization through partnerships with universities, foundations, think tanks, and corporations, and on its own accord.

Curriculum. The Institute encourages faculty to consider appropriate ways to incorporate spiritual entrepreneurship and globalization perspectives in the courses they teach and research they undertake.

Courses. The Institute works with schools to develop appropriate courses that specifically deal with spiritual entrepreneurship and globalization and works with university centers to integrate it into existing courses.

Conferences. The Institute sponsors seminars, forums, roundtables, and larger conferences to which academic, corporate, political, social sector, and other leaders from around the world come to discuss, learn, and share perspectives.

Lectures. The Institute sponsors an annual series of lectures by nationally and internationally known leaders in academia, business, and politics.

Executive and distance education. The Institute specializes in executive education programs in the area of spiritual entrepreneurship and globalization.

Awards. The Institute offers a number of global prizes and awards to those selected as luminaries and exemplars in this field in the private, public, and social sectors, in the United States and globally.

The Spiritual Enterprise Institute developed projects that had a clear purpose and that had significant strategic impact on the fields of science, business, religion, and culture overall. The results were considered in a strategic manner: how they furthered the field, influenced opinion leaders, impacted decision makers, appealed to the media, and opened up dialogues on campuses and in companies, worldwide. The Spiritual Enterprise Institute enhanced a commitment to a global outlook, testified to by its well-known international programs, and the overseas participants it attracted. The Institute's orientation extended quality and mission across disciplines. As such, it offered a firm basis for understanding and evaluating the phenomenon of spiritual entrepreneurship within the context of globalization. As such, the Institute looked west and east, north and south. Big themes were at the nexus of business and government, the public, private, and social sectors.

Nothing ever quite works out as planned, and things naturally evolved. The first breakthrough for SEI came indirectly through a $1 million grant from the Ford Foundation and matched by seven others, made through one of its partners in the humanities to "rebuild the public humanities."

A large conference was held in Aspen on the future of the humanities that was organized in concert with the National Endowment for the Humanities and their Indiana Center. Some 250 luminaries from around the country, including leading public intellectuals, such as

Michael Novak (AEI), Jean Elshtain (University of Chicago), and Steven Carter (Yale Law School), attended the meeting.

The second prong involved a major book coauthored with Scott Massey, titled *Renewing American Culture: The Pursuit of Happiness*. We spent a summer writing it at a villa outside of Florence, Italy, and gave a paper based on its themes to an international symposium. The book was well received, with book openings at both the Library of Congress and at Lincoln Center. The foreword was written by librarian of Congress James Billington, and endorsed by many on the right, left, and center, as "the way forward." The book was then made into a vignette-style PBS sixty-minute documentary with the same title. Massey and I were the executive producers, and Todd Gould, an eighteen-time Emmy winner, produced the film, which aired nationally to an audience of 11 million in November 2007. The documentary premiered at the Heartland Film Festival, where an entire evening was dedicated to its showing and an hour-long panel discussion with a distinguished group of scholars, journalists, politicians, and businesspeople hailed its cry for building more spiritual capital.

SEI also released a Gallup Poll called the "Spiritual State of the Union," which came out just before the president's own State of the Union. It got large press, and George Gallup and I gave a presentation at Washington's Metropolitan Club to a full house. Michael Lindsay, the sociologist of some acclaim, was our consultant.

Other books were readied for publication. One was *Thrift: Rebirth of a Forgotten Virtue*, and another, *Being Generous*, I outlined in the previous chapter. It seemed that the world was more and more interested in recovering the lost virtues and making them a part of the public vocabulary, again. With speeches at many colleges and universities, and in places as far as away as Scotland, where we commenced an annual Malloch Lecture on spiritual capital, and China, then India, there was growing evidence of interest in morality and the market. Liberty Fund asked to partner with SEI on more than a dozen colloquia for businesspeople on related topics. And they were held at places such as

Forbes Trinchera Ranch; Big Sky Ranch in Montana; Naples, Florida; and Jackson Hole, in Wyoming.

One of the biggest projects SEI undertook was the research and publication of the comprehensive *Religious Freedom in the World.* It was done with my friend of twenty-five years, Paul Marshall, and in conjunction with Freedom House and the Hudson Institute. Religious persecution affects all religious groups. There is no group in the world that does not suffer to some degree because of its beliefs. *Religious Freedom in the World* published at the end of 2007 and profiles 102 countries and territories, which between them contain more than 95 percent of the world's population, and uses a clearly comprehensible numeric scale to rank the level of religious freedom found in each. It also provided separately derived measures of government regulation of religion, government favoritism of religion, and social regulation of religion. The countries in the survey represent each continent, major religion, and geographic area, cover countries with the largest populations, describe particularly egregious violators of religious freedom, and illustrate variations within regions. The essay contributors over and above the seventy-five researchers from around the world who compiled the data, included Habib Malik, Willy Fautré, Tom Farr, and Brian Grim. After a major conference and a smaller working group in Washington to the press, the report got thousands of pages of news coverage and television the world over. We were asked to brief both the State Department and the National Security Council.

With conferences at Wake Forest and Yale and consultations in many companies, the concepts of spiritual capital and spiritual enterprise were well on their way into the public vocabulary and international awareness. I penned entries on the topic for the *Oxford Encyclopedia of Economics, The Handbook of Faith and Business*, and many more. I appeared on television and radio regularly, from CNN to ABC to Fox to CBS to NewsMax. We did more than two hundred radio broadcasts, from NPR to drive-by shows to televangelism. I spoke to some sixty-five business schools or showed our Emmy-nominated documentary around the nation and the world. We had visitors from many countries, the economic advisor to the then shadow prime minister of Great Britain, and an entourage from Canada's new PC government visited. Large and smaller privately held companies were asking us about virtues in business. Newspapers and magazines wanted interviews and quotes, and television shows wanted to know what this was all about. We certainly got the word out! One where I received a standing ovation for five minutes was the Freedom and Markets Forum hosted by Hillsdale College and the Consortium of Christian Colleges and Universities.

In many respects, history is occupied with the invention and development of what we today know as forms of financial, political, human, social, and tangible capital. But it is fair to say that originally the dominant form of capital in the world was spiritual capital. And it was spiritual enterprise—putting spiritual capital to work—that was largely responsible for originating and developing human civilizations.

In recent centuries spiritual enterprise has cycled in and through an increasingly secular society. It has at various times been rediscovered, rebuked, redefined, and has stimulated the core tenets of modern economic theory and the creation of remarkable wealth and prosperity. In the eighteenth and nineteenth centuries, spiritual enterprise was brandnamed the "Protestant work ethic" and stimulated much of the thinking by the moral philosopher Adam Smith and the social observer Max Weber.

Today, in the wake of 9/11 and in concert with the influences of globalization, spiritual enterprise is again emerging as a topic of keen interest to economists, the media, religious leaders, and many in business and politics. And it is credited anew with being a fundamental driver for individuals, communities, and whole economies.

According to the latest research by Professor Robert Putnam at Harvard, religious practice is named the largest generator of social capital—and that social capital is a critical catalyzing agent for civil engagement, strong democracy, philanthropy, and increasingly, best business practices. The proposition then quickly emerges: if social capital promotes important civic and economic enterprise, and religious practice is the largest generator of social capital, then there is a great benefit in investigating and developing the religious components that drive the creation of such capital.

Unfortunately, some dubious folks, critical left-wing evangelicals along with most far leftists, don't like my work on spiritual capital. This came to a head when I published a piece on James Hunter, the University of Virginia sociologist (we knew him as "hippy Jimmie" in college) in the conservative paragon the *American Spectator*.

It didn't end with a flurry of exchanges, as do most such insignificant (academic) disputes. The stakes were too low. A person with whom I was friendly and had worked on numerous joint projects (including staying at my house in Palm Beach for free), took particular umbrage. He wrote to me saying he had taken all the many copies of my books I had given him to the local dump and burned them in revenge. This sounded like a Nazi approach, I thought—burning books?

His brother-in-law (they were missionaries in Korea), who studies evangelicals at the Ethics and Public Policy Center in DC, took offense and talked behind my back—even though he had hypocritically endorsed these *very* books and is quoted on the back flap!

So this book burner and a schlocky New York failed former investment type who stood all of about four feet nine inches tall (like Napoleon, he suffered a complex), but was a Yale graduate at that, wrote to me saying I should be "fired from Yale" and that he would "ruin my career."

Now, my career is already *very* far down the road, so I didn't see that as very possible. I got my lawyers to rattle the book burner and to settle for a modest award and a written promise that they would cease and desist. Nice people, these thin-skinned pretenders that parade as holier-than-thou but amount to a pile of human dung; there is nothing all that new in vile and loathsome people, I suspect. It just hurts when you have allowed them into your inner circle and they turn and bite you.

Back to my story line, I argue that the religious components that drive the creation of social capital have been called "spiritual capital," and that capital put to work is, in essence, spiritual enterprise. But having arrived at those definitions, a flood of questions arises:

- Precisely what are spiritual capital and spiritual enterprise?

- Can spiritual capital be measured?

- How do you invest in spiritual capital?

- Is there negative spiritual capital?

- Can it be bought, borrowed, or traded?

- What erodes such capital and destroys such enterprises?

- What builds and sustains spiritual enterprise(s)?

We are only just discovering what questions to ask. In the same way the astronomers know a black hole exists by the behavior of light and matter around it, so too, thoughtful observers acknowledge the important existence of spiritual capital and recognize it by the positive movement of communities around concentrations of the spiritual enterprises it stimulates and creates. We wrote a case book, complete with teaching notes about such companies, entitled *Practical Wisdom in Management*, which grew out of a relationship with the Academy of Business in Society based in Brussels and their very sharp president, Gilbert Lenssen, who was himself a senior executive at BP, besides being a professor of strategy at INSEAD, the business school outside Paris, and a profoundly Catholic thinker.

It appears Adam Smith, in his *The Theory of Moral Sentiments*, published long before the more famous *Wealth of Nations*, got it right. He knew more then than we know today about virtue. He said, and I repeat in closing:

> Wise and judicious conduct, when directed to greater and nobler purposes, is called prudence. Prudence, combined with valor, benevolence, a sacred regard to the rules of justice, and supported by a proper degree of self-command—necessarily supposes the art, the talent, and

the habit of acting with the most perfect propriety in every possible circumstance (and) necessarily supposes the utmost perfection of all the intellectual and of all the moral virtues. It is simply, *the best head joined to the best heart.*

The lesson of this account is to follow your heart, but know that others will attack you mercilessly for it.

MY THIRTEEN BIGGEST TROPHY FISH CAUGHT

1. 125-pound Wahoo off of White Sands in the Bahamas

2. 195-pound Mako Shark off of Ocean City, New Jersey

3. 230-pound Swordfish in the Gulfstream, seventeen miles off Hobe Sound, Florida

4. 52-inch Barracuda off Jupiter, Florida

5. 32-pound Salmon in the River Dee, Scotland

6. 115-pound Black Marlin off the Ocho Rios coast of Jamaica

7. 295-pound Tuna off of the Berry Islands, the Bahamas

8. 6 foot 7 jumping Sailfish off of Palm Beach, Florida (sixteen in a day)

9. 80-pound Dorado off of Cat Island, the Bahamas

10. 26-inch Rainbow Trout, Adirondacks, New York

11. 95 Bluefish off of Nantucket, Massachusetts, in a day

12. 27-pound Cod off of Beverly Farms, Massachusetts

13. 38-pound Rockfish, Chesapeake Bay, Maryland

EPILOGUE

THE TAKEAWAY(S)

These words are trustworthy and true. The Lord, the God who inspires the prophets, sent his angel to show his servants the things that must soon take place. "Look, I am coming soon! Blessed is the one who keeps the words of the prophecy written in this scroll."

—REVELATION 22:6–7

Historically, what were called "morality plays" were a type of theatrical allegory in which a protagonist was met by personifications of various moral attributes who tried to prompt him or her to choose a godly life over one of evil. The plays were quite popular in Europe during the fifteenth and sixteenth centuries. Having grown out of the religiously based mystery plays of the Middle Ages, these plays represented a shift toward a more secular base for European theater. I still like them!

Morality plays only gradually died out as tastes changed toward the end of the sixteenth century. Throughout his career the bard, Shakespeare himself, made references to morality characters and tropes, suggesting that the form was still alive for his audiences, at least in memory, long beyond the period of their flowering.

Most of these plays had a protagonist who represented either humanity as a whole, the so-called *Everyman*, or an entire social class. Antagonists and supporting characters were not always individuals but rather personifications of abstract virtues or vices, such as the seven deadly sins. You get the gist. Morality plays were typically written in the vernacular, so as to be more accessible to the common people who watched them. They learned and discovered how to live from watching these enactments.

My chapters are in an *extreme* sense twenty-first-century equivalents of morality plays, if such can even be deemed politically correct in our postmodern and post-Christian era of total depravity, complete relativism, and worst of all, non-judgmentalism. I do take the transcendent seriously and believe in spiritual capital that is built up over the generations and institutionalized, shared, and hopefully, renewed. My travails are unique to me, and the times that I have inhabited, but they are instructive to others as well. I am a person of faith who has stuck his toe or whole foot into the world, into the globalism that is so rampant, and I have tried to be *salt and light,* to use a biblical illustration taken from Matthew 5:13–16.

I have for business, pleasure, school, and mostly, country, traveled to 145 countries; some travels split into multiple parts since my visits (for which I claim no responsibility). I have worked in every sector of modern reality: academe, politics, finance, diplomacy, research, think tanks, philanthropy, and for the past twenty-five years, in strategic management and a term I first used way back, "thought leadership." I fought the Cold War and won and kept the faith while renewing our culture (see my book coauthored with Scott Massey, *Renewing American Culture: The Pursuit of Happiness*, or the one with Nicholas Capaldi, *America's Spiritual Capital*).

The PBS documentary I made, *Doing Virtuous Business*, was viewed nationally by 15 million viewers and was nominated for an Emmy award. More recently, after joining the first and former secretary of homeland security on a presidential mission to China for goodwill and stronger trade relations, I was dubbed by Ridge America's first "secretary of offense." If Tom ever becomes US president (quite unlikely), I may hold him to that impressive title and demand an appointment.

I have written books on thrift (*Thrift: Rebirth of a Forgotten Virtue*) and generosity (*Being Generous*). My book (and PBS documentary) *Doing Virtuous Business* was a huge best seller and gained acclaim worldwide. It was translated into Spanish, Portuguese, and Mandarin. Most recently, I co-penned a book on economic vice, entitled *The End of Ethics*, which describes not just the worst companies (economic vices) of the past decade, but "a way back." It has received overwhelming attention and gotten me on TV shows all over, from Fox to BBC to CNBC.

But if after all I have seen and lived I can be so bold as to offer some hints or slight rudiments of normativity from all my experiences, here it is, contained in *thirteen* (why not an "unlucky" number to go with my various lists, since WASPs don't believe in luck or fortune?) *suggestions*.

I say "suggestions" because when working with Ted Turner in 1992, I vividly recall his strict lecture against the Ten Commandments and everything hinting at the biblically dogmatic religious, saying, "why couldn't He have at least made or offered them as the Ten Suggestions?".

Here then are my ten—okay, *Thirteen—Suggestions* for your closest deliberation, even memorization (win a free week to summer camp). Take note: I am thinking of naming them *The Book of Ted* (after me, of course) and having them inscribed on some antique (perhaps golden) scrolls and then finding them buried in my backyard. This would allow me to found a new American religion, as Joseph Smith did Mormonism. I have taken www.Tedism.org just in case. So they are copyrighted and possibly inerrant (still to be determined) as well. No one would ever say they are not inspired, but they are truthfully likely not inerrant.

The problem with "new" religions is that the old religions generally don't like them, since most are monopolistic, exclusive, or strive to be all-powerful. They try to rub them out and eradicate them as Gnostic, unholy, schismatic, or divisive.

Picture Luther standing before the Diet of Worms. Religion is a very competitive force (read Gary Becker, the Nobel Prize–winning economist on this), and wars have in the past been fought over such beliefs, for one hundred years or longer in some cases. Indeed, even in this very modern world, much energy and terror are still expended over revived old religions (jihads) and certain newly emergent ones, which are sometimes called "cults," usually by people who see them as a threat. Cults are interesting because they either fade away quickly or survive and themselves turn into old religions. It all has to do with what some sociologists call "institutional capacity" and, I suppose, sustainability. Clever religions find adherents, adapt, and change to fit new circumstances and epochs. Generally, I think superstitions become heresies, then, if followers abound, take over old faiths. But that is just my theory.

Like Sir John Templeton, with age I have become more and more tolerant, open, respectful of others. Still and forever a WASP, I find myself respecting every tradition and race (heck, they lasted, so who am I to knock them?). We should honor all religions (even civic ones) or none at all. Very libertarian, I suspect.

John Locke was right in his famous *A Letter Concerning Toleration* of yore. So on my top shelf in my home library I have: the Buddha, Ganesh (for prosperity), a crucifix, two Eastern Orthodox icons, the Shinto shrine and cherry blossom, a Zen garden, an Islamic lamp, a yarmulke, an African animistic dagger, the menorah, a Thai dancer, the Hittite goddess Artemis, a Balinese Hindu dragon god, a statue of Saint John, a relic of Mary (Mother of Jesus), a statue of Hercules, a bust of Aristotle, another of George Washington, the American flag (of course) from my fathers twenty-one-gun-salute military funeral, a bronze of TR, and a wooden Indian god Vishnu given to me for rendering the C. K. Prahalad Memorial Lecture in 2011 at the Indian Institute of Management, in Kerala. So my bases are pretty much covered. Would you not agree?

Truthfully, I grew up singing old and new hymns. The songs I most recall include the likes of "Jesus Loves Me" and "Deep and Wide," besides all the classic, favorite seventeenth- and eighteenth-century hymns. For me, faith was and remains the ultimate purpose for living and serving. Each summer my family would travel from the heat and humidity of the inner city of Philadelphia where I was raised to vacation at a camp in the Adirondack Mountains, on what is literally called Lake Pleasant. The image still reverberates in my over-educated mind, especially on sleepless nights. It was as cool, calm, and refreshing a place as is a heavenly breeze. That is because it likely was.

It was a religiously inspired but nondenominational Protestant setting. They called us "gospel volunteers"—as if we were free and roving ambassadors for Christ. I guess I still am to large degree. I recall my last summer there, then as a counselor. Every Sunday morning at chapel, set high on a hill overlooking that ever-pleasant pristine blue lake, we would march in carrying more than a hundred different flags. They were from nearly every country around the globe—from America to Zimbabwe, Canada to Zaire. As they paraded forward to the stage, the orchestra would play and the ebullient choir would sing in the loudest and most melodious voices I have ever heard, "Crown Him with many crowns . . . Thy praise and glory shall not fail for all eternity."

My final word—actually, prayer—for you as readers is that you too will find your Lake Pleasant, as a reservoir of strength; and that you too will remember special places of education (literacy and numeracy), the character *and* friendships formed, so that you too can give *all* the glory to God. Because in the end, brothers and sisters, life is a calling, and taking on your challenge is nothing more than a personal doxology; from Him all blessings flow and to Him they shall return.

When my young daughter, Morgan, was about three or four years old and certainly not yet schooled or tainted by the ills of contemporary society, she told our then nanny, a wonderful older woman of Jewish background and an artistic soul, named Aunt Jeannie, that her father was a "small god" (which is why I am using a lower case *g*). She fully believed it and could defend her belief, using (childish) reason and experience both. My Princess Morgan has since unfortunately come to lose some of those sentiments as she entered her teen years and was polluted by other factors, but we continue a beautiful and close, devoted father-daughter relationship that I hope and trust will go on for a long lifetime.

So please do take these few "Suggestions" seriously, as they are handed down by a still small (and likely getting much smaller) not even semi-god, who has nonetheless fought the good fight "in the arena."

In humility, as my father used to remind us, "you put your pants on one leg at a time—just like everyone else." And I would be remiss if I did not leave you with a Bible verse, as was the custom whenever we visited my grandmother. Here is one for the ages, from Isaiah 40:31 in the King James Version: *"But they that wait upon the LORD shall renew their strength; they shall mount up with wings as eagles; they shall run, and not be weary; and they shall walk, and not faint."*

THIRTEEN SUGGESTIONS FROM THE "BOOK OF TED"

1. Thou shalt not worry about terminal degrees, just perpetual learning.

2. Behold, power corrupts, so get some and use it before the other guy does.

3. Verily, you can't buy squat without capital. Buy, borrow, and earn all you can get (in all its forms).

4. I say unto you, Black is black and white is white, but alas, most things are some shade of gray.

5. Try to find the highest common denominator and always shoot high.

6. Honorable people like to be around important people; get there too, but be nice.

7. Do not cross the media, for they can make or break you and just about everything else, so befriend and beguile them.

8. Realize going into any action that the best intentions (often) go wrong.

9. Leaders do best when they shut up and act.

10. What you don't know can hurt, even destroy/kill you.

11. Be hungry and enterprising or you are likely to be poor and/or dumb.

12. Beware of that which is free, as there are sure to be strings attached.

13. Alas, be your own best career counselor and personnel director. Follow your conscience.

ABOUT THE AUTHOR

Theodore Roosevelt Malloch has since its inception been chairman and chief executive officer of the Roosevelt Group, a leading strategic advisory and thought leadership company. He also started Global Fiduciary Governance LLC. He was a research professor at Yale University and a supernumerary fellow of Wolfson College, Oxford University. He was as well the founder and chairman of the not-for-profit Spiritual Enterprise Institute (SEI), created in 2005. He is a senior fellow at Said Business School, at the University of Oxford in England.

In 1994 he cofounded and has since directed the CEO Learning Partnership for PricewaterhouseCoopers LLP. Ted has been a senior fellow and vice president of the Aspen Institute, where he previously directed all of its national seminars and ran the Wye River Conference Centers. He was also president of the World Economic Development Congress sponsored by CNN, the common frame of reference for the world's power elite. That Congress focused on "building the integrated global economy" and offered some twenty-five hundred chief executive officers, ministers of government, investment, and economic leaders from around the world, a forum where new business relationships were established. At that meeting Margaret Thatcher, the congress chairperson, called him "a global Sherpa."

Dr. Malloch has served on the executive board of the World Economic Forum, which hosts the renowned Davos annual meeting in Switzerland. He held an ambassadorial level position as deputy executive secretary in the United Nations in Geneva, Switzerland (1988–91), where EDI was founded; he headed consulting at Wharton-Chase Econometrics; has worked in international capital markets at the investment bank, Salomon Brothers, Inc.; and has served in senior policy positions at the US Senate Committee on Foreign Relations and in the US State Department. He has taught and lectured at a number of universities in the United States, Canada, and abroad.

Ted earned his PhD in international political economy from the University of Toronto, where he held the Hart House Open University Fellowship. He took an MLitt degree (with honors) from Aberdeen University in Scotland on a St. Andrews Fellowship and earned a BA from Gordon College. He was awarded an honorary LLD degree from the University of Aberdeen in 2008. He is a research professor at the Claremont Graduate School and the Drucker School of Management. He has authored thirteen books, numerous journal articles, and corporate and governmental reports and has appeared frequently on television and web casts and as a keynote speaker.

He has served on numerous corporate and mutual fund and not-for-profit/educational boards. He advises numerous international and US governmental advisory bodies and think tanks.

NOTES

INTRODUCTION

1. Conor O'Clery, Moscow, December 25, 1991: The Last Day of the Soviet Union (New York: Public Affairs, 2012), 27.

CHAPTER 2

1. See Charles Mackay, *Extraordinary Popular Delusions and the Madness of Crowds* (London: Wordsworth, 1999), 1–82.

CHAPTER 4

1. Adam Smith, *Wealth of Nations*, Book V (London: J.M. Dent & Sons ; New York : E.P. Dutton,1910).

CHAPTER 12

1. "The Aspen Institute—Justice and Society Program," idealist, accessed August 26, 2015, http://www.idealist.org/view/nonprofit/8589GgxKJ874/.

CHAPTER 13

1. Lionel Barber, "Transcript: Wen Jiabao," Financial Times, February 2, 2009, accessed September 2015, http://www.ft.com/intl/cms/s/0/795d2bca-f0fe-11dd-8790-0000779fd2ac.html#axzz3lMF5Fdv6.

2. See, for example, http://www.transparency.org/country#CHN and http://www.economist.com/node/3203266.

CHAPTER 16

1. "Dead Man's Float," by Stephen Roderick, *New York Magazine*, February 10, 2008, http://nymag.com/news/features/43914/

CHAPTER 17

1. Yale University, About › History, accessed August 28, 2015, http://www.yale.edu/about/history.html.

2. Ibid.

3. See http://www.yaleherald.com/archive/xix/3.24.95/news/bass.html.

4. See John Winthrop's sermon "A Model of Christian Charity," at the Winthrop Society website, http://winthropsociety.com/doc_charity.php.

5. See Howard Zinn's essay titled "Myths of American exceptionalism" at http://www.ufppc.org/us-a-world-news-mainmenu-35/2959-essay-howard-zinn-on-myths-of-american-exceptionalism.html.

6. V. S. Naipaul, "Our Universal Civilization," November 5, 1990, on the website of *New York Times on the Web*, http://www.nytimes.com/books/98/06/07/specials/naipaul-universal.html.

7. From Washington's letter to the Hebrew congregation of Newport, Rhode Island, August 18, 1790. http://www.heritage.org/initiatives/first-principles/primary-sources/washington-s-letter-to-the-hebrew-congregation-of-newport-rhode-island

8. From Adams's letter to Zabdiel Adams, June 21, 1776. http://www.thefederalistpapers.org/founders/adams/john-adams-foundation-of-a-free-constitution-is-pure-virtue

9. From Eisenhower's 1952 address to reporters http://spectator.org/articles/38107/eisenhowers-religion

INDEX

N

X

Y

Z